Also by Anjelica Huston

A Story Lately Told

WATCH ME

A Memoir

ANJELICA HUSTON

**SIMON &
SCHUSTER**

London · New York · Sydney · Toronto · New Delhi

A CBS COMPANY

First published in Great Britain by Simon & Schuster UK Ltd, 2014
This paperback edition published by Simon & Schuster UK Ltd, 2015
A CBS COMPANY

1 3 5 7 9 10 8 6 4 2

Simon & Schuster UK Ltd
1st Floor
222 Gray's Inn Road
London
WC1X 8HB

www.simonandschuster.co.uk

Simon & Schuster Australia, Sydney
Simon & Schuster India, New Delhi

A CIP catalogue copy for this book
is available from the British Library.

ISBN: 978-1-47113-341-1
eBook ISBN: 978-1-47113-342-8

The author gratefully acknowledges permission from the following
sources to reprint material in their control: p.103, "Walter of Battersea,"
courtesy of Jim Harrison and Joyce Bahle; pp. 110-12 from *Palm Beach Post*,
October 24, 1979, © 1979 *Palm Beach Post*. All rights reserved.

The author and publishers have made all reasonable efforts
to contact copyright-holders for permission, and apologise
for any omissions or errors in the form of credits given.
Corrections may be made to future printings.

Printed and bound by CPI Group (UK) Ltd, Croydon, CR0 4YY

For Bob Graham

CONTENTS

PART ONE

LOVE

Photographed by Bob Colacello

CHAPTER 1

My old life ended and my new life began as I was standing next to a baggage carousel in the customs hall at LAX in March 1973. It was there, at the age of twenty-one, that I parted ways with Bob Richardson, the man I had lived with for the last four years, a bold and provocative fashion photographer twenty-four years older than I, with whom I'd been involved in a tempestuous affair. Until this moment we had been sharing an apartment in Gramercy Park, New York. Had it not been for the presence of my father and his latest wife, Cici, with whom Bob and I had just been vacationing in La Paz, Mexico, I doubt that I ever would have had the final stroke of courage it would take to leave him.

I would be staying temporarily at the ranch house in the Pacific Palisades that Cici had owned prior to her marriage to Dad and that she was redecorating to accommodate some treasures from our old life at St. Clerans, a pastoral estate in the west of Ireland where I grew up with my brother Tony— before we moved with our mother to London; before the birth of my half siblings, Danny and Allegra; before I acted in a movie at the age of sixteen with my father directing; before my mother's death by car crash in 1969, a cataclysmic experience that for me ended that beautiful, hopeful decade, when I moved from England to America.

One morning early in my stay at Cici's, I ordered a taxi and told the driver to take me to Hollywood. "Do you mean Vine Street?" he asked vaguely. I had guessed that Hollywood wasn't really a place but rather a state of mind, with a great many parking lots sandwiched between shops and storefronts advertising sex and liquor.

But oddly, there was a sense of coming home to California. Although I had grown up in Europe, I was born in Los Angeles. The desert skies were clear blue and untroubled. Living with my father again felt strange, but he would be leaving soon to resume work on *The Mackintosh Man* in New York.

I was eager to buy some marabou bedroom stilettos to match the pink swan's-down-trimmed negligee that Cici had generously just given me. Driving along Sunset in the pale sunshine, I noticed that the panorama was bare and garish, mostly warehouses and two-story facades. There were rows of tall palm trees and purple jacarandas. The air was windy and dry and sweet-scented. Beverly Hills, it seemed, was all about who you were, what you were driving, your pastimes, and your playgrounds.

A few days before, Cici had taken me shopping on Rodeo Drive, where there was a yellow-striped awning above Giorgio's boutique, with outdoor atomizers that puffed their signature Giorgio perfume. Indulgent husbands drank espresso at a shiny brass bar inside as their wives shopped for feathered gowns and beaded cocktail dresses. For lingerie, the local sirens went to Juel Park, who was known to seal the deal for many aspirants based on the strength of her hand-stitched negligees and satin underwear trimmed with French lace. We lunched at the Luau, a Polynesian watering hole, the darkest oasis on the street, where you could hear rummy confessions from the next-door booth as you tucked behind your ear a fresh gardenia from the scorpion punch. Los Angeles was a small town then; it felt both incredibly glamorous and a little provincial.

Cici, who was in her mid-thirties, had a son, Collin, by a former marriage to the documentary filmmaker and screenwriter Walon Green. Cici had gone to private schools in Beverly Hills and Montecito, and her friends were the hot beauties of the day, from Jill St. John and Stefanie Powers to Bo Derek and Stephanie Zimbalist—glamorous sportswomen and great horseback riders who had grown up privileged in the western sunbelt. She had played baseball with Elvis Presley at Beverly Glen Park in the fifties and roomed with Grace Slick at Finch College in New York. Cici also had a lively retinue of gay friends who were sportive and gossipy and informal.

Cici's energy was buoyant. She cursed like a sailor and loved a bit of illicit fun, as did I. Our practice, at least a couple of times a week, was to do an impromptu raid on other people's gardens in the neighboring canyons. I would wield the shears, and with a trunkful of flowers and branches, Cici would drive her candy-apple-red Maserati like a getaway car, burning rubber to peals of laughter; although we tempted fate, for some miraculous reason we never got caught. Sometimes Allegra would accompany us on these forays.

After the sale of St. Clerans, Allegra had moved in with her Irish nanny, Kathleen Shine, whom we called "Nurse," to share a rented house in Santa Monica with Gladys Hill, Dad's co-writer and secretary. Heartbroken by the death of our mother and still painfully loyal to her, Nurse had been a staple of Tony's and my childhood. Gladys was calm, deliberate, intelligent, and kind. A pale-complexioned woman with ice-blond hair from West Virginia, she was devoted to Dad and shared his passion for pre-Columbian art. She had worked for him in the previous decade and was part of the family in Ireland when I was growing up.

Allegra was going on nine and was extremely smart; it was already her intention to go to Oxford University. From the time she was a baby, she'd had an innate, deep wisdom and a sweet formality about her.

I looked up Jeremy Railton, a handsome Rhodesian friend from my former life, when I was going to school in London. He had been designing the sets for a play by Ntozake Shange, *For Colored Girls Who Have Considered Suicide When the Rainbow Is Enuf*, and was living in an apartment on Fountain Avenue. We picked up our friendship where we'd left off five years before. He introduced me to his social circle, which included the comedy writer Kenny Solms and his collaborator, Gail Parent; the talent agent Sandy Gallin; Michael Douglas and Brenda Vaccaro; Paula and Lisa Weinstein; and Neil Diamond. Kenny and Gail wrote for *The Carol Burnett Show* and numerous television specials for Mary Tyler Moore, Dick Van Dyke, and Julie Andrews.

Cici knew that I was still shaken from my split with Bob Richardson. She did her best to take me out and introduce me to people, but I was more interested in riding her horses and walking in the next-door garden. She and Dad had just celebrated the completion of a new Jacuzzi, and one afternoon I found the actor Don Johnson and a male friend of his floating in it. Though I was grateful to Cici for her efforts, I was somewhat embarrassed and ran back to the camellia trees.

A Swedish friend of hers, Brigitta, who owned Strip Thrills, a dress shop on Sunset, told Cici that she was going to a party at Jack Nicholson's house that evening and invited her to come along. Cici asked if she could bring her stepdaughter, and Brigitta said fine, that it was his birthday, and Jack loved pretty girls.

I borrowed an evening dress from Cici—black, long, open at the back, with a diamanté clasp. Brigitta and another Swedish girl picked us up, and the four of us drove in Brigitta's car to Jack's house on Mulholland Drive, on a high ridge separating Beverly Hills from the San Fernando Valley on the other side. It felt like we were on top of the world.

The front door of a modest two-story ranch-style house opened, and there was that smile. Later, after he became a superstar and was on the cover of *Time* magazine, Diana Vreeland was to christen it "The Killer Smile." But at the time I thought, "Ah! Yes. Now, there's a man you could fall for."

In 1969, when I was still living in London, I had gone with some friends to see *Easy Rider* in a movie theater in Piccadilly Circus, and had returned alone some days later to see it again. It was Jack's combination of ease and exuberance that had captured me from the moment he came on-screen. I think it was probably upon seeing the film that, like many others, I first fell in love with Jack.

The second time was when he opened the door to his house that early evening in April, with the late sun still golden in the sky. "Good evening, ladies," he said, beaming, and added in a slow drawl, "I'm Jack, and I'm glad you could make it."

He motioned for us to enter. The front room was low-ceilinged, candlelit, and filled with strangers. There was Greek food, and music playing. I danced with Jack for hours.

And when he invited me to stay the night, I asked Cici what she thought. "Are you kidding?" she said. "Of course!"

In the morning, when I woke up and put on my evening dress from the night before, Jack was already downstairs. Someone I came to recognize later as the screenwriter Robert Towne walked through the front door into the house and looked at me appraisingly as I stood on the upper landing. Then Jack appeared and said, "I'm gonna send you home in a taxi, if that's okay, because I'm going to a ball game."

The cab took me back the half hour to the Palisades. When I got out in the backless evening dress, Cici was at the door. She looked at me and just shook her head. "I can't believe you didn't insist that he drive you home," she said. "What are you thinking? If he's going to take you out again, he must come and pick you up and take you home."

Jack called a few days later to ask me out. I said, "Yes. But you have to pick me up, and you have to drive me home." And he said, "Okay. All right. How about Saturday?" And I said, "Okay. But you have to come and pick me up." Then I got a follow-up call on Saturday saying he was sorry, he had to cancel our date, because he had a previous obligation. "Does that make me a secondary one?" I asked.

"Don't say that," he said. "It's not witty enough, and it's derogatory to both of us." I hung up the phone, disappointed. That evening I decided to go out with Jeremy and Kenny Solms and Gail Parent. We were dining at the Old World café on Sunset Boulevard, when they started to whisper and giggle. When I asked what was going on, Gail said, "You were supposed to see Jack tonight, right?" And I replied, "Yes, but he had a previous obligation," and Kenny said, "Well, his previous obligation is a very pretty blonde, and he just went upstairs with her."

I took my wineglass in hand and, with heart pumping, climbed the stairs to the upper section of the restaurant and approached Jack's booth. He was sitting with a beautiful young woman whom I immediately recognized as his ex-girlfriend Michelle Phillips. I had seen them photographed together in magazines when I was living in New York. She was in the group the Mamas and the Papas. As I reached the table, a shadow passed quickly over his face, like a cloud crossing the sun. I lifted my glass airily and said, "I'm downstairs, and I just thought I'd come up to say hi." He introduced Michelle to me, not missing a beat. She was charming. I guess they were at the end of their relationship at that point. One morning, some weeks later, she drove to his house on Mulholland Drive to collect something she had stored there. Upon discovering that I was with Jack, she came upstairs to his bedroom with two glasses of orange juice. From that moment, we became friends.

On one of my first dates with Jack, he took me to the races at Hollywood Park. He wore a beautiful cream wool suit with an American flag in rhinestones pinned to his lapel. He got a hard time at the gate to the grandstand for not wearing a tie. Jack gave me fifty dollars' betting money. I won sixty-seven and returned his fifty.

I was still wrapped up in thoughts of Bob Richardson and the suddenness of our parting. I wrote in a diary I was keeping at the time that I didn't know what was me and what wasn't anymore, that I'd been Bob's possession and his construct, saying the things he might say, even smoking his brand of cigarettes. I thought it must be planetary, all this disruption and indecision. Someone said it was fragments of helium floating about the atmosphere, because everyone I met at the time seemed touched by a peculiar madness. Even Richard Nixon had lost his moorings and was on his way to being impeached. In the overture to our relationship, Jack sent mixed messages. Alternately, he would ask me to stick around or would not call when he said he would. At one point he told me he had decided that we should cool it, and followed that up with a call suggesting we dine together. Sometimes he called me "Pal," which I hated. It implied a lack of romantic feeling. I didn't want to be his crony but, rather, the love of his life. I thought he was still very involved with Michelle, who seemed to have made up her mind to move along.

Jack gave me a variety of nicknames. I started off as "Fab." As in "The Big Fabulous," which became, with a German accent, "Ze Bik Fabuliss." This was because when I first came to Los Angeles, Jeremy and Kenny used to say "the *most* fabulous" all the time, a habit that I had adopted. Then, I don't know why, my name developed into "Toot," rhyming with "foot," or "Tootie," which became "Tootman Fabuliss." Then it became "Ze Bik," and then simply "Mine," or "Minyl." Jack had nicknames for most people. Warren Beatty was "The Pro." Marlon Brando was "Marloon." Fred Roos was "The Rooster." Arthur Garfunkel was "The Old New G." Jack had a thing about names. He liked Harry Dean Stanton's name so much that he wrote it somewhere in every film that he did. So, whether it was his initials on a prison wall in graffiti or carved into a tree in a Western, if you look closely at this period of his movies, you'll see HDS somewhere. He called Michelle "Rat" in the nicest way possible. His car, a magnificent Mercedes 600 the color of black cherries, was christened "Bing."

One of the first things I noticed about Jack was that he had a great many people around who performed all sorts of functions for him. On Saturdays the guys would all sit in the TV room at the back of the house and drink beer and eat hot dogs and watch sports all day. Jack might leap up to demonstrate a slam dunk. As long as he had a friend sitting by, nodding his head, a smile decorating his face, life was good. I think, for the most part, that's all Jack needed. In some ways, he was a man of simple tastes. A receptive and appreciative audience always charmed him.

Others had the job of helping Jack keep his life running smoothly. He called his assistant, Annie Marshall, "My staff." The daughter of the late actor Herbert Marshall, Annie was tall, dark, and pretty, brilliantly funny, neurotic, and smart as a whip. There was Helena Kallianiotes, who was a complete mystery to me at the beginning. Helena was "Boston Blackie"; born in Greece, dark and brooding, she had mahogany eyes, a waist-length snarl of black hair, and a compact, lithe body, and had been a belly dancer in Boston. She was also a great cook, and provided the Mediterranean food at Jack's party. She was a fascinating woman, complicated, intense, and secretive. The writer of *Five Easy Pieces*, Carole Eastman, a very good friend of Jack's, had seen Helena dancing in the late sixties and had been so impressed that she'd introduced Helena to Jack and the director, Bob Rafelson, who gave her a small but memorable role in the movie. Knowing she was at loose ends afterward, Jack offered her a position looking after his house. She was living there when we first met, at his party, and eventually moved to a house that he acquired next door.

Helena wasn't really a housekeeper. She was Jack's chief

of staff, to a degree, although there was often confusion about the running of the house, as Jack would appropriate many people to perform the same task. Helena was also the keeper of his confidences and trust, and always had Jack's best interest at heart. Sometimes they had fights, and he would blame her if something broke down or went missing; she took some heat but was always fiercely loyal to him.

During my first months in L.A., I spent a lot of time at Kenny Solms's house, alternately nursing and bullying my friend Jeremy, who had developed a very high temperature but refused to discuss his ailments. At one point, Kenny and I decided to drive him to the nearest emergency room, at Cedars-Sinai. He was terribly ill and ultimately needed an operation.

I was riding Cici's horses in the mornings up at Will Rogers Park, then going into Beverly Hills to visit with Kenny while Jeremy was in the hospital. Sometimes I would stay at Kenny's house, and together we would enact scenes from *A Little Night Music* for our own personal amusement. We liked to believe our version of "Send in the Clowns" was nonpareil, and our performance became something of a daily ritual that I greatly enjoyed.

After Jeremy recuperated, I decided to rent a place with him high up on Beachwood Drive under the Hollywood sign, opposite a rustic little riding school that, for ten dollars an hour, would rent you a horse you could ride on a trail over the pass to Glendale. There you could hang a feed bag on the horse and halter it to a post while you ate tacos and drank beer. The house itself was Spanish, with white walls and yellow trim around the windows, cool inside, with tiled and wooden floors, alcoves, rounded portals, and French doors leading to a central courtyard. Upstairs there were balconies overlooking the garden, and my bedroom was a perfect little white box. Cici gave me a selection of housewarming presents, including a Sony record player, beds, chairs, tables, and lamps. We had a lot of fun parties in Beachwood Canyon, but because it was the beginning of my relationship with Jack, I was spending my nights more often than not at his house on Mulholland Drive, then taking taxis in the early morning down Coldwater Canyon across town to Beachwood. My practice was to arrive at the house and start washing the dirty dishes soaking in the sink from the previous night.

Allegra came to visit with me sometimes at Beachwood Drive on weekends. Once I dressed her in my grandmother Angelica's Edwardian gown that I had salvaged from St. Clerans, and tried to take her picture in a hammock, but she was reluctant and camera-shy; even at nine, she reminded me so much of Mum—loyal, sensitive, sweet, and wise, but without the advantage of having had our mother for long.

Jeremy and I planted a pretty garden at Beachwood, full of foxgloves and forget-me-nots, wisteria, chrysanthemums, passion flowers, and dahlias. Jeremy started to keep quail in the back yard, and we had a lovely pair of resident raccoons and their babies. We vowed one day to have a farm together, a place where we could be totally free and creative, and make a haven for animals.

One morning when I entered the kitchen, I met an extremely handsome young man with black hair and dark eyes. His name was Tim Wilson. We smoked some grass and bonded instantly. He told me that he was studying Transcendental Meditation. That summer Jeremy, Tim, and I planned out our dream farm on paper, drawing a map describing where each of us might live, what our animals might be, where each of us might have ponds and plant gardens. Eventually, this would become a reality.

There was a nascent western branch of the New York clan in Los Angeles. A lot of people were making the shift—Berry Berenson, Pat Ast, Peter Lester, Juan Fernández, Dennis Christopher. European friends, too, were making the journey west. There were about ten places to eat in town—the Bistro, Trader Vic's, Perino's, Chasen's, the Cock'n Bull, La Scala, Scandia, the Old World, the Source, the Brown Derby.

Things happened at a leisurely pace. Unlike New York, where the pavements abounded with energy and purpose and everyone seemed to have an objective, Los Angeles was filled with friendly people who seemed content to hang out at home in tracksuits and kaftans, waiting for good things to come to them, or those who relied on whimsy for advancement: A girl in a pink Corvette had her own billboard opposite Schwab's pharmacy. Her name was Angelyne; she had blow-up breasts and seemingly did nothing other than advertise herself. Andy Warhol had just originated the idea that everyone in the world could be famous for fifteen minutes.

Up on the Strip, the hot clubs of the moment—the Roxy, the Whisky, and the Rainbow Room—were all owned by Jack's best friend, Lou Adler, who was president of Ode Records, and his partner, Elmer Valentine; they catered to a young, hip crowd. But we also celebrated Groucho Marx's eighty-second birthday at the Hillcrest Country Club. Groucho had a companion and secretary, a woman called Erin Fleming who, along with the young actors Ed Begley, Jr., and Bud Cort, was helping him to come out of retirement. As I recall, he sang "Animal Crackers" and made a pass at me before he temporarily lost consciousness.

CHAPTER 2

During the four years I spent in New York, I had achieved top status as a model and worked for the best photographers and designers in the world. I had grown used to hearing that I was "exotic" and "high-fashion." These were not necessarily attributes that would work to my advantage as a model in Southern California, where tanned blondes with big smiles were the order of the day. I did not think it was likely that I'd be booked for toothpaste ads or Clairol commercials, and decided I would not offer myself up to rejection and disappointment. I was still smarting from the collective drubbing I'd received for Dad's movie *A Walk with Love and Death*, in which I had starred with Assaf Dayan. But I believed that at some point I would take up the reins and become the actress I had always wanted to be. So, grateful to Dad for helping me out for a few months, and to Cici for her generosity, I, too, joined the ranks of the cheerfully unemployed—but not for long. If I was out of place as a model in L.A., I still fit the bill in New York: a few months after my move to California, I accepted an invitation to go back east to do shows for Halston and Giorgio Sant'Angelo.

On the day of my departure, Jack offered me a ride to the airport and took me to lunch before my flight. We arrived at the airport early, and he waited until I boarded the plane. He was going to join me in New York in a few days, and from there he would go on to Europe to make *The Passenger*, with Michelangelo Antonioni.

Jack and I were both going to stay at Ara Gallant's apartment in New York. Ara was a friend to the boys and the girls alike. I hesitate to call Ara a hairdresser—he was more an artist who worked with hair and a creator of high-fashion fantasy; he would put three wigs on your head, and two of them might be blue—this before anyone else was dyeing their hair primary colors. Later, Ara became a photographer. He was a party giver, the center of the disco scene in New York at Studio 54. From the mid-seventies to the mid-eighties, he went dancing every night with Apollonia van Ravenstein, one of the most sought-after models of the time. Ara's apartment was on West End Avenue, with high-gloss black-patent walls and blacked-out windows, where he lived like something out of Huysmans's *Against Nature*. I gave him the charm of Jonah in the whale's mouth that Mum had given me so many years before, to sew onto the Kangol Spitfire hat that was his trademark.

It felt odd to arrive in New York and not ask the taxi driver to take me to my old apartment in Gramercy Park. It was evident that my state of mind was fragile; even though I knew it was absurd, I was terrified of running into Bob Richardson, worried that he might learn I was in town and show up at Ara's to claim me. But the cab took me to West End Avenue without incident, and Ara and I stayed up talking until four in the morning.

I had a fitting at Halston's just a few hours later, at 9:30 A.M., and walked across the park to Madison Avenue. It was great to see everyone, and Halston showered me with gifts of dresses and coats and cashmere—it felt like Christmas. When

I returned to Ara's, I woke him up and replaced him in his bed, where I slept for hours. I awakened to music, and there ensued a haircutting session before dinner. Annie Marshall was paving the way for Jack's arrival, and the legendary model Veruschka von Lehndorff had come over to the apartment for Chinese food. When Apollonia arrived toward midnight, having missed her Grand Marnier soufflé, we stayed up talking and telling stories. I almost overslept again the next morning but made it across town for the show at Halston's. My modeling agency, Wilhelmina, called to say that I would be traveling to Europe the next week to work in London, Paris, and Milan for British *Vogue* with David Bailey. Since Jack was going to be filming in Europe, the timing was perfect.

After Jack arrived, the days and nights continued to overlap in the timeless vortex of Ara's apartment. I did a catwalk for Giorgio Sant'Angelo, which Jack and Annie attended. It was fun showing off for them. The music was "Rocky Mountain High," the first time I ever heard John Denver. We went to a Carole King concert in Central Park with Lou Adler; A&M Records was her label at the time. Joni Mitchell was there, and she sat on the ground between Jack's legs throughout the show. I was hurt and jealous, but I said nothing about it until later on, when I confronted him. "Come on," he said with a sigh, rolling his eyes as if I were boring him to tears, "she's just an old friend."

Ara's was a refuge for many of us; he was a fantastic host. He introduced Jack to beautiful models, and in turn Jack would go to Ara's parties. Of course, after I met Jack, this posed a not inconsiderable problem for me. But those evenings could be extraordinary, resembling dream gatherings that people conjure up, in which they say, "Oh, I'd want Churchill and

Gandhi and Elizabeth Taylor to be there." Like when Mike Nichols brought Jackie Onassis over for dinner, and when Veruschka, Carol Kane, the beautiful model Susan Forristal, Art Garfunkel, Joni Mitchell, Lou Adler, Annie, Jack, and I would all be seated in the mirrored dining room eating delicious Szechuan food prepared by Ara's chef, Billy. Billy pronounced Mike's name "My Nichols," which we all found hilarious; needless to say, it stuck. In that short week, I met people whom I would know for the rest of my life.

Mike Nichols had a party at his apartment for the cast of *Uncle Vanya*, starring the British actor Nicol Williamson. I had known Nicol in London when he played Hamlet and I was understudying Marianne Faithfull as Ophelia. But we did not reacquaint; he played piano downstairs all evening as the cast sang along, "Won't you come home, Bill Bailey, won't you come home?" I wore a Fortuny dress of Mum's that night and showed Mike a picture of her that I kept in a silver locket around my neck.

Before I departed for London, Ara threw another party. Joni Mitchell came and wrote a song about it later, "People's Parties." Apollonia van Ravenstein was there. Jack called her "Apples only." Apollonia and I were quite good friends and had often modeled together in London and New York. She had been crying that night—laughing and crying, it was hard to figure out which or why. She had balanced a lampshade on her head; tears were pouring down her cheeks. The night before I left, Jack and I spoke about Bob Richardson and Mum and Michelle Phillips and us. He held me in his arms, and I told him that I loved him and he said that he loved me, too. After I left for London, Jack was to stay at Ara's for several days before heading off to Munich to start filming.

* * *

A few days later, Apollonia arrived in London and came to see me. During dinner, she let slip that she'd slept with Jack at Ara's the night I'd left. She told me they had been in a relationship before he met me. Now I understood the reason behind the lampshade hat and the tears. I hadn't understood that she loved him. When I confronted Jack on the telephone, distraught, sad, mad, he said, "Oh, Toots, it was just a mercy fuck." That was the first time I'd heard copulation described as an act of compassion—not that he'd ever vowed to be faithful to me, but somehow he thought it was an acceptable answer.

I met with Grace Coddington, the fashion editor of British *Vogue*, and David Bailey at his studio in Primrose Hill, and we left for Jean Shrimpton's home in Berkshire, where we worked all day doing pictures with horses and rabbits. I returned to London just in time to do a big show for Zandra Rhodes at the Savoy Hotel. Jack arrived from New York, and we stayed together at the producer Sam Spiegel's apartment at Grosvenor House. We were out every night. We went to the opera and to a Paul Simon concert at the Albert Hall, followed by jazz at Ronnie Scott's. Lou Adler's girlfriend, Britt Ekland, gave birth to a beautiful baby boy, Nicolai, at a private maternity hospital in Hampstead, and demanded caviar and champagne upon delivery. Lou, Annie, Jack, and I were all a bit unruly in the waiting room, and the matron almost got nasty.

Jack was still preparing for Antonioni's *The Passenger*, which would span four countries—England, Germany, Spain, and Chad. Meanwhile, I was flying to Milan, where I would ride dangerously in a Missoni cloak on the back of

Oliviero Toscani's Harley-Davidson, at night on the auto route, with Bailey hanging out the window of a big black Mercedes, taking photographs. Bailey had been drinking heavily the night before. His hands were shaking. "Wanker's colic," he called it. I was doing my best to keep up, but Bailey was on a roll.

From Milan we proceeded to Paris, where Jack was holed up at the George V. We went dancing; Bailey and Penelope Tree came by, and I met Nelson Seabra, a lovely older Brazilian gentleman whom Jack had seemingly adopted, and an attractive couple called the Le Clerys. Jack had met them the year before, when he was in Rio for Carnival. The following day, I worked again with Bailey, who photographed me with Yves Saint Laurent, a shy, sweet, timid creature, in his beautiful apartment on the rue de Babylone, surrounded by a stunning collection of chinoiserie, deco, lacquer, and art nouveau. Then we went on to Karl Lagerfeld's house—much in the same style and very beautiful, though not quite as grand—to take more pictures. When I returned to the hotel, Jack announced that he was going to a garden party with Nelson, who was very much a part of the social scene in Paris. It surprised me and hurt my feelings that I was not included. After they left, I called my friend Tony Kent, who came over on his high-handled chopper and drove me all around Paris at top speed—over the bridges and through the tunnels by the Seine. If I couldn't get a commitment from Jack, at least I was going to have fun on my own terms.

Bailey and I left for the little town of Cognac the next day on the train. When I talked to Jack on the phone that morning, I asked if I'd ever see him again. Jack was defensive. He asked me what I was talking about; he'd followed me all over the place already! I asked if I should follow him. He said no, which hurt. Unrequited love is painful. If you give less, they give more, I thought. I should try to cool it.

A week later, when I returned to London, Jack and I met at San Lorenzo's for lunch, and by that afternoon I had moved in with him at Andy Braunsberg's apartment in Albion Close. So much for cooling it. Annie Marshall was staying there, too. We went to see Paul Scofield in *Savages*, and Jack took me to Glebe Place, in Chelsea, for tea one Sunday, at the home of Hercules Bellville. When I first heard that name, I thought it sounded like a sea captain's. One knew one was in for something important. And not for a second did Herky disappoint. I instantly loved him; the perfect antithesis of his namesake bronze ogre in Hyde Park, Herky stood tall and poetic, eerily thin, with straw-gold hair waving to his shoulders. Herky had worked with Roman Polanski since 1965, when he had been hired as an assistant on *Repulsion*, and was now working as production manager for Antonioni. He was one of those rare beings who are well informed about almost everything; he had a vast knowledge of and affection for art, cities, music, movies, and people.

Herky became a dear friend and would always call to make a date when I was in London, or later, when he came to L.A. He had a penchant for rare perfumes, scarves from Antiquarius, and country music. An aficionado of out-of-the-way burger places, Herky liked specificity in all things; it was always a challenge to identify the least popular restaurants of South Kensington and the Kings Road, where we would meet for lunch. The date would be fixed in stone, and woe betide you if you were a moment late.

Herky was a kitten of the first order. Whenever I saw him, he presented me with a miniature object; I have an eclectic collection of gifts from him, often presented in little brown envelopes—framed Chinese stamps, tiny baguettes, thumb-sized pagodas, prints from his Pre-Raphaelite or orange-label collections, a lithograph by Sir Lawrence Alma-Tadema.

On the Sunday that Jack introduced me to Herky, tea was in the garden. Herky's cats, Kitty and Pussy, wandered to and fro, and we drank mint tea and ate cake, and ran indoors when it started to rain. It was very British. Everyone was asking, "What are you reading?" And "Where's that book I lent you?" Bernardo Bertolucci and his wife, Clare Peploe, were there. Clare's brother, Mark, had written *The Passenger*. Mark's wife, Louise, was doing the costumes. It was something of a family affair. Michael White was also there. A dear friend of Herky's, he was the most important new theater producer in London, with *The Rocky Horror Picture Show*. Michael's girlfriend was the beautiful Lyndall Hobbs, an Australian who starred in her own television show.

One evening there was a party for Barbra Streisand given by Ryan O'Neal. Ryan stared at me from across the room. Jack was a little in his cups and refused to eat. We took a walk the next day in Hyde Park; there was a solitary runner, two white bodies swimming in the Serpentine lake, a military man arguing with his horse, a man on a bike surrounded by swans. The dew was heavy on the grass, drenching my espa-drilles. Jack told me he was "broken up" about leaving me, which sent a thrill through my heart.

Annie and I saw Jack off at Heathrow Airport when he left for Munich, and I went to work. It was a miserable day; I was modeling furs in a hot studio. Annie and I stayed on at the

Braunsberg flat for a few more days, then Jack said he would like me to come to Germany. Ara would be coming, too.

Soon I was on my way to visit Jack in Munich. When I arrived, it became evident that he was an altered character. Jack was one of the least pretentious people I had ever met, but he was capable of the greatest actual pretense—of assuming the mantle of another character without reservation and with, to the smallest detail, a fearless, dedicated commitment to that identity. Sometimes it was an uneasy balance, and he didn't much like it when real life intruded.

That night found us at a restaurant called the Weinerwald, then at a discotheque. Uschi Obermaier, a very sexy German model, joined us, along with Ara, Annie, and Veruschka's boyfriend, Holger. Uschi and Jack were flirting. I stood up. Jack pulled me down by the wrist. "Don't ever stand up like that to leave." I enjoyed his brief flash of possessiveness.

The next day we went to visit Veruschka in the country. It was a beautiful ride down into Bavaria, the ripest, greenest landscape. It made Ireland seem almost pale by comparison. Veruschka's home was a large terra-cotta farmhouse and barn. We spent the afternoon in a Moroccan tent pitched on the lawn. Veruschka, wearing a loose kaftan, had painted herself blue from head to toe. Upstairs, her sister was painting a self-portrait. Her mother showed us around. Straight out of a painting by Tamara de Lempicka, Countess Lehndorff wore riding britches, a tweed jacket, a riding stock, and high black boots. She smoked a chain of cigarettes. It was my birthday, the eighth of July. We listened to Van Morrison on a tape recorder in the tent, visited the dairy cows, and went for a swim by the last rays of the sun, our bodies rosy in the light.

Jack swam well, far out in the lake. We hauled ashore and sat on the grass, pulling off our wet swimsuits. It was chillier out of the water, the deep evening dropping off to dark. We were close, speaking in low tones as we walked back to the house for dinner.

We were staying at the Bayerischer Hof in Munich, an extremely pricey hotel. The bathroom had obviously been recently redone. It had canary-yellow furry nylon pasted half-way up the walls, and an enormous Jacuzzi bathtub. We'd been in it a couple of nights before, and Jack had left a cigarette on the edge of the bathtub that had made a little nicotine spot. He had received something like a three-thousand-dollar bill from the hotel and was outraged. He was complaining about this the following morning over breakfast, before going to the set, where Michelangelo Antonioni was waiting for him. As he ranted away, I noticed a pool of water creeping under the door of the sitting room, which only could have meant that it was coming through from the bedroom. I thought, "That's odd." When I opened the door, the water just gushed out. The entire big grand bedroom was soaked. Jack had turned on the tap and forgotten all about it.

In the bathroom, the huge Jacuzzi tub was flopping over with water. Jack took one look at this and said, "I'm late for work. Don't call nobody," and off he went. Whenever he was in a spot, Jack would use the double negative, Jersey-style, for emphasis. I was left to bail water with a wastepaper basket, and it took hours for the Jacuzzi to drain.

But if Jack could be inconsiderate, he also could be wildly generous—he might buy you a Rolls-Royce off the cuff. When we got back to California, he actually did buy me a beautiful Mercedes-Benz sports car. I took a few driving lessons and passed the test (I don't know how), and when I picked it up from the garage, I immediately rear-ended a woman going up Laurel Canyon. The brand-new Mercedes got mashed on its first day. I never admitted it to Jack. I told him it must have happened in a parking lot. He chose to believe me.

From Munich I traveled with Jack and Annie to Barcelona. I remember Jack having an explosive temper tantrum at the airport because our combined luggage was overweight and he had to pay the excess baggage fees. If you screamed like that these days at an airport, they'd arrest you.

On our first morning in Barcelona, I dressed all in white, and when I walked outside the hotel, a pigeon shat on my head. I think it was a flying cow, actually. My outfit was ruined. These things can be embarrassing when you're newly in love, but Annie said it was lucky.

Jack, Annie, and I went to the beach and lay under the fierce Costa Brava sun amid empty beer cans and bleached plastics. Jack read, and Annie and I turned our towels south and tried to shoo away the sand fleas. Then Jack had the idea of going to a bullfight. I went with him but lasted only five minutes. I saw one bull killed and dragged from the ring, and the next bull seemed intent on goring a horse. I went to sit outside the arena to wait for Jack and missed the high point of the day, when another bull ripped into a matador and cut his leg badly. When we returned to the hotel, Jack got a call from Nelson Seabra. Their beautiful Brazilian friend Regina Le Clery had died in a plane crash at Orly Airport.

Jack and I talked for a long time that night about Mum and Regina and ghosts. He took a sleeping pill and I held him in my arms; I was wearing my mother's pearls, and he went to sleep playing with them. The next day we rented a boat. It was, however, incapable of making it out to the high seas, so we chugged around the oily Barcelona harbor and looked at the pleasure liners, the tankards, and the vessels of the Spanish navy. We ate a lot of fishy paella. Jack was beginning to look and sound like Michelangelo Antonioni; he had adopted Antonioni's tic, a wince and simultaneous half-shrug, for his part in *The Passenger.*

Annie and I had become friends in Spain, particularly when the company moved to Almería, where we'd spent an exuberant evening at a local bar meeting the bullfighter Henry Higgins and downing tequila sunrises. I have a recollection almost as vivid as the drink, of Annie driving down a winding road over precipitous cliffs in the black night and me singing loudly and off key to Joni Mitchell on the tape player: "Went to a party down a red-dirt road / There were lots of pretty people there, reading *Rolling Stone*, reading *Vogue.*"

Jack was less than enchanted when, upon arriving at the hotel, I began to serenade him in our room. He was not feeling particularly well, having received that day in the mail a gift from Lou Adler of eight-day-old green corn tamales covered in mold from his favorite Mexican restaurant, El Cholo, in L.A., and having devoured them, green mold notwithstanding. And he had an early call.

Maria Schneider, the actress from *Last Tango in Paris*, was playing his lover in *The Passenger*; I didn't fear Maria as a rival, despite her sexiness. She was having a wild, volatile affair with Joey Townsend, another beautiful and interesting girl, largely conducted beside the hotel swimming pool. David Bailey had asked me to go on a trip to Corsica for British *Vogue*, but I was very torn about leaving Jack, even briefly. Ara counseled me with a quote from the *I Ching*—to paraphrase somewhat, "If he belongs with you, the horse shall return," or some such sage advice. Since the Apollonia incident, I was sure that Jack would forget me instantly and have an affair with someone else. However, I followed Ara's counsel.

It was only after my bags were packed and the car that was taking me to the airport was idling downstairs that Jack looked deep into my eyes and said, "Please stay." But it was too late. I left for Paris.

There was evidence after Spain that Jack had slept with a script supervisor. Whenever I was suspicious and I'd start looking around for evidence—in his wallet, his bureau, his bedside drawer—there was never a time when I did not find some telltale item, some scrap of inflammatory confirmation, so at a certain point I stopped snooping, but I also stopped trusting him.

I went off to the South of France to do a series of pictures for British *Vogue* in Nice and then Corsica, with Manolo Blahnik, photographed by David Bailey. I wasn't getting the kind of attention I needed, and Jack had allowed me to leave. He had not regretted my imminent departure until the very last minute. And Bailey was seductive.

En route to Nice from Barcelona via Paris, I holed up for one night alone at the Esmeralda, the most romantic little hotel on the Left Bank, with Notre Dame framed in the window in amber light. That night I received flowers from both Jack and Bailey and felt good with the world. My room was on the top floor—wallpaper with green birds and butterflies on a sepia background, antique mirrors hung on the walls, my flowers in big jugs on a marble-topped chest, and in the morning peach sunlight seeping through the open window overlooking the Seine. The birds sang; there was little traffic. I looked out over the top-hat chimneys, the gray slate domes with attic windows. Breakfast came, coffee and croissants. I was in a Colette state of mind, alone with my roses and lilies. August in Paris.

When I arrived in Nice the following day, I met up with Bailey, Grace Coddington, and Manolo Blahnik. Manolo and I were meeting for the first time, and I liked him instantly. To Manolo, everything was "amusing." He was prone to short sound bites, yelps of contrasting hysteria and humor, in moments of outrage or pleasure. I remember some photographs at the Negresco Hotel as the first we shot in the series. Grace procured fresh orchids and pinned them to my hair and the shoulder straps of my dress. I was lounging on a bed with Manolo in the foreground on a telephone.

It was Bailey's idea that we go to Helmut Newton's house the following day and also try to fit in a visit to David Hamilton's farm in the same area. David Hamilton's photography was generally of very young girls provocatively posed in soft focus. Bailey decided to do a takeoff on David's work, at David's farm. It was an inside joke, and the same went for the picture at Helmut's: I stood in the doorway of his cottage like a Newton model, in shades and a black beret. Helmut and his wife, June, even posed in some of the pictures. Later on that evening, June attempted to hypnotize me.

Bailey and I were drinking a fair amount of wine in the evenings. Before the morning departure to Corsica, we shared a couple of Fernet Brancas in the departure lounge to dispel our collective hangovers. When we actually took our seats on the flight, we were slightly unhinged by the presence

of a large group of nuns heading home in what turned out
to be a lightning storm. The flight was extremely turbulent.
We gleaned from the steward that this group was in fact taking a deceased sister home. When we landed, the storm had
abated, although the runway was flooded and the clouds were
scattered and gray in a cold lemon glow off the horizon. A
man from the travel agency met us in a station wagon. When
he opened the trunk of his car, I was surprised to see several
repeating rifles, a sort of traveling garrison of machine guns,
which he moved aside to make room for our luggage.

The hotel staff was almost entirely West African. The
waiters in the hotel didn't speak a word of English, nor, did
it seem, French. They had a fleeting-eyed, nervous look, like
boat people who didn't know where they had landed. They
always seemed to be on the verge of suggesting a deal one
might not want to partake in.

That evening we decided to go into the capital, Ajaccio,
for dinner, but the hotel told us that for some reason it was
possible to eat only between the hours of seven and eight—
otherwise, we would go to bed hungry. As we descended the
hill into town, three Black Marias flew past us. The main
square was filled with riot police in uniform, and the doors
to all business establishments, including restaurants, were
firmly locked and bolted. So much for dinner.

The following morning I was awakened by a strange chor-
tling noise from an adjacent balcony. This turned out to be
Manolo chanting, "Vive la Corse!" to no one in particular. I
joined in this exercise for a while, and then we got a call to
pull ourselves together; Bailey wanted to hit the road early.

Several hours later, we were in the mountains. On each
hairpin turn, a pile of stones, a crucifix, a bunch of flowers—

some faded, some fresh. It seemed that people were careening off these cliffs regularly, given the profusion of roadside shrines. Up and up we went. The scrub turned to dark green and the mountains peaked around us. There was no one on the road. No cars. No buses. Eventually, we arrived at a citadel of white barracks and a surrounding cobblestone village of whitewashed concrete blocks. When we got out of the car and walked into a café, we noticed that the sole occupant wore a white uniform with a kepi. He was heavily scarred, had a facial twitch, and was armed with a pistol. We didn't see many soldiers, but the ones we did see were shaved-headed, introverted, strange. It turned out we were at an outpost of the French Foreign Legion. All were dressed in white, as though they were fighting a ghost war up there in the mountains.

Evening fell as we made our way back to Ajaccio precisely on time for dinner at the harbor. As we were sitting by the bollards lining the dock outside the restaurant, waiting to be allowed in, Bailey said something like "You'd be mad not to marry me." And I said, "Don't be ridiculous." And that subject never came up again, although we enjoyed a short but most pleasant affair. I was still in love with Jack, but I was in a replica of my parents' relationship, during which both of them strayed—the "If that's what you want to do, then I can do that, too" syndrome. I wasn't going to hang around and let Jack treat me badly.

The next day we buried Manolo in the sand for a photograph. He claimed to have the unpleasant sensation of being entombed. I was fascinated at how many shotgun shells I found on the beach and, oddly, how many pairs of shoes, as though their owners had suddenly just airlifted out of them.

Grace joined us in another picture, putting on a cloak and a black beret with her red hair flying in the wind, and Manolo dressed like Picasso in a striped shirt and espadrilles. Manolo and I toasted the sunset with champagne, and Bailey took the photograph, which later got to be on the cover of the magazine.

CHAPTER 3

Two days after finishing *The Passenger*, Jack started *China-town*, arguably the most beautiful and authentic film ever to be made on location in Los Angeles, about Los Angeles. From the seamless pairing of the city's little-appreciated but fabulous original architecture with Richard Sylbert's inspired interiors, to the costumes and wardrobes for the actors by the great designer Anthea Sylbert, to the creative cinematography of John Alonzo, to the masterly direction of Roman Polanski, the movie looked like a classic black-and-white film magically transposed to color. Everything was right, from the shots of the orange orchards to the vintage cars; indoors, the photography was deep and saturated, and the exteriors, by contrast, were baked and dry as a desert. It's a movie about water, and about the corruption that lies beneath the surface of the city. The performances are veiled and mysterious. Faye Dunaway, fine as an Italian greyhound, portrays Evelyn Mulwray, the haunted heroine who carries a terrible secret, and Jack, the private detective J. J. Gittes who follows the trail of corruption that leads to the character Noah Cross, played by my father.

Jack and Roman were already friends, and Dad and Jack got on really well, sharing some philosophical conversations and a lot of laughs. It was during *Chinatown* that I moved out of Beachwood and into Jack's house. My furniture from my mother's house in London was still in storage, so the stuff I was moving was mostly clothes. Since we had returned to Los Angeles after *The Passenger*, I had been spending every night at Jack's. By this point, I had developed more of a sense of etiquette insofar as visiting sets was concerned, or so I thought. I had never enjoyed visits to Dad's locations as a child, because there was always that feeling of being extraneous and in the way, but when Dad asked me to come visit him on the *Chinatown* set, I agreed. At a long table outdoors, having lunch, Jack on one side, my father on the other, Polanski at the head of the table, I sat down quietly beside Jack. Out of nowhere, my father, eyeing him malevolently, said, "I hear you are sleeping with my daughter"—long pause—"Mr. Gittes." I went bright red, and then I realized: they were rehearsing. Everyone burst out laughing.

Later, the word from set was that Roman and Faye had gotten into an altercation because he had plucked a stray hair from her head before a scene. This story became magnified and amplified in the retelling, but I believe it held up filming for a day or so.

On my father's last night of shooting, I came to set again. Annie had agreed to meet me at the Luau in Beverly Hills before going out to location. We ordered a fortifying cocktail and headed for Chinatown. Night had fallen, and when we arrived on set, I could see through the window of Dad's trailer a half-empty bottle of Stolichnaya on a table. I knocked on his door and he called for me to enter. As soon as I did, I was met with a cold reception. What had taken me so long? What had I been up to?

They were taking a long time to light the scene. It was

to be the horrible denouement of the film, involving Noah
Cross and his daughter. Fact and fiction sometimes blur, and
it began to dawn that Dad was practicing on me. The crew
broke for supper. It was about one o'clock in the morning.
Dad and Annie and Jack and I were in the back booth at a
café, having egg foo yung for dinner. Dad dropped a noodle
on his lapel but didn't seem to notice. Jack reached over deli-
cately with his chopsticks. "Let me help you with that, John,"
he said good-naturedly. They wrapped the final scene at 5 A.M.

Jack took me to Aspen in the winter of 1973. There were no
ostentatious mega-chalets or dress codes, makeup was considered corny, and we never dreamed of putting on a snow-
suit. We lived in blue jeans and stayed at the beautiful rustic
mountain home of Bob and Toby Rafelson in Castle Creek.
Bob had directed Jack in several films, including *The King of
Marvin Gardens* and *Five Easy Pieces*. Jack called Bob "Curly"
and Toby "Bums," names that have stuck to this day.

It was through them that I met Paul Pascarella, an artist
who drew birds and buffaloes and burned and tooled leather
and deerskin. Jack bought me a poncho painted like a thun-
derbird, which I wore with the gray fox-fur stole and Borsa-
lino hat he gave me for Christmas. Paul was one of the best
chefs I have ever come across. His dinners were a harmoni-
ous assortment of ingredients shopped, picked, hunted, and
found. He was a shaman in the kitchen, and a lovely skier.

I hadn't skied since I was sixteen, in Klosters, where Tony
and I went on winter holidays with our mother as children. I
remember following Paul downhill in the still, cloudy silence
of the mountains when the visibility was flat or when snow
was falling and the moguls were hard to see. He'd make wide

arcs and long, sleek traverses, as though moving to music. Occasionally, I would fatigue and totally lose control skiing, humiliating myself once in a doubleheader by crashing into Teddy Kennedy and then crossing over Martina Navratilova's skis as she was preparing to descend; to her credit, she simply arched an eyebrow. Roman came to Aspen that winter as well. He wore red-and-white racing spandex and was an excellent athlete.

Jack was introduced to Aspen by the fourteen-year-old daughter of his acquaintance Art Pfister, who owned Buttermilk and Ajax mountains. Her name was Nancy, and she was a wild child, a free spirit, and an amazing skier. A few years later, Nancy found a perfect house for Jack above a beautiful beaver pond in the Maroon Bells. In those days there were at least eight pubs on Main Street. After our last descent of the evening, we'd go to the bar at the Jerome Hotel for Irish coffee. Ads proclaiming Hunter Thompson's run for sheriff were prominently displayed on the forest-green walls.

I liked Hunter, but he frightened me, and there were myriad stories about his wild behavior out at Owl Farm in Woody Creek. And yet Hunter might make an appearance on a winter's evening, shuffling through the snowbanks into the house, legs bare to the freezing cold, in flip-flops and madras shorts, for a quiet Jacuzzi or a gentlemen's conversation with Jack and Bob Rafelson over a good bourbon, without incident. I always considered this a miracle, having heard of his vast capacity for mischief. I respected his girlfriend, Laila Nabulsi, a beautiful Palestinian-American girl, for her bravery living with him in the wilderness in Woody Creek, where at one point later in life he accidentally shot his assistant in the buttocks, thinking she was a bear.

Jack and I returned to L.A. after New Year's on a Learjet with David Geffen and Cher, his new girlfriend.

The first time I saw Las Vegas was through the open window of a limousine with Jack. It was a black velvet night, the strip still baking from the blazing sun of day, a reddening of the sky over a gash on the desert floor, ahead of us a ribbon of colored lights flashing like a gaudy fault line. On both sides of the street, an effulgent avenue of kitsch—the Flamingo's shocking-pink casino, the Roman columns of Caesars Palace, and on the pavement the transients, adrenaline junkies, hawkers, hookers, dancers, gangsters with their girlfriends and their bodyguards.

Jack and I were there to see Frank Sinatra, basking in the afterglow of a comeback album, *Ol' Blue Eyes Is Back*. Onstage at Caesars Palace, he ambled from the wings with a whiskey in one hand and a cigarette in the other and settled in front of the audience like the king of his domain. His eyes were indeed as blue as periwinkles; his voice was slightly mocking but still sounded like the silken tone from the record player at St. Clerans, on the album *In the Wee Small Hours*, its cover depicting Frank standing under a blue streetlamp wearing a gray fedora. After the concert, we went upstairs to the penthouse suite, an open-layout space with white shag and gold mosaic, and a thin veneer of glassy marble on the floor. After a wait of some twenty minutes and some speculation as to whether he would appear at all, the door to the suite was flung open. Surrounded by bodyguards, Sinatra swept through the foyer, calling out, "Tina!" His entourage hard-shouldered everything in their path, leaving a note of bewilderment in their wake.

On another occasion we flew back to Las Vegas with Lou Adler and his new girlfriend, Phyllis Somer, to see Muhammad Ali fight at Caesars Palace. The ring was elevated in a pool of golden light, and all around us, a magnificent display of jewels, sequins, and plumage glinted in the audience. The women were dressed to the nines, some with gardenias in their hair, and the atmosphere was high-tension. Many of the older fighters were there; we said hello to Joe Louis. I loved going to the heavyweight fights with Jack: the audiences and the entourages, the women and the athletes, stunning and adrenalized, like a four-ring human circus.

In the spring of 1974, we went to Cannes when Jack was nominated for best actor for *The Last Detail*. The festivities took place at the old opera house, the Palais des Festivals on the boulevard de la Croisette. We were escorted indoors, past a throng waiting in a light rain. Inside, the theater was humid and packed with people. As soon as we got to the circle upstairs, before we took our seats, they called out Jack's name. He dropped my hand and proceeded to the stage to collect his prize, a pair of gold cuff links with an olive peace branch—the logo of the festival. The dress circle rose to its feet in thunderous applause. I was alone in the mob, barely able to glimpse, through the thicket of bodies, Jack's big white happy smile. He was comfortable in the public eye and seemed to have forgotten I was there.

I remember screenings of two movies—*The Holy Mountain*, by Alejandro Jodorowsky, and Bert Schneider's heartbreaking documentary about Vietnam, *Hearts and Minds*. After the screenings, we walked down the Croisette toward the Majestic, where we were staying—Jack, Bert, Annie, Joan

Buck, and the director Henry Jaglom. Joan and I were both wearing white. She was my childhood friend, and we were like sisters. She had come in from Rome, where she was bureau chief for *Women's Wear Daily*. When we entered the lobby of the hotel, Josephine Baker saw us and called out, *"Regardez! Mais elles sont des anges!"* It thrilled us to be deemed angels by this goddess.

Even though Jack and I were by now a couple, pretty French girls would come up on motorbikes and say, "Oh, Jack, you want to ride on my bike with me?" And he'd get on the bike and leave me standing on the sidewalk. Finally, I would just retire to our hotel room in tears. I remember another year, during a particularly awful week there, when everyone was going on Jean-Pierre Rassam's boat. One of the most powerful producers in Cannes, he wore black silk Chinese pajamas and looked nefarious. His aide-de-camp, who trawled the harbor and picked up girls, was an unsavory guy called Joe Le Porno. Whenever Jack and I would wind up on Rassam's boat, I felt uncomfortable. I didn't like the milieu; it brought out the convent girl in me. But it was part of what went on at movie festivals.

As far as I guessed, no one cared about me, and my way of coping was to retreat to my bed. Jack would trot in from the Croisette between screenings and the attentions of beautiful, forthright Frenchwomen, and toss onto the duvet the odd little oil painting or trinket he'd bought for me, hoping I'd lighten up. And I would sulk, jealously hoping he would linger long enough for me to forgive him for enjoying all that attention.

Above Cannes, for respite, there was the lovely Nid du Duc—Tony Richardson's house, set high in the hills. Tony was always surrounded by friends, wives, partners, and daughters. On one visit, Jack and I stayed there in a little cottage below the swimming pool. The first vision of the morning was David Hockney, in a pistachio-green suit with pink shirt and bow tie, under a fine white panama hat, painting alfresco with palette and easel. He was amazingly prolific. By lunch—as shopped for, cooked, and served by Tony's partner, Grizelda Grimond, and his beautiful daughters, Natasha and Joely—the morning's painting was completed, with its title in block letters on the canvas: *La Piscine*. Sir John Gielgud was also a guest.

Nearby were Arles, Les Baux, and Grasse, where they distill the flowers for all the perfume in France, the Matisse Chapel, and the Maeght Foundation in St. Paul de Vence, which houses a remarkable army of Giacometti's standing figures. I had last seen the pieces on a trip to Vence in the sixties with the Bucks, when I stayed at Cap Ferrat one summer with Joan. One always made the pilgrimage to La Colombe d'Or restaurant, where they have a very good collection of Impressionist paintings dating from the days when artists who couldn't afford to pay their bills exchanged work for food.

That first time in Cannes, Sam Spiegel was trying to persuade Jack to work with Elia Kazan, who would be directing Sam's next movie, *The Last Tycoon*. Sam's yacht, the *Malahne*, was docked in prime position in the harbor at Cannes; it was a gorgeous boat, not ridiculously ostentatious, just pure luxury. Its interiors were tasteful beige and maritime navy blue, the fittings all brass and teak. Sam was a generous host, albeit a touch controlling. Once when I was there, he lashed into Sophie, the stunned widow of Anatole Litvak, for lighting up a cigarette in the dining room; this in an era of smokers, while all the men were puffing on cigars and Sam, himself no puppy in his middle to late seventies, was entertaining a seventeen-year-old girl and her midwestern parents, who seemed somewhat bewildered but not displeased to have fallen into Sam's lair. After the festival, Sam loved to sail to the Italian Riviera down the Amalfi coast, overnight to Portofino. We were expected on deck for bullshots before dinner, rain or shine; if it was inclement, you could choose from a selection of blue wool pea coats with brass buttons. Sam didn't take no for an answer. On the way out of the harbor one day, we passed Stavros Niarchos's boat, a white shark the size of a small battleship, rumored to be the world's largest floating art gallery, idling in deep waters. After sailing through the night, waking up to find ourselves docking in Portofino, the walls of the town blushing as the sun rose over the sea, was a most lovely sight. Mum first brought me to Italy when I was a small child, and I always feel close to her there.

CHAPTER 4

On July 8, my twenty-third birthday, Jack started work on *The Fortune*. The script was written by his friend Carole Eastman, and Mike Nichols was set to direct. When I told Jack that I would like to work in movies, he shook his head, declaring that he hated actresses, but later suggested that *The Fortune* might be a good vehicle for us to do together. He put forward the idea to Mike Nichols. I was reluctant to make the same mistake I had made on *A Walk with Love and Death*, working too closely with my family. As I remember, Mike and Jack wanted me to try out for the female lead. But I thought the situation was dangerously nepotistic, and I didn't feel brave enough to participate. My reluctance was ultimately a boon to everyone, as the picture became the debut of a young actress called Stockard Channing. Jack and Warren Beatty were sharing the screen on *The Fortune*, and they spent much of their time, when not together, speaking to each other sotto voce on the phone. They seemed to have a lot to talk about. Warren was dating Jack's old flame Michelle Phillips.

Jack chose a very unsightly hairstyle for himself in *The Fortune*—a disastrous, frizzy permanent wave. I couldn't help feeling this commendable sacrifice of vanity might not be a good decision on his part. But Jack, a natural egotist, did not harbor fears to that end and managed happily to render himself quite unattractive, which was a real accomplishment for one of the world's best-looking men.

One morning I was in Jack's trailer when the telephone rang. Someone at the house had received a message asking him to call a number in New Jersey. Jack's sister Lorraine and brother-in-law, Shorty, were the two remaining members of his family living there. His mother, "Mud"—who owned a beauty parlor in Neptune, New Jersey, and had put curlers in his hair when he was a child—and his sister June, a beautiful brunette Earl Carroll showgirl, had both died from cancer some years earlier, as had his father, who, from what I gathered, was an enigmatic alcoholic figure who dropped by the house very sporadically in Jack's youth. Jack was slightly thrown off by this message, but he called the phone number in New Jersey even though he didn't recognize it.

A woman answered, claiming that she was married to Jack's real father, the former lover of his sister June, and that he wanted a word with Jack. She continued, telling him that June, who hitherto he had thought was his sister, was in fact his mother. "Mud," the woman claimed, was his grandmother. Jack was in shock. He called Shorty later that evening. Shorty denied everything at first, then Jack got to the bottom of the story with Lorraine. She confirmed the truth. The damage was already done: all those years, all that deception, all that was left untold and unexplained.

By the time Jack found out that he was in fact his sister's son, both she and his grandmother had died, so there was no one to confront about these past events. Jack seemed to have no interest in starting up relations with his "new" family and seldom spoke of the situation.

* * *

Jack was not fazed by much. He liked his creature comforts and had a real zest for life. He liked to travel, especially to Europe. He loved to collect people. Paternally, he would call us "my people." This designation included Annie, Helena, and whoever else was in close attendance. At the time the generality of it bugged me; I wanted to be special, and I felt a loss of identity. "Where are my people?" But there was very much a sense with Jack that one was on his team. And it was a good team to be on. A strong team. The winning team. Jack held on to his friends, many of whom he'd known for a long time. He kept a special place in his heart for fellow journeymen from his early days in Los Angeles or, reaching further back, favored pals from Manasquan High School in New Jersey.

Jack had a temper and an extremely good command of the language, but he didn't have my father's vodka edge. They were both literate. Jack was reading Freud, Jung, Nietzsche, and the Princeton psychologist Julian Jaynes's *The Origin of Consciousness in the Breakdown of the Bicameral Mind*.

My father and Jack were a lot alike. They both loved personalities—sometimes freakish or irritating people if only because they possessed an uncommonly interesting trait, like looking a certain way or reminding them of someone else, or people who were regional types. It was like casting your life with character actors.

Jack could be awfully generous, as with his kindness toward Allegra, his inclusiveness. It was not long before Allegra told Dad that she didn't need Nurse to tie her shoelaces anymore, and moved in with Dad, Cici, and Collin at the Palisades, and Nurse returned to Ireland. At the time, I was more upset than anyone by this change. Nurse had been with the family since I

47

was two years old. Dad asked Tony and me to invest some of the money that would be coming to us in his will to help buy a house for her on the outskirts of Dublin, in Roscommon, which we were grateful to do. We had all agreed that Nurse was the closest thing to a saint there was.

Jack's daughter Jennifer, from his marriage to the actress Sandra Knight, was a sweetheart. Jack called Allegra "Legsy" and Jennifer "The Bimbereen." Jennifer was a year older than Allegra, and often came to Aspen with us at Christmas, or to London—wherever he was traveling to work.

There was a profound and devoted sense of loyalty with Jack. If he invested in you, or if he placed his heart with you, it meant something for life. Jack had a very healthy aware-ness and a self-approbation that you could enjoy with him. He saw the lunacy in situations and was generally at the cen-ter of it. Jack could wear clothes like no one else on earth. I walked into Harrods one day and bought him the yellow silk jacket he wore later in *Prizzi's Honor.* There was a sense of festival and holiday to the way he dressed. Jack could have the greatest fun with clothes of anybody I knew. He could wear something that on any other man would make you cringe. Something about the way Jack took on color and shape in clothes kind of exalted what was unique and great about him.

I remember going out to dinner one evening with Jim and Holly Brooks in New York. Holly was a big girl. And Jack, at some point, contrived to have her lend him her stiletto heels, in which he proceeded to walk through the Carlyle Hotel lobby—clickety-clack on the marble floor in the toniest hotel in New York. On another outing, Susan Forristal was walk-ing with us on Fifth Avenue when Jack decided he was going to act like an infant. For the whole walk down Fifth Avenue back to the hotel, he would run halfway across a street, then jump up and down on the curb and flap his arms—stupid toddler stuff.

There had been a time when Jack courted Susan, whom he had rechristened "The Admiral" or, for short, "Addo." On a previous trip to New York, I had been put out when he booked a lunch alone with her. Some months later, Suze and I were in my car going up Coldwater Canyon, and she said, "Anjel, I want you to know, I love Jack dearly, but he is with you, and I respect that and would never attempt to subvert it in any way." It was a thoughtful thing to say, and I was always grateful to her. When I was with Jack, there were very few women I trusted.

Jack was prompt at sending flowers, and chocolates on Valentine's Day. Annie covered him well. He liked to give beautiful presents. He often thrilled me with generous gifts of jewels and furs. We thought fur was just great in those days. He even gave me a drawing by the eighteenth-century painter Giovanni Battista Tiepolo.

Jack's enthusiasm for certain things, like basketball, was joyously unrestrained. The first few years I was with him, I was determined to love the Los Angeles Lakers. Several times a week, I'd watch these guys with huge feet squeaking as they thundered up and down the floor at the Forum. It was relentless, and they'd always lose. Heading to the car, Jack would be momentarily despondent. Chick Hearn would be on the radio, rehashing the game. Lou Adler would be in the passenger seat, and I'd be sitting there in the back of Bing, staring out at Inglewood, thinking, "Why in God's name am I here?" The only reason I was there was because I was in love.

Women will do strange things for love, as I learned in childhood, like pretend to know how to ride horses to impress my father, or stand alone and humiliated in a backless evening dress in a freezing marquee as my mother did, or, like me, go to basketball games in downtown Los Angeles to watch a team they don't care about lose miserably three times a week.

Jack had tickets to a UCLA game in Portland, Oregon, once, and he said, "You're coming, Toots." I hated flying, and I had no idea how far it was. The flight was bumpy and lasted three or four hours. When we finally got to the game, the team fell behind instantly and was crushed. At a nearby motel that night, Jack was going on and on about a UCLA player whose athletic prowess had fallen short when I finally said, "Jack, this is unbearable. Let's turn on the TV." A show called *The Newlywed Game* was on. We watched for a few minutes in silence, then Jack said mockingly, "Oh, little marriage. Little tiny marriage game." And I replied, "If you had any balls, you'd marry me." And he said, "Marry you? Are you kidding?"

I wept all the way back to L.A. and sobbed for three more days after that. Jack just didn't get it. He'd say something innocently, and I would plunge into a sea of tears, go to my bed, and turn my face to the wall—something I'd possibly learned from my mother and honed through my years with Bob Richardson.

At a certain point, I decided I just couldn't bear basketball anymore. One night I begged off. I said, "Jack, I've got a dinner with the girls I can't get out of." Naturally, the Lakers won that night, so I was never invited again. "No way. No, Toots. You can't come. You're bad luck." I'm sure it was just an excuse. He probably had some other bird on his arm.

People think, "Jack the joker"—Jack's all about fun. And he pulls it off successfully, but it is a one-dimensional view. He is emotional. Life touches him, and moves him, and upsets him. He is a deep and serious person. He takes things harder than you'd imagine or than he would want you to know. On the other hand, perhaps in part because of the early experience of everyone in his family lying to him about his birth, it is not surprising that he's quite cynical.

Jack's house was a gray stucco bungalow typical of California in the early sixties. In my first year with Jack, my model friend Phyllis Major came over from Paris to visit. Those days she was dating the singer Jackson Browne and planning to marry him. She suggested that we should have Jack's outside walls repainted barn red, which was a big improvement. The property overlooked both the Valley and Beverly Hills, and at night the view of the city lights in the Valley was a vast sea of fluorescence. On the other side of the house, a canyon sheltered a large reservoir, where Jack and I would often go running.

I was spending my days at Jack's house, very much in love with him but feeling thwarted professionally. There was a degree of absurdity to my position in that I was the girlfriend of the world's most famous actor, but I didn't want parts to come to me because I was with him. I had contempt for that idea.

Every day scripts arrived for Jack and he complained that he didn't have the time to read them all. Everyone was pressing him to do this or that. Every phone call was a proposition or a proposal. I announced to Joan that I had decided to become a lady of leisure. Joan Buck, to whom work was something of a religion, was clearly horrified.

51

When I moved into Jack's house, it seemed there really was no niche that I could fit into other than his bed. The food was cooked, the flowers arranged; he was more than catered to. I had a bad habit of popping open Coca-Cola cans, taking a couple of sips, and leaving them around the house, two or three at a time. Someone complained to Jack about that, and there were little asides from Annie and Helena as to why I shouldn't draw on the notepads by the telephone. I found this irritating—why couldn't Jack tell me himself? I was embarrassed by the criticism. It made me feel like an errant child. But as soon as I got over it and realized that they were just attempting to follow Jack's direction, both women became my lifelong friends.

My attempts to imprint on Jack's territory occasionally proved disastrous, as when I insisted on the hiring of Cici's Jacuzzi builder to make a similar one in Jack's back yard. Unfortunately, a key element was omitted, the pipes became clogged with hard cement, and the contractor went on a bender and disappeared. Eventually, the whole mess had to be drilled out of the ground, very loudly and at great expense. Jack and I were not too lucky with bathtubs.

Jack loved his house on the hill, its walls plastered with paintings. He knew a good deal about art and learned more as he accumulated a diverse and eclectic collection, for the most part building it on his own instinct. He had a personal affinity for pigs and a prime collection of porcine artifacts—photographs and porcelains, which overflowed the bookshelves. People sent pigs to Jack on a regular basis.

A few of our best fights centered on picture hanging, as he was even more averse than I was to changing what was already on a wall. It was a problem, given that he was prone to augmenting the collection with no particular regard for the lack of space, and to setting up a visual potpourri mixing styles and dates, which made me crazy. Ultimately, he solved this problem by acquiring other real estate properties next to his own, which helped in part to accommodate the artwork.

Marlon Brando lived farther up the hill from Jack, and they shared a driveway. At one point, having gone very green and eager to recycle the contents of his sewage tank, Marlon redesigned his watering system to irrigate the pepper trees Helena had planted along the driveway. So although the trees thrived, there was, for a short while, the low-lying odor of human waste on the property.

Marlon had several children, and the two eldest, Christian and Miko, would often pass Jack's house to go next door to see Helena. She was sympathetic to them. Christian was very handsome, but he was troubled and seemed somewhat adrift. He had his father's charisma and wanted to act, but Marlon never condoned it. Often, Christian would bring his crossbreed pit bull–German shepherd, Feisty, through the property with several other half-breed mutts who had taken to running in a pack.

Feisty and our Labrador mix, Big Boy, got into it a few times, and I usually wound up yelling at Christian to keep his animals under control. Helena had a little white bichon frise called Sasa, and I feared for her life, with good reason: Feisty went after her and killed her. One morning after I walked down the driveway to the post box with Big Boy at my heels, I had turned back to retrace my steps to the house when Feisty and three other big dogs approached us in a pack and crouched around Big Boy and me, as if they were circling game. I was frightened and stopped in my tracks. I heard a deep growl low in Big Boy's throat. I held on to his collar, and one by one we passed them all, with Feisty backing down like the coward he was.

When I first met Marlon, in Ireland, he seemed to like me more than he did when we met the second time around in Los Angeles. I daresay it was because I was no longer a child and had become shyer and more solemn and harder to talk to as a young woman.

Marlon loved to make practical jokes and generally engaged Helena to put them into effect on April Fools' Day. Once Marlon instructed her to report to Jack that he had decided to sell his house to Sylvester Stallone, claiming that having been offered so much money for the property, he simply couldn't afford to turn it down. While Stallone in those days traveled with a small army of bodyguards and lived a notably opulent lifestyle, Jack prided himself on his talent for privacy, moving under the radar whenever he wished, even though he had one of the most famous faces in the world. The thought of all those Stallone fans at the gate worried him to no end. Marlon thought that was just hilarious.

CHAPTER 5

I got a call from Michael Douglas, asking if I would give Jack a script. It was a film he had wanted to do with his father, Kirk, from a novel by Ken Kesey called *One Flew Over the Cuckoo's Nest*. They had rethought the movie and wanted to recast with a younger actor. Michael felt that Jack was the perfect choice to play Randle P. McMurphy, a criminal who pleads insanity to get himself moved from prison to a psych ward. McMurphy is one of the last of the literary American rebels, before everyone descended into pallor and angst. It was an iconic role, and Jack brought to it insolence and animal intelligence. Even in a lunatic asylum—maybe especially in a lunatic asylum—Jack is robust. The film was shot on the grounds of the state hospital for the mentally ill in Salem, Oregon. To an outsider, it appeared that there was an invisible thread, an artery, that bound the members of that community to the asylum. Everyone living in town, it seemed, had a history with it or a connection to it.

When I was still in L.A. and Jack was already ensconced in Salem, I invited Nancy Pfister to accompany me and Big Boy in my little bullet-gray Mercedes on a three-day road trip to Oregon. There was a detour in getting there—I awakened from a deep sleep to find us pulled over on the side of the road by the Arizona Highway Patrol, Nancy having been apprehended for going over 100 mph in a 55 zone. She had also traveled ninety-five miles in the wrong direction. Eyeing my tweed hat, which happened to be sitting on Nancy's head, I hoped the officer wouldn't search us for marijuana. The last time I'd seen it, the bag was sitting on the dashboard. The cop was a kindly sort and offered to show us the way to the local police station so we could just pay the fine off the bat; we followed him there, paid our ticket, and walked to the parking lot. "What did you do with the grass?" I asked when we got back into the car. Nancy lifted my hat from her head, pulled out the stash, and gave me a wink.

Eventually, we got to Salem. Jack was occupying a model home on a lake filled with swans and mallards, next to two other model homes: on the right, Michael Douglas, who was producing *Cuckoo's Nest*, and his girlfriend, Brenda Vaccaro, the hot actress from *Midnight Cowboy*; on the other side, Milos Forman, the director of the film, and his companion, the lovely French actress Aurore Clément, François Truffaut's last muse. When Nancy and Big Boy and I moved in on Jack, his blood pressure rose. Big Boy started to misbehave, eating most of the ducks on Hidden Lakes in one fell swoop. Although I would try to restrict him to the leash, at some point I would start to pity him and let him off for a romp and he'd be gone, running up to the top of the city dump, or off to the supermarket to sniff up some woman's skirt. After one such escape, it took an army of dogcatchers from the local shelter to eventually capture him. He was generally listed as a Newfoundland because he was so large, but in fact he was half Labrador, half golden retriever. Jack had chosen the puppy from a litter belonging to his ex-wife, Sandra Knight. And he was a truly fantastic dog, but up until two years old, he was nothing but trouble.

One night all hell broke loose when Jack and I came home from a dinner out, having left Big Boy alone in the house. It looked as if we'd been invaded by swamp alligators. The white shag rugs were filthy, the curtains all chewed off at two feet. For several days after work, Jack holed up with Big Boy in the garage for a series of exercises to bend a dog's mind. Big Boy made a turnaround and became a saint among Labradors. Except for drinking paint thinner and getting hit by multiple cars on public holidays, he was a dream of a dog.

Aurore cooked local crab for the whole crew one night, and everyone declared it the best dinner they ever had. A few days following her triumph, I drove the nearly fifty miles to Portland to purchase live crab, as she had done. I wound up buying some natural deerskin boots that were too small for me, loading bushels of desperately clawing live crustaceans in buckets into the back seat of my car, and heading back to Salem in the relentless rain. Unfortunately, when it came to cooking them, it had never occurred to me that you had to gut the crabs, and I was terribly embarrassed, as they were totally inedible. I'd made nothing else for dinner. An ear of corn, perhaps. The company left disgusted and hungry.

Things had become a little strained with Jack, who by this time had fully taken on the role of Randle P. McMurphy and had little time for me. When I read in the newspaper that he had been nominated for an Academy Award for Best Actor in *Chinatown*, I went shopping for a bottle of Cristal and a bunch of yellow gladioli, and headed over to the set to congratulate him. It was lunchtime. I climbed the steps into his trailer, pulled some water out of the tap for the flowers, and propped them in the sink, at which point Jack walked in, grim-faced from his morning in the asylum.

"Congratulations!" I said cheerily.

Jack waved his hand in disdain. "I don't have time for this," he said irritably. I brushed past him on my way out and got into my car. I stopped at Hidden Lakes to dry my tears and to collect Nancy and a few items of clothing on my way out of town, and then we headed off on a 627-mile nonstop ten-hour drive to Sun Valley, Idaho, to stay with some pro ski racer friends of hers, leaving Jack and Big Boy to ponder each other for a full week at Hidden Lakes.

As the road to Sun Valley became ever more frozen, we found ourselves skidding on a skating rink of black ice somewhere near Ketchum, Idaho. Finally, we located the chalet and hooked up with Nancy's ski racers, who shared their magic mushrooms with us and took us to spectacular runs on the mountains where the snow was fresh but not too deep and you could carve an arc like an angel's wing.

In 1975, Dad was directing *The Man Who Would Be King* in Morocco, with Michael Caine and Sean Connery. Cici had gone with him for a holiday and stayed at La Mamounia in Marrakesh, but fell ill and returned to Los Angeles early. Soon after, Collin and his nanny, a young Mexican woman called Maricela Hernandez, went to Morocco to visit Dad. Maricela was a quiet, mysterious girl with dark almond-shaped eyes and a short haircut; her features were primitive, like those of a jade mask from Veracruz.

When Dad got home to Los Angeles, something gave way between him and Cici; apart from fights they'd had related to the sale of St. Clerans, something had broken. Cici sneered at him and called him an old man, a fossil. Cici had seduced him with her amber eyes and tawny hair and tanned cleavage, and he couldn't believe that she had the audacity to turn against him. Cici was anything but half-measured. She could be your dearest friend or rise up against you like a lioness.

I received a call from Dad one morning some weeks after his return to the Palisades. He sounded terrible. "I want to see you," he said. "Meet me for lunch at the Brown Derby." I walked off the street into the restaurant's dark interior, my eyes adjusting to the light. I followed the maître d' to a table at the back of the room. Seated on a banquette, I watched Dad enter some few minutes later, moving stiffly forward to a seat opposite my own. I was struck by his grayish pallor. We ordered a bullshot.

"What is it, Dad?" I asked, fearing his reply with every corpuscle in my body. "What's going on?"

"It's Cici," he said, wincing. His eyes were red and downcast. "She is accusing me of having an affair."

"With whom?" I asked.

"Maricela," he replied.

"Is it true?" I asked. "Where there's smoke, there's fire sometimes."

Dad, a legendary ladies' man, looked at me as if, by asking the question, I'd openly betrayed him.

"Absolutely not," he said.

I read later in a book about the Huston family that my brother Tony had walked in on Dad and Maricela in Morocco—as quoted, "wrapped around each other like pretzels"—but I never asked him about the matter. However, there is no doubt that Maricela had become Dad's constant and intimate companion, his partner and confidante. After my conversation with Dad, I never needed or wanted to know the extent of their physical relationship.

When Cici told Dad that she wanted a divorce, he left for Xalapa, on the coast in Jalisco, Mexico, where he started a whole new chapter with Maricela. She was there for him and cared for him throughout the last twelve years of his life. Gladys moved to nearby Puerto Vallarta. I think Dad left Ireland, even though later he largely blamed Cici for the move, because his lungs couldn't take the cold anymore; he needed warm weather. He knew that in order to extend his life, he'd have to change climate. Allegra continued to live at Cici's.

Chinatown had an impressive eleven Academy Award nominations. Its producer, Bob Evans, hosted a small party for the film at his house in Beverly Hills, with Cristal and beluga caviar. For the ceremony, I wore a Halston dress with transparent sequins over painted silk that looked like fish scales. Jack wore black tie, shades, and a black beret. Faye Dunaway was in a bat-wing satin dress with her husband, the musician Peter Wolf, also in a black beret, by her side. If memory serves me, Robert Towne, who wrote the movie, also wore the ubiquitous beret, as did Lou Adler, who brought Lauren Hutton, bronzed and resplendent in Halston rainbow chiffon. The costume designer Anthea Sylbert was elegant in black and white with pearls. There was an atmosphere of expectancy. We were very excited. Everyone was convinced the movie would win.

It soon became evident that *Chinatown* was not doing well in competition. *Godfather II* won Best Picture, and Francis Coppola won for Best Director. Finally, the wind gone from our sails, we got into the car to leave the Dorothy Chandler Pavilion. Robert Towne was the lone member of the group holding a statue, for Best Original Screenplay. In the back of the limousine, embarrassed, he jokingly pretended to hide it under the armrest, as if it were not the highest accolade his industry had to offer but, rather, an object of shame. Jack was philosophical and Evans despondent. The highlight of my evening was meeting Fred Astaire. The following day, Hal Ashby came by the house on Mulholland and very sweetly gifted Jack the Oscar he had won for directing *In the Heat of the Night*. Hal was aptly named: he was a prince.

The state of Montana stretched out under an endless expanse of blue—Big Sky Country. It was July 1975 and Jack was making *The Missouri Breaks* with Marlon Brando costarring, along with Jack's traveling academy of favored actors, including Harry Dean Stanton, Freddie Forrest, Randy Quaid, and John Ryan; the film was produced by Elliott Kastner and directed by Arthur Penn. We were living in Billings, not a large town, so it was easy to maneuver my big rented Ford truck. I loved driving it, dressed up like a cowgirl, listening to Waylon Jennings on the radio.

Joan had left her job at *Women's Wear Daily* in Italy, had broken up with her boyfriend, and was looking for a new life when I sent her a postcard: "Come west, rest." She flew with me up to Montana from L.A. and we brought Allegra. Jack's daughter Jennifer was also there, so we were a happy little clan. Jack was renting a bungalow belonging to a Mr. Ikkes. Upon arrival, I found some love notes from a girl saying how much she missed Jack and how tender their lovemaking had been and how she couldn't wait to hear from him again. I was in floods of tears when I confronted him, but he told me a wild story about how they were really letters meant for Harry Dean, who had been impersonating him. For a sophisticated girl, I could be tragically gullible—maybe that's why acting has always appealed to me; if I want to, I can believe almost anything. I must have wanted desperately to buy this story, because it was so clearly far-fetched.

Early on in our stay, the plumbing in Joan's bathroom burst and the ground floor was covered in bilge water. Within minutes, Mr. Ikkes arrived and proceeded, somewhat to our surprise, to check his militia-sized arsenal, with everything from pistols to body armor and hand grenades hidden in a room-sized vault behind a slab of fake wood paneling in the basement.

Meanwhile, Jack and I were in the back yard having our picture taken by Harry Benson from *People* magazine, beside an aboveground swimming pool bubbling with mosquito larvae. The house was an exposed bungalow in a suburban neighborhood, and the bedroom windows looked out onto the street. Sometimes at night, giggling girls would come to spy on Jack, poking around in the bushes and peering through the blinds.

Joan remembers my cooking a lot of roast chicken, and when she wasn't catching up on reading the John Birch Society handbook or *The Total Woman* by Marabel Morgan in the Ikkes library, she was going out in my big truck to buy supplies for me at the local supermarket. Once she asked for veal from the butcher. "Hell," he said, "we don't kill 'em that young!"

I used to like to go to Skaggs, the drugstore, or down by the railroad tracks to the pawnshops on Second Street, full of wampum beads and steel guitars. On one of his days off, Jack and Annie and I took Joan and the girls to the Crow reservation and rented a boat to take us downriver, past marshes and wetlands to a verdant place called East Rosebud Lake. Other than on this strip of water, the state was in a severe drought, and grasshoppers were piled up in the doorways on the streets of Billings. I stood on a big rock by the highway and Joan took pictures of me as the Marlboro Man. Montana was a marvelous place to ride horses. I'd ridden in the mountains and in Irish stone wall country but never on the American prairie, with the vast blue sky above like a heavenly fishbowl. As a friend from Aspen used to say, "And not a cloud from here to Guam!"

One day I picked up a local newspaper to read about a runaway, a pregnant girl who had tried to steal a farmer's truck. Before she turned the key in the ignition, she'd written him a letter, explaining that she was desperate and needed to get out of town. The farmer shot her dead through the window when he saw her pulling away. The next day there was a picture of her parents in the paper, shaking hands with the guy.

Marlon had taken to residing in his Winnebago and eating alfresco under the stars. He had decided that, as the villain of the film, he was going to be experimental regarding how to send the other characters to their final end, and was thinking up various novel methods of incapacitating and slaughtering them. One device was a Catherine wheel with edges like a Ginsu blade. Along with this weapon, to give a necessary element of surprise, he had chosen to wear a frontier woman's costume, from wide cloth bonnet to layers of skirts and petticoats. Thereafter, we would watch Marlon bumping along, driving back and forth to set, his skirts billowing, perched like a great mother hen atop a little green Honda scooter. When Annie spotted him, she raised an eyebrow and remarked wryly, "From *The Wild Ones* to this?"

One weekend, Harry Dean Stanton called up and said to me, "Come over to the Red Dog Saloon. There's someone I want you to meet." When Annie and I walked into the café, a large man with a fixed eye and a black walrus mustache stood up. Harry Dean introduced him as the writer Jim Harrison.

Harry Dean was recalling a scene he'd shot the previous day with Marlon. In the movie, Marlon's character, the mercenary Clayton, wearing his dress, has tracked down Harry's character, Calvin, intent on killing him. Harry Dean, a Method actor, was taut with tension before the scene, as, wounded by the Catherine wheel, his character staggers to the riverbank, where he is to receive his coup de grâce. Arthur Penn called, "Action." The cameras rolled. Marlon dismounted from his mule, wagging, skipping, inventing snatches of dialogue, mugging through the death scene, which was meandering on. He was obviously having a whale of a time. Suddenly, the unexpected happened. Harry Dean lurched to his feet in the muddy river and lunged at Marlon, bringing him facedown in the water. A brief skirmish followed, a lot of white water, kicking and petticoats, and finally, they emerged, soaked from bonnet to boots, laughing hysterically. "Seriously, he was taking too long," Harry Dean explained. "He won't make that mistake again."

CHAPTER 6

It was October 29, 1975. Annie was packing Jack's bags; he was flying out to New York the following day.

"What's up with you?" he asked me. "Why are you so mad?"

I explained that it was because he had not invited me along.

"Evans is getting the key to New York!" he exclaimed. "None of the wives will be there." He was referring to Bob Evans, and there was a tone of civic loyalty in his voice.

I reminded Jack that we were unmarried and retreated to my room to sulk. Jack left shortly thereafter on the Paramount plane without much further ado.

I rang Jackie Bisset, who had invited us to a party at her house on Coldwater Canyon that night. I told her that Jack was in New York and that I was alone.

"Come anyway," she said. "I'd love to have you."

A few hours later, I was at one of several round tables in her living room, having dinner, when Ryan O'Neal came by. He knelt by my knee and motioned for me to lean close so he could whisper in my ear: "I've been wanting to talk to you all night. I need to talk to you." I should have known then that I was playing with fire. But I was just self-centered and egotistical and needy enough to follow up with him the next day. He had arranged with Lou Adler to invite me along to a

Lakers game on Jack's season ticket. I drove my car to Ryan's house in town, and after we smoked a joint, we set off for the Forum. We were late getting there, because we were high and talking and laughing along the way, getting lost in the cloudless wasteland of Inglewood. We arrived in the third quarter, giddy. The Lakers were losing and Lou was in a bad mood. I think he had suddenly realized his mistake in giving Jack's tickets to Ryan and allowing Ryan to invite me. I could see he felt we were violating his trust. He said good night to us coldly in the parking lot. I went with Ryan in his magenta-maroon Rolls-Royce Corniche, with the license plate PRO 3, back to his house off Tower Drive, and kissed him for six hours straight on the dining room table.

In my memory of Ryan, I see a golden specimen, always in motion, an Apollo. His red-brown skin was darker than his mane of yellow-blond hair. He was an athlete, a runner, a boxer, and a bully. He loved to play Frisbee on the beach. He was a gorgeous California native, born and bred in the Palisades, overlooking the Pacific Ocean, a peaceful name for a tumultuous sea.

When Jack returned from New York a few days later, I told him the news: I was in love and I was leaving him for Ryan O'Neal. Jack's reaction was not to criticize or attack me. He was by turns confident and horrified; this event was sudden and surprising to him. For me, too. It came totally out of left field. I had no idea such a thing might occur. In truth, I found it quite ridiculous. How could this have happened? After *Cuckoo's Nest* premiered on November 19, to great acclaim, Jack left for Aspen. There was never a confrontation between him and Ryan.

Although at first I stayed on at Mulholland Drive, I began

to go out to Ryan's house in Malibu on the weekends. Lou's girlfriend, Phyllis Somer, was my confidante. A California blonde with a great smile and a beautiful tanned body, she was living at Lou's house in Malibu, close to Ryan's on Broad Beach, and she gave me a song recorded by Mary MacGregor called "Torn Between Two Lovers." I said to Lou, "I know that after a couple of weeks, I'll be dragging home to Jack with a Frisbee around my neck."

I spent New Year's Eve with Apollonia, Ara, Lou, and John Phillips and his daughter, Mackenzie. Ryan was not with us. He and I had fought, as was to become our habit. He was demanding my attention by trying to hurt me. After the parties, we ran out onto the beach from Lou's house; the sunrise was luminescent, like the glass in his collection of Gallé lamps. We were all in evening dress. Lou said, "I've always wanted to walk down a beach in a tuxedo." He and John played football and made wonderful passes and catches, and on the way back to his house, Lou put his arm around me. I was grateful to him for that; I had always respected his friendship with Jack and had not meant to compromise his position. In a way, I was embarrassed, too, because I'd always found Ryan too eager socially. He had a rueful, self-deprecating charm. There was a molten quality to him, as if his engine ran too hot.

Ryan was very concerned with his daughter, Tatum, then about twelve, with whom he had filmed *Paper Moon*, with Peter Bogdanovich directing, and he brought her everywhere. Tatum was the youngest person ever to win a competitive Oscar, and I did not realize at first that they were almost a couple unto themselves; he seemed to have few boundaries with her when it came to taking her to clubs and parties.

She was included in many of the finer details and decisions regarding his life.

Ryan had amassed a list of gorgeous conquests, from his wives—Joanna Moore, the mother of Tatum and her brother, Griffin; and his second wife, Leigh Taylor-Young—to his girlfriends, who included Barbra Streisand, Bianca Jagger, Diana Ross, Nathalie Delon, Ursula Andress, and Anouk Aimée, with many broken hearts in between.

The truth was that there were two Ryans. He could be fun and gregarious, including Allegra on weekends and taking us shopping and for haircuts (I cut mine off to half an inch and Tatum followed), or energetically running Tatum, Allegra, his Belgian Shepherd, Jada, and me up and down the sand at Malibu, throwing Frisbees as we leaped and dove into the surf to catch them. Or putting on a pale blue Hawaiian shirt that matched his eyes and driving us up to Moonshadows or Hal's or Giorgio Baldi's in Santa Monica for dinner. But then there was a dark side. He could be critical, pugnacious, jealous, demanding, and deceptive.

On Fridays, we'd drive out to the beach house and sometimes I'd cook spaghetti and meatballs. Griffin was pretty much living out there all week long. He was only eleven, surfing and smoking weed, and although this seemed a matter to warrant concern, the attention was mostly centered on his sister. Ryan had gained custody of the children when Tatum was six, because of their mother's substance abuse. I felt bad for them, these tough little survivors. They had charm, but poor examples to follow in life, and in the big picture I don't believe that Ryan had much of a conscience, guilty or otherwise. He could go from Jekyll to Hyde in a heartbeat.

Ryan had recently returned from Ireland when we first met. It was part of a bond he ventured to establish between us, calling me "Big Irish" and telling me all about his adventures with Stanley Kubrick, the director of *Barry Lyndon*. He was very proud that he had been chosen for that film. It was the mark of artistic validation he had been seeking.

Ryan bolstered himself with two friends from his days as a student at Palisades High, Greg Hodell and Joe Amsler. Joe had the dubious distinction of having been one of the jesters who in the sixties kidnapped Frank Sinatra, Jr., as a prank, an offense for which he was lucky to have done only three years and nine months of time at Lompoc Prison, and not lost his neck. Joe and Greg were cast in Ryan's image, muscled and tall and athletic, but just a little rougher than he was. They say you wind up looking like who you really are. Joe and Greg took the rap first.

One day we were up in the Malibu Mountains. Joe and Greg were jumping from rock to rock above a chasm; the terrain was very steep, perhaps a two-hundred-foot drop. Joe was carrying a beer and missed a foothold on the rock and plummeted backward. I thought for sure he was a goner. At the last second he grasped a little bunch of weeds and saved himself from a deadly fall. These guys were literally living on the edge. It was part of their makeup. There was often the sense with them that you'd made it through another potentially hairy situation but that it probably wouldn't be the last.

In time I was to learn that there was something distinctly perverse about the O'Neal household. When I went to see Ryan in Amsterdam, where he was filming *A Bridge Too Far*, Greg and Joe were there with him; there was a strange atmosphere, and I could sense Ryan's distance. Tatum's demeanor had altered toward me as well—she loved me but was now expected to lie to me on Ryan's behalf.

Even though my pride was hurt, there was a modicum of relief when I found out Ryan was sleeping with another girl. I don't think Ryan was capable of love without some kind of downside.

Ultimately, it was revealed that a young actress had just left for the airport and that she had been sharing Ryan's bed. She was a playmate of Tatum's and another kind of playmate to Ryan. And yet I stayed on after a confrontation. I knew that Tatum cared for me, and Ryan's sleeping with her friend must have cost her a wealth of divided loyalties. When Ryan took me to the location, I saw that Dirk Bogarde had a part in the film, and I asked Ryan to knock on the door of his trailer. Dirk had been a friend of my mother's, and we had spent many Sundays at his house in the English countryside when I was a teenager. When Dirk appeared in the doorway of his camper, he was delightful to Ryan but sour to me, and only later did I realize he hadn't recognized me. I retreated, feeling hurt. He wrote me a note the next day, apologizing for his mistake and calling me a "silly goose."

I regretted leaving Jack. I hated causing him pain. Yet despite the way things were going with Ryan, I returned from Holland via London with him. One night a photographer jumped out from a dark side street in Knightsbridge as we came out of Mr Chow, but we outran him. In the year and a half I was with Ryan, I never had my picture taken with him in public. His innocent blue eyes, his automatic, coy smile for the cameras, his compliments, those big warm boxer's mitts that seemed ready to punch or stroke—I was beginning to mistrust everything about him. Soon he was telling me about unfinished business with Ursula Andress and confessing to phone calls with Bianca Jagger. Things were getting ugly; I was holding on longer than I should have, and I decided to return to Jack.

CHAPTER 7

The Last Tycoon, based on the novel by F. Scott Fitzgerald, follows the story of Monroe Stahr, the young head of one of the biggest movie studios in the Golden Age of Hollywood, during a time of industry turmoil due to the creation of the Writers Guild of America. The character of Monroe was inspired by the life of Irving Thalberg, the onetime boy-wonder production chief of MGM. It was evident that Sam Spiegel and Elia Kazan very much wanted Jack for this role. Maybe that was why they agreed to let me read for the female lead.

I had gone to Mr. Kazan's address on Beverly Drive, below Wilshire, to read with an actor called Cliff DeYoung. Sam Spiegel and Kazan stood up when I walked into the office. Sam called Kazan "Gadge." I had met him when he came over to Jack's house for dinner and had liked him immediately; he had been forthright and inquisitive and had asked me a good many questions about myself. Now he suggested that I read through a couple of scenes with Cliff, but afterward there was no sense that I'd gained any ground. There was no direction from Kazan. As I prepared to leave, he abruptly said, "I'll walk you downstairs."

We stepped out into the fierce midday sunlight. Kazan motioned to a bench by a bus stop. "Come," he said, "sit down with me a minute." An older woman was seated on the bench. "Excuse me," said Kazan, turning to her. "May I ask you a question?"

"Okay," the woman said.

He indicated me and asked, "Do you think she's beautiful?"

I blushed.

The woman appraised me. "No," she said. "Interesting, perhaps, but not beautiful."

I watched the part disappear forever in the ether.

"What do you think our relationship is?" asked Kazan, pushing it further.

She threw him a dirty look. "Don't be disgusting," she said, and got up to take the bus.

Soon I learned that Ingrid Boulting had been cast as the female lead, the "right" girl, Kathleen Moore, in *The Last Tycoon*. Jack had agreed to play Brimmer, a supporting role in the film, with Bobby De Niro starring as Monroe Stahr. Graciously, Sam Speigel and Elia Kazan offered me the part of Edna, the "wrong" girl, who shows up for a date with the hero only to have him reject her.

We were rehearsing at Paramount, and in the center lot a great pond had been created to contain an enormous bobbing fiber-glass head of the goddess Shiva, from which Ingrid and I were to dismount in an early scene in the movie.

Early that morning, Kazan had come by the bungalow I was using as a dressing room on the lot. He wanted Ingrid and me to do an improvisation. He set up the scene, explaining that my character needed something to wear under a transparent blouse for a hot date that night, and that Ingrid's character might have something for me to borrow. He told me to take a few minutes to get into character, then to come to another bungalow a few streets down on the lot.

As I made my way past the backdrops and facades, I found the house that he had indicated and knocked on a door. I had worked a few times with Ingrid when we were models in our previous life in New York. She was a very beautiful girl, with even features and huge eyes in a gentle moon face. I had always thought of her as self-contained, remote, and very British. But when she opened the door, what I saw was quite different. Ingrid was choking back tears, with black mascara pouring down her cheeks, hardly able to contain herself. It was utterly shocking. Until that moment I had been living in my own head. I had not even considered the other character's state of mind. It was a great lesson in drama, as given by Kazan. Sadly, even though the movie was full of promise, it was not a success. I was, however, always grateful to be able to work with its brilliant director.

On my first day of work, Jack sent me flowers, as he did on all my first days of work throughout our relationship.

In January 1976, *Cuckoo's Nest* was nominated for six Golden Globe Awards, with Jack for Best Actor. Michael Douglas had been calling on the hour to make certain Jack would attend; Jack had decided to skip the awards ceremony. Finally, in frustration, Michael came to the house and pounded on the front door. Jack and I hid and giggled in the TV room until he was gone. It was just a taste of old-fashioned rebellion, as far as we were concerned. Jack and I watched it all on television with a limo parked outside that Michael had ordered to stay in the driveway, in case Jack changed his mind. The film won six awards straight. Everything. We turned to each other after the show and Jack said, "Well, Toots, it looks like we'll be going to the Oscars."

Jack was right. *Cuckoo's Nest* received nine Academy Award nominations. He was going on a big promotional tour for the movie, from Paris to Hamburg to Copenhagen to Japan, and asked if I would come, too. But I said no. I had other plans. I wanted to find a place of my own; I still had unfinished business with Ryan. As Jack left for the airport, I handed him a letter that I hoped would explain. I asked what he was going to do.

"I'm going to work on being tied up," he said.

That February I flew to New York to stay with Ara. I was feeling unmoored and indecisive. Whenever things went from horizontal to vertical with Ryan, we had bad fights. I had begun to suspect that, for all his flattery and bravado, he didn't really care for me. On Valentine's Day, Jack sent me flowers.

I modeled for Saks with Pat Cleveland and Apollonia and did a show for Halston. Ara had decided to become a photographer and had asked me to shoot some pictures with him for *Viva* magazine. One morning as we were traveling across town to see the editors at *Viva*, we noticed a palmist's storefront near Lexington in the Fifties. I asked Ara if we could go in after our meeting. The woman who greeted us was obviously a gypsy. She spoke to Ara alone for a short while and afterward took me into a small room behind a curtain. She took a reel of turquoise thread and knotted it seven times and asked me to make a wish. I closed my eyes and wished for peace of heart and watched the knots unravel as she pulled the thread straight. "Your wish will be granted," she said. "But there are several things you have to do."

Before I knew it, the gypsy had me flying to L.A. for forty-eight hours to pick up, from its security box at the bank, a ruby ring my grandmother had left to me in her will. Helena came over to the house in the morning and observed that I was not meant to be back in town so soon and, noticing that I was acting mysteriously, asked what the heck was going on. I realized abruptly that I had been in the gypsy's thrall and that she was probably intending to rob me. But the truth was, I was unbalanced, in love with two men at once, under the influence of a lively assortment of drugs, and following Ara's questionable advice.

On the twenty-ninth, Jack came to New York for the screening of *The Missouri Breaks*. I stayed on for a month, pining for Ryan. On March 11, I was with Ara in his kitchen, and he was dying my hair red, when the NYPD called to tell him that his brother had been murdered. I think that was the beginning of Ara's descent.

I flew home to L.A., where, despite my better judgment, I continued to see both Ryan and Jack. On March 22, the day after the ski racer Spider Sabich was shot, I flew to Aspen. Jack met me at the airport with three pink roses tied up with a cherry ribbon. He appeared different, clean-shaven and shorthaired and healthy-looking. He drove me up to Maroon Creek. Annie Marshall had introduced Jack to a decorator, Jarrett Hedborg, and the house had been redone in my absence—mushroom walls and taupe carpets, grays and browns and luxurious austerity, some artwork I hadn't seen before. Jack was very sweet to me. There were presents at dinner, with a full moon shining down on the snowy-peaked mountains.

We flew back to L.A. for the Academy Awards. Richard Tyler made me a white wool suit, very Marlene Dietrich, with satin lapels and a floor-length pencil-thin skirt with a big box pleat. I loved when Oscar night wasn't all about skin. Jennifer came with us. She wore a white lace dress and a little cape, just as I had at Dad's premiere of *Freud* when I was eleven. That night *Cuckoo's Nest* brought down the house and swept the major categories, including Best Actor for Jack as Randle P. McMurphy, volatile, proud, and heroic; it was one of the great performances ever. We celebrated that night at Warren Beatty's house; he was living with Michelle Phillips.

Three weeks later, we celebrated Jack's birthday in Vegas—Lou, Michelle, Warren, Art Garfunkel, Harry Dean Stanton, Annie, and me. We watched Bette Midler perform at midnight, and Brenda Vaccaro, Kenny Solms, and Jeremy Railton flew in to join the fun. Everyone was relieved that Jack and I were together again, but I was still not finished with Ryan.

CHAPTER 8

Cici told me in February 1977 that she had introduced Allegra to her biological father, John Julius, Second Viscount Norwich, a traveler, writer, and historian with whom our mother had fallen in love when we were living in London in 1963. John Julius's father was Duff Cooper, minister of war under Neville Chamberlain, and his mother was Lady Diana Cooper, Cecil Beaton's favorite society muse, whose blond hair and blue eyes Allegra had inherited. Allegra was not surprised by the information that she was not Dad's progeny, as by then she had suspected as much. She continued to live at Cici's for the next year, until she moved to the home of Cici's parents. I continued to have her with me most weekends.

On March 9, Roman Polanski called and asked if I'd like to go to the movies. I was flattered. I had always found him extremely charismatic, with a quicksilver intelligence. I met up with him at Nate 'n Al's delicatessen, on Beverly Drive, had chicken matzo ball soup, and then got into his car to go see Lina Wertmüller's film *Seven Beauties*. Afterward, when Roman dropped me off in the parking lot behind the restaurant, I wondered, as his taillights receded down Beverly Drive, if it was true that everything in Roman's life turned to tragedy.

I had been around the set occasionally on *Chinatown*.

Roman was restless, opinionated, urbane, brilliant, impatient, and mercurial. I felt that perhaps he was always on the verge of being bored or irritated. You had to work to keep up with him. His passage had been marked in so many ways, it was hard to imagine surviving what he had endured in life—his family's tragic decision to move from France to Poland just before the German invasion and the beginning of World War II; the imprisonment of his father and the death of his mother at the hands of the Nazis; the murder of his wife, Sharon Tate, by the Manson "family" in 1969 in Los Angeles.

In the afternoon of the following day I went to Jack's house to pack up some boxes. I entered through the kitchen and saw, on a banquette, some cameras and a denim jacket that I vaguely recognized as the one Roman had worn to the movies the night before. I walked into the dining area and around the corner to the living room. The open layout afforded me a view of the outdoors and the pool. The living room was empty. The house was quiet. I called out, "Is anyone here?" I made a phone call to a friend and then walked toward the back of the house. The Jacuzzi was outside a downstairs bedroom suite, and farther up the hall was the television room. The door opened a fraction.

A voice I recognized as Roman's called back, "We'll be right out!" I returned to the living room. A short while later, Roman and a girl came around the corner; he introduced me to her and said they had been taking pictures. Big Boy was sitting on the carpet and got up to greet the girl, wagging his tail. She asked whether he was a male or a female. She was wearing platform heels and appeared to be quite tall. Roman collected his jacket and cameras, and they left together. I thought no more of it.

The next night I was again upstairs at the house on Mulholland, alone with Big Boy. My attention was suddenly focused on what seemed to be flashlights below the window, in the garden. Jack had installed a big gate in recent months, replete with cameras and barbed wire, so it was odd that there were people on the property. As I moved to a long window at the top of the stairs, I got a clear view of a group of men below, standing under the porch light. Roman was among them. I heard him knocking at the door, ringing the bell. Concerned, I descended and opened the door. "What is it?" I asked.

"It's nothing," Roman said. "Just some confusion about last night—these gentlemen want to have a look around, if that's okay." I was surprised and didn't think to ask if they had a search warrant.

I held the door open, and three or four of them came in. They were plainclothes detectives. One, a sandy-haired cop, was more aggressive than the others. Another was younger and seemingly more sympathetic. They spread around the downstairs rooms, shining their flashlights, and then the sandy-haired one shone his on a pack of rolling papers in an ashtray. "You better show me the drugs," he said to me. "Otherwise we'll take this place apart." They followed me upstairs, and I showed them some grass in a drawer. At that point, they started to go through my handbag, where they found a gram of cocaine. That seemed to be enough evidence for them. Roman and I were bundled into the back of two separate police cars. We were under arrest.

Although it was March, I had put on a lynx coat that Jack had given me, because my blood was running cold. As the arresting officers walked me down the corridor of the West L.A. precinct, there were some interested glances from the cops going off duty. It was about 10:30 P.M. and I couldn't believe my circumstances. Up on the hill at Jack's house, they may have read me my Miranda rights, but I was scared and believed that if I were truthful and cooperative with them, they might let me go. When my arresting officer asked who was my next of kin, I said Dad and Allegra. The worst was having to drag Dad and Allegra into this. The seriousness of the situation hit me hard—that they would have to suffer for my sake. That I had shamed our family name.

Roman's path and mine crossed as we were taken to be booked. He said, "I'm sorry for this, Anjelica." They took me to be photographed, and the cop in the booth gently helped me take off my fur coat before I was fingerprinted. They had allowed me to call Jack's business manager, Bob Colbert, to ask for bail. They told me he'd better arrive fast, because otherwise they would have to send me downtown to county jail. By then, it was two o'clock in the morning. Mercifully, Bob Colbert showed up with the cash. It had been all but impossible for him to procure thousands of dollars in the middle of the night, but bless him, he had succeeded.

After that there were newspaper articles, photographs, repercussions. Roman was charged with the sexual assault of a thirteen-year-old girl at Jack's house. It was an awful time. On August 9, the morning newspaper reported an account of the Polanski matter and stated that my anticipated testimony of seeing both Roman and the girl in a bedroom likely would be a crucial factor in bringing about a change of plea in the case. This hurt most of all; I had witnessed nothing untoward and had never seen Roman and the girl in a bedroom. Throughout the proceedings, the district attorney's office was reported to have suggested that I would be a witness for the prosecution in exchange for dropping charges of cocaine possession—an unfortunate impression, since it was an illegal search and seizure in the first place. Roman later accepted a plea bargain and my testimony was never required. When Roman learned that he would likely face imprisonment and deportation, he fled to France in February 1978, hours before he was to be formally sentenced.

During all this, I received a letter from Elia Kazan:

Anjelica darling,
   I think of you and hope you are all right. I read all the stuff in the papers. I know how painful that kind of thing can be. I hope it wasn't too bad in your case. You know you have a big hug from me any time you need it.

                                          Yours,
                                          Elia

Jack and I were off and on, and Ryan had a bad temper. It did not serve me to take my troubles to him. I moved to a little studio on a hill behind Cici's house in the Palisades. It was located directly between Jack's house on Mulholland and Ryan's house on the beach, and it gave me the advantage of being close to Cici, who was protective of me and whom I loved, and also the chance to be close to Allegra.

One night Ryan and I went to a party at a Spanish mansion in Beverly Hills. There was a belly dancer in the middle of an open floor and tables all around. I had left Ryan's side to go to the bathroom. When I reentered the dining area, I could not get to him without crossing the dancer's path and decided to wait until she stopped. As I looked on, I could see Ryan becoming agitated. Suddenly, he stood up and left the room, exiting by an outside stairway. I ran after him down to the parking lot. The attendants were bringing him his car. "Ryan!" I called out. "I'm here, it's okay!"

He turned on me, grabbed me by the hair, and hit me in the forehead with the top of his skull. I saw stars and reeled back. Half blind, I ran away from him, upstairs to a bathroom. Soon there was a knock on the door; his brother, Kevin, had come to talk to me. Another knock—this time it was security, standing behind a red-faced Ryan.

"He wants to speak to you. We saw what happened. Is that all right?"

"Yes," I replied. "You can let him in."

No sooner had I complied than Ryan was in the bathroom, batting me about the head with open hands. Then, abruptly, he left. I realized I had no one to turn to. I had given up my friends when I was with Ryan; they were too close to Jack, and I didn't want them to know what was going on. Lou disapproved; I couldn't call him, or Phyllis, or Cici. So I asked Kevin to drop me off at Ryan's. It was by now about two o'clock in the morning, and all the lights were on. When I walked into his bedroom, Ryan was sitting up in bed with an ice pack on his forehead, chuckling ruefully. "I've got quite a headache," he said.

The next morning, with Allegra in the passenger seat of my car, driving on the Pacific Coast Highway, I asked her, sobbing, "What shall I do, Allegra? What can I do?"

She looked over at me coolly. She was thirteen years old. "Leave him," she replied.

When I ended my affair with Ryan, I returned to Jack but began to look for a house near his, so that we could still be close but I could also be independent. I found a little cottage on Beverly Glen, close to Mulholland, and painted it pink. Jack bought it for me. It was tiny but perfect, and Jarrett Hedborg took me to Robertson Boulevard to choose fabrics and some pieces of furniture. Jack came over only once. I knew he hated it. It was a liberation for me, yes, but it was also the beginning of a change for us. It was hard to admit that our relationship was no longer hopeful or innocent; I no longer had stars in my eyes. Now there was a wry note, an irony, an irritation. Both of us had crossed a line.

Neither of us was any good at confrontation, and we were living "Life in the Fast Lane," as our friends in Aspen, the Eagles, put it so succinctly. We were spending our winters at Maroon Creek, but we had developed our own agendas.

CHAPTER 9

I think when children are without their parents at an early age, they find things to stimulate memories of them, or they look for areas of comfort that remind them of their parents' presence. A perfume, or a blanket, or a taste, something tactile or sensory that draws them, captures their essence. For my father, the scent I most fondly remember is what eventually killed him, his cigar smoke. I could always tell where he was in any hotel just by following the smell of Monte Cristo through the hallways like a bloodhound—except one didn't have to be nearly as acute as a bloodhound in order to track him down. He was always surrounded by that smell. He was smoking little brown Mexican cigarillos before he started on cigars. It was when he was working on *The Bible* that he had the first signs of emphysema and saw a doctor. He was starting to lose his oxygen, and the doctor said, "You have to give up smoking. It's enough now." So Dad went to Rome and found himself a new doctor, who said, "Yes, you have to give up cigarettes, but you can have a cigar once in a while." Dad immediately interpreted this as an invitation to chain-smoke them. And they were good cigars, but nevertheless.

I was there for a lot of big, challenging moments in my father's life—among them, the news that he would need heart-valve-replacement surgery. There was always the underlying deficit of emphysema, the ever-present threat that the doctors would be unable to get him off the breathing machines that took over this function during the operations for various other problems, such as an effort to salvage a bungled repair of his elbow after *The Man Who Would Be King* (which had been performed with whiskey as anesthesia and a machete somewhere in the Moroccan desert) or surgery to reduce a hernia in his groin. Once he was in the hospital, the problems always seemed to intensify, and former solutions ceased to apply. I remember Dad one morning, terribly thin, lying flat on his back, his face, for the first time ever, looking small and fine-boned on the pillow. I could see his cranium beneath the skin. He had a number of Band-Aids on his forehead and scalp. "Dad, what's that?" I asked.

"Oh, nothing much, honey," he said, smiling ruefully. "Just a little skin cancer."

The most primitive of all tortures were the times when Dad's oxygen levels were so low that going to sleep actually carried a risk of death. We would have to keep him awake for hours on end, haranguing him to keep his eyes open. When finally he would come out of intensive care after these unbelievable struggles, the experience would have made him afraid to sleep. He'd close his eyes and think immediately that he was dying.

The hours of waiting. Waiting for tests, waiting for the results from the tests, the good news, the bad news. The corridors, the nurses' stations, the violet phalaenopsis on the bedside table, the Mylar balloons, the smells of Lysol, food, medication, and bodily fluids, the language of hospitals and how to negotiate them. Put on your freshest shirt, your brightest lipstick (just enough to look less gray and anxious should he be alert), cook up something at home to take to your beloved, try to think of some story to tell him, something to distract him from what is going on in both your minds.

"Will Dad die from this disease?" I asked a nurse one day.

"Our respiratory patients usually come back to the hospital," she replied. I don't know why it came as a shock, but it confirmed my greatest fear—that Dad's emphysema was chronic.

It was terrible to see him so sick. The attack on his system by the disease was relentless. He was wracked with coughing, struggling for breath, incapable of sleeping. I would try to visit him every day when he was in the hospital. I noticed that if I missed a day, his condition would deteriorate. If I took my eyes off him even overnight, he was more prone to fail.

With emphysema, it becomes harder to exhale than to breathe in; it feels like drowning. Later on, as it progressed, there'd be terrible episodes when we'd have to keep Dad up for three days straight in the hospital. We couldn't let him sleep because the doctors were scared that if he did, his carbon dioxide would rise so high it could damage his heart or his brain. For the last decade of his life, he was in and out of hospitals with respiratory failure. He was in hell with this disease. When his oxygen would get low, he'd suddenly get very acquiescent, tired, and dreamy, and then we'd know—that was our sign that we had to take him in. Generally, this would follow days when he didn't eat well or sat in a draft. He became very fragile.

In the fall of 1977, Dad's doctors discovered that he had an abdominal aortic aneurysm, the same condition that had killed his father, Walter, one day after his sixty-sixth birthday.

Ironically, Dad learned the news while staying at the Beverly Hills Hotel, where Walter had suffered his deadly stroke. Dad called and asked us to come see him, and Tony, Allegra, Danny, and I followed the smell of Havana cigars to his room, where he told us the grim news. Soon afterward, there were the visits to Cedars-Sinai, appointments with the doctors, and efforts to have Dad cut down on his intake of tobacco.

At first Dad's doctors were worried that his lung capacity was too compromised for him to survive surgery, but they determined to see how much they could improve his thoracic function by keeping him off cigars for a week. Dad was basically surviving on one lung. He would need to be transferred to a respirator for the operation, and it was more than possible that he would not be able to transfer back to his own damaged respiratory system. We all knew Dad would rather be dead than hooked up to a breathing machine permanently. Bad enough that he relied so much on the ubiquitous canisters of oxygen. Amazingly, giving up cigars for a week produced an improvement of more than fifty percent, and the doctors decided they could go ahead with the operation.

The night before surgery, I walked in on Dad attempting to hide under the mattress a stack of girlie magazines that the producer Ray Stark had brought over to the hospital to make him laugh. The next morning found his children clustered around his bed as he waited for his medical team to come talk to him, and for the nurses' aides to transfer him to the gurney to go down to the operating theater. Finally, they came to his room—his heart doctor and internist, Dr. Gary Sugarman, and his lung specialist, Dr. Rhea Snider.

"Well, helloo, Gary," Dad greeted Dr. Sugarman warmly. I almost expected Dad to offer him a drink. Then, smiling broadly at the assembled doctors, aides, and interns, with the lightest note of challenge in his voice, Dad said, "Well, gentlemen, let's get this under way—my life is in your hands." He was transferred to a gurney and wheeled out of the room.

Nine hours after the operation, I visited Dad in the intensive care unit. He was alive, alert, off the breathing machine, and writing messages on a chalkboard. The next day he was already out of the ICU and in a private room on the eighth floor; when I walked in, he was in a marvelous mood. "Well, it looks like I made it after all."

I returned to the hospital after lunch to find him doubled over at the foot of his bed. "Something's wrong, honey. I survived the surgery, but now I've got the worst bellyache."

By that afternoon, he was hooked up to a machine that had taken over the function of his stomach. Impossibly, a nurse had offered him shredded wheat on the morning following surgery, which had caused severe intestinal blockage. As a result, we had to hire private nurses to watch him every moment. One morning about three weeks into this purgatory, they came to me and suggested that I insist on surgery. They said that Dad was dying. It was true that his skin had fallen away from his bones. I could see the outline of his skeleton on the pillow. And so the doctors operated again; having cut him from breastbone to groin, they now cut him again from side to side.

If I could have sacrificed a part of my own body to help my father, I would have without question. To watch him undergo the often painful indignities of the various medical procedures was horrendous. One morning I walked into the ICU as the doctors were suctioning his chest. The panic in Dad's eyes stopped me short in the hallway outside his room, and I felt my own heart constrict at the sight of it.

When Dad came off the feeding tube, we worked hard on getting him to eat. His appetite was almost nonexistent anyway. When I went to his hospital room the first morning, they were allowing him to drink fluids after a full three weeks without any food or beverage. A slow-moving nurse was stirring liquid in a plastic cup. "What's that?" I asked.

"I'm just stirring the bubbles out of the 7Up," she said. From that moment, I set up a virtual juice bar in his room. It is extraordinary to me that the importance of nutrition is still so largely unaddressed in hospitals in America.

One day my voice joined the chorus of others, and I said, "You have to eat, Dad."

He stopped me cold. "Anjel," he said, "please don't ask me again. The consistency of the jelly is unflinching." After that, I prepared some fresh fruit jelly to take to him for lunch; they had told me he was not yet ready for solid foods.

When he was finally allowed to get out of bed, Dad would make us walk up and down the corridors at Cedars, assessing the donor art. It is strange for me to think that so many years before I met the sculptor Robert Graham, Dad was, even then, absorbing his drawings on the walls of the hospital.

After Dad was on the road to recovery, all of his astute characteristics came back into play. He would be in a penetrating, inquiring state of mind, which always threw me into apprehension, because I would have to tell him what I was thinking and what I was up to. I always felt put on the spot. I'd talked to a therapist about my inability to calm my fears when I went to visit Dad, and she said, "Why don't you just go in and say nothing until he does? See what happens." Although I was nervous, it seemed like a good idea.

I sat by his hospital bed, and he told me stories. I hadn't

come in with my whole defense on my lips, and surprisingly, it felt great. After this, I thought, "Well, maybe I'll ask him about the time he confronted me about dancing suggestively—doing what he called 'the bumps.'" So I said, "Remember the bumps, Dad?"

"The bumps?" he said. "What do you mean?"

And I said, "Yes, Dad, remember the bumps, when I was fourteen and you slapped me in the face?"

He said, "Honey. That wasn't the bumps. That was about you being belligerent because you didn't want to go to l'École du Louvre." He'd entirely rewritten the scenario.

A few years earlier, I had cut out a picture of First Lady Betty Ford at the Republican National Convention, with the caption "BETTY BUMP—Mrs. Ford dancing the bump with TV personality Tony Orlando at Uptown Theater in Kansas City." I kept that picture forever, but I never had the courage to show it to Dad.

Danny and I were seated on either side of Dad's hospital bed one evening. Dad was lying back on the pillows, inhaling oxygen through a green plastic tube. We were exhausted after another weeklong intensive fight for his survival but relieved that he still had the will to go on. The room was quiet and dark but for the sound of his labored, vaporous breathing.

Dad broke the silence. "When I was your age, I was just like both of you. I could stay up all night, and the following day I could go longer and harder than anyone. But there is a certain vulgarity in thinking you can get away with smoking. It got me in the end, and it will get you, too, if you continue." Danny's eyes met my own.

The sound of the oxygen pump filled the room, and Dad drifted into sleep. Minutes later found Danny and me on the roof of the hospital, inhaling Marlboro Reds for all we were worth, in full and accurate knowledge of how fleeting and precious this thing was that we were getting away with.

Before the doctors would release Dad from the hospital, they generally pumped up his system with a blood transfusion as we heaved a collective sigh of relief and packed up his room. Then we'd go down in the elevator, through the lobby and the sliding glass doors, and out onto the pavement in the hard light of day, with Maricela pushing Dad in a wheelchair attached to a large canister of oxygen. At first he might stay at the Beverly Hills Hotel or out at the beach house of his friend the actor Burgess Meredith, in the colony off Malibu Canyon Road. Even though Dad was in such poor health, I think they shared some good times there, he and Buzz. On one occasion, Dad rented the main house and moved into the master bedroom and had a fine view of the Pacific Ocean as it rolled over the pale Malibu sand outside the windows. Buzz took up temporary residence in a little guesthouse next door, often dropping in with a fine vintage from his wine collection for them to share and enjoy.

Soon Jack offered his ranch house in Ventura, and we moved Dad out there. The property was remote, however, and proved too far from the hospital. Allegra was stalked by someone following her car in the canyon one night, so we decided to rent a place for Dad in Beverly Hills. On subsequent occasions, Gladys and Maricela rented houses and apartments for Dad in the area, in order to be close to his doctors until he regained his strength and could return to Mexico.

Gladys was spending more time in Puerto Vallarta, having adopted a baby, Marisol. She stayed there to take care of the business of Dad's houses, his work, his correspondence, his many obligations, plans, appearances, dependents, and friends. Maricela had been doing all the traveling with Dad and was with him at all times when he was in the hospital—that is, until someone she didn't like would enter the room. Danny's beautiful mother, Zoë, was a frequent visitor, and when she arrived Maricela usually disappeared.

On one occasion after Dad had come out of the hospital and was installed in a rented home in Beverly Hills, an attractive Irish nurse came to look after him. Maricela took to sleeping on a hall bench outside his bedroom with a loaded shotgun in her lap and Diego, their Rottweiler, by her side. She suspected the nurse was taking advantage of "Papi." Maricela seemed utterly devoted to Dad and he to her.

Dad's life was constantly moving, even when he was not. After every health crisis, the painful efforts to reclaim life followed. Filled with drugs, unable to sleep, with no appetite, he always held on to his regal bearing. On one occasion, having narrowly escaped death and hovering on the brink for five days in the respiratory intensive care unit of Cedars-Sinai, he awoke asking for beluga caviar and a glass of very cold Château d'Yquem.

Later that same day, Dad's agent, Paul Kohner, came to see him in the ICU. Paul, at this point, must have been eighty-five—almost blind, walking with a cane, and his skin had the quality of a mille-feuille. He had to be assisted over to Dad's bedside by aides on either elbow. Tears were running down his cheeks as he beheld his old friend and client. "John!" he exclaimed in a whisper, close to Dad's ear. "John, it's Paul!"

Dad opened his eyes and fixed Paul with a cold stare. "You sold out," he responded weakly from the pillow.

As a wave of wonderment and shock crossed his already stricken expression, Paul asked if Dad would repeat that statement.

"I told you I wanted Sam Shepard for *Revenge*," Dad continued, "but you went and agreed to another plan with Ray Stark." He was on his back but clearly on the attack.

By now poor Paul was apoplectic. "I was led to believe you were dead, John!"

"Well, I'm not dead yet, and you can tell that to Ray, the son of a bitch."

Contrary to Dad's wish to cast Sam Shepard, Ray had sent the script to Kevin Costner. Dad was angry; he'd been in a life-or-death situation just hours before, but he was damned if he would let them think they could get away with disrespecting him. When he eventually got out of the hospital, he allowed Ray to send Kevin Costner to see him. As I've heard the story told, Dad just gazed out the window and whistled throughout the meeting. He never really forgave Ray afterward. Dad didn't like that Ray had doubted he would live. Later, when Dad got seriously sick in Fall River, Massachusetts, he asked Ray to get him Nancy Reagan's plane to fly him back to his doctors at Cedars-Sinai. This was a steep request even for Ray, and he wouldn't or couldn't come through, but it was as if Dad knew that and wanted him to feel bad. Theirs was a complicated relationship to the end.

Dad went on to make seven more movies. Because of his emphysema, the insurance companies refused to allow the studios to continue hiring him for films—a sad state of affairs and a very depressing moment in his creative life, given that at this point he was one of America's most celebrated and esteemed veteran filmmakers. But soon he would meet a couple of young producers, Michael Fitzgerald and Wieland Schulz-Keil, who would provide him the means to make the small-budget but vital films that described his new trajectory—films like *Wise Blood*, *Under the Volcano*, and *The Dead*. He also had another friend and admirer in the producer John Foreman, who, having completed *The Man Who Would Be King* with Dad to great success, went on to produce *Prizzi's Honor*.

CHAPTER 10

My friend Jane Buffett and I had gone on holiday to Hawaii for several weeks in August 1978 and were staying in Kipahulu in a cabin on the Lindbergh estate. When I returned to L.A., the phone was ringing—it was Joan Buck, encouraging me to go to London to be with Jack, who had started work on Stanley Kubrick's *The Shining* at Pinewood Studios. I took her advice and flew to England. Entering the house Jack had rented on Cheyne Walk felt like stepping into the interior of a box of Turkish delight—an odd combination of remodeled Regency and Arabic. The dining room, in the basement, had a monolithic refectory table and medieval benches, church pews with straight backs—like something out of a Bela Lugosi movie. Upstairs, Jack lay supine on a bed of balsa wood. The explanation was that for several days in a row, he had accidentally left his keys inside and had been forced to scale the fourteen-foot wall surrounding the property to get back in the house. The last time, he had landed on his heels in a manner that had jammed his spine and slipped his discs, resulting in major back trauma. He had been in consultation with Her Majesty the Queen's back doctor and had been recommended absolute rest on a plank. Jack looked terribly depressed as I entered the bedroom, a riot of red velvet curtains and gold-and-black-embossed wallpaper. A couple was standing sympathetically by his side.

"Hello, Tutti!" the woman greeted me effusively with a British accent. She had a tumbling mane of red curls and was wearing a purple leather pantsuit with eye shadow to match.

"This is Nona," said Jack. "And this is All-England," he added, gesturing toward a polished gentleman—Nona's husband, I presumed—who introduced himself as Martin Summers. "Nones and All-England are the greatest! They've been taking care of me in London."

"I can see that," I replied. My initial wariness about Nona and Martin faded in about twenty-four hours. Their house on Glebe Place in Chelsea was the center for amusement, and Nona was a fantastic hostess; by day she was designing exercise attire with padded shoulders, and the girls were meeting at her house for white wine and aerobics, then going out at night to the great parties Nona and Martin threw. All kinds of people came; everyone was young and beautiful. There was delicious Thai food under an Arabian tent all done up in Fortuny fabric in one of the long living rooms, and the furniture was a fantastic collection of bohemian art nouveau by Carlo Bugatti, the father of the car designer and manufacturer Ettore Bugatti.

Martin was a co-owner of the Lefevre Gallery on Bruton Street. Nona was of Austrian-Hungarian descent, educated in Switzerland. Their circle of friends ranged from theater and movie people to Greek shipping magnates and Jordanian princesses. One morning Nona called me up, her voice bursting with excitement. "Flagrante delicto!" she cried. "Flagrante delicto!"

"What on earth are you talking about?" I inquired. It

seemed that Martin had been spotted by Nona in Berkeley Square in the embrace of a pretty secretary. I was surprised that this event, as opposed to provoking a negative reaction from Nona, seemed instead full cause to celebrate, and celebrate she did, heading straight to Browns on South Molton Street for some serious retail therapy in the form of a new fur coat.

Our circle expanded in London, and I made many dear and lifelong girlfriends—among them Sabrina Guinness, Jerry Hall, Penelope Tree, the British actress Anne Lambton, Diane von Fürstenberg, Lyndall Hobbs, the model Marie Helvin, and the photographer Carinthia West. Sabrina was seeing Prince Charles, and there was little respite from the British press. I admired how coolly she coped with finding herself under a magnifying glass when so much was being made of it.

One afternoon Nona had a bunch of us come over to the house in Glebe Place to watch a live black-belt demonstration by a judo master called Steve Seagal, who had operated an aikido dojo in Japan. This before he met Hollywood agent Michael Ovitz of CAA and was transformed into an action star and married the British model Kelly LeBrock. He was flying around barefoot in a linen happi coat, doing great leaps and jumps in the hallway. The men were all pretty blasé about it, but couldn't resist poking fun, probably because of a sense of inadequacy about their own physical prowess. The girls were transfixed, if a little bemused.

Allegra had come to London to be with me and was staying with us on the top story of the house. It was a quite spacious attic, and she rarely came out of that room, staying alone and reading all day. She was studying for her tenth grade at Marymount with a tutorial equivalent, and at fourteen she was reserved and, to my thinking, antisocial. I charged her with overspending on taxis, which was rich, given that I used to steal from Mum's handbag to take them and had not troubled to teach Allegra the London bus or subway system. I was on a health regime and forced her to come out to jog with me along the Thames embankment one day. She remembers my expounding on the freshness of the air as diesel engines passed us, spewing noxious fumes. We wound up going to Hyde Park in short shorts to play Frisbee, but it felt wrong—too much like the era of Ryan O'Neal—so we didn't do that again.

Jack was very honored to be working with Stanley Kubrick; evidently he was a taskmaster, but for Jack he was all genius. It took weeks for Jack's back to repair even to the point of his standing up. Since Kubrick owned most of the equipment—including cameras and lights at Pinewood—the fact that insurance was paying for the hiatus was bearable, but the workload was immense for the actors. There was talk that Scatman Crothers had exceeded one hundred takes on a scene in an afternoon, and Shelley Duvall had moved out of London entirely and was staying at Pinewood so as to be within a stone's throw of the studio. Everyone worked late and looked exhausted.

Jim Harrison came to stay while Jack was working in London. Jim's luggage had gotten lost, so he went off to look for a shop to buy clothes. When he returned in a pair of stitched-pocket boot-leg jeans, he thought he looked nifty.

I asked, "Where did you get those? Walter's of Battersea?" And Jim wrote a poem:

WALTER OF BATTERSEA
For Anjelica

I shall commit suicide or die
trying, Walter thought beside
the Thames—at low tide and very
feminine.

Picture him: a cold November day,
the world through a long lens; he's
in new blue pants and races the river
for thirty-three steps. . . .

Jim and I took to having long lunches at Osteria San Lorenzo, a haunt from school days when my mother first took me at twelve years old and introduced me to the owners, Lorenzo and Mara. Jim would have risotto with squid ink, and I'd always have mozzarella pomodoro, because in those days you still couldn't get fresh mozzarella in Los Angeles. Then we'd progress to fishes or meats or pastas and desserts, washed down with a fine Barolo, a possible Chianti Classico, and a little grappa or Sambuca to polish it off. With just enough espresso to get us home from our boozy lunches, we'd weave our way through Chelsea to our respective naps before "Dad," as we had taken to calling Jack, got back from the set.

We tried to appear perky, but Jack would take one look at us, still hungover from lunch at seven-thirty in the evening, and shake his head. He was always gray in the face when he got back from work, with a blood clot of dried red sugar from special effects stuck to his temple. After the endless hours he was spending on set, he wouldn't bother to wash it off in the hair-and-makeup trailer, preferring to shower when he got home to Cheyne Walk. So it was often touchy when he'd stagger in with his bad back, looking like the ax murderer of Pinewood, with a mood to match. He was so busy being good for Kubrick that he had no room for nice for the rest of us. He wouldn't spend long over the well-done lamb chops that his cook, Annie Marshall's nephew Tim Bourne, had prepared. Jack had a special disdain for garnish, and he would pick out parsley from his plate with unveiled contempt and toss it aside. Jim and I would push our food around and pretend we weren't still stuffed from lunch. The atmosphere in the basement dining room felt monastic and chilly. Combined with Jack's appearance, it was, it seemed, the nature of the day—cloudy skies but rarely bad weather.

One weekend Mick Jagger brought his wife, Bianca, and his daughter, Jade, to see us. They were living a few doors down. I'd known Bianca since Halston days, but I hadn't seen Jade since she was a toddler and had told me to go away because she wanted to be with Jack. When I asked her what she wanted to drink, she said, "Fresh strawberry juice." I thought that was pretty good for a seven-year-old in November in England.

On November 18, 1978, my brother Tony married Margot Cholmondeley in a ceremony in the chapel on the grounds of her father's estate, Cholmondeley Castle, in Cheshire. The wedding was held over the course of a weekend, with lovely dinners and a long night of dancing and revelry. Dad flew in from Mexico, Danny and Zoë came down from London, where Danny was in film school, and Allegra came with me.

The following morning, with dew on the grass, we walked to the chapel through an ancient graveyard. Margot was a perfect Pre-Raphaelite bride, with her translucent ivory skin and a lace veil pinned to her wild red curls. She looked like a Rossetti. I gave Tony and Margot a Philippe Halsman picture of Mum from *Life* magazine in a silver frame. Tony seemed surprised. He said he didn't expect that.

Margot was to give our family three of the most beautiful children on earth—my nephews Matthew and Jack, and my first niece, Laura.

Jeremy Railton came through London on his way to Rhodesia to see his parents. There was unrest in Zimbabwe, with Robert Mugabe at the helm of what looked to be a nationalist uprising. Local people from the townships were attempting to take over many of the white-owned farms, so there was a threat of violence. Jeremy was second-generation Rhodesian, and the bush was home to him. He was going over to help his parents set up an information center and museum at their game park.

Jack and I thought we would be going back to the U.S. for the holidays, but the schedule for *The Shining* was running over. I was upset because it was too late to buy Christmas lights or decorations. So Jeremy began to draw and make cutouts to inspire me to make my own. I begged him to stay for Christmas, but he insisted he had to go. "I might not see my parents again," he said. Jeremy said this with such simplicity and conviction that I stopped badgering him.

On Christmas Eve there was a winter storm. Jeremy left for the airport, and Jack, Jennifer, Helena, Allegra, and I had an all-out snowball fight on Cheyne Walk, ducking behind parked cars, running and sliding on the Chelsea embankment.

When Jeremy and I reunited in Los Angeles some weeks into the New Year, he showed me photographs of a small but beautiful museum and visitors' center that he had built at his parents' game park. It was the last time he ever saw his mother and father. Intent on recovering the land his parents had settled a full generation before, a militia in Zimbabwe murdered them.

CHAPTER 11

On the occasion of my twenty-eighth birthday party, Jack really put on the dog, hiring Chasen's to cater—the caviar sat in tubs and the Cristal flowed—and writing me a poem:

> It's Tootie's day,
> Hoorah! Hooray!
> A Bigger Fairy dress she'll want
> No surprise please, just girls and guys, please
> Perhaps a jool* to flaunt
> Party could be her middle name
> But then she's had so many.
> Like—Tootman, Fab and Mine and Big
> You know, my dear, this doggerel here
> Is written all in fun
> 'Cause in my heart, and every part
> You're simply called "The One"
> Happy b'day
> Yr Jack

I was sitting on the gray wool carpet on the floor of the living room at Mulholland Drive, wearing a Norma Kamali

*jewel

black satin flamenco skirt, and opening a box containing a fabulous set of diamond-and-ruby clips from the estate of the artist Tamara de Lempicka, when I turned to my brother Tony, who happened to be there on a layover back from London to New Mexico, and said, "Well, this is a bit over the top!"

"Yes," Tony replied, "it certainly is."

A very pretty, natural-looking girl with ice-blond hair came into the room on the arm of Harry Dean Stanton. She gave me a piece of carved sandstone and introduced herself to me as Greta Ronningen. Greta was just in from Kalamazoo, Michigan, by way of Albuquerque, New Mexico. We were to become very close friends. It was, as she remembered it, a moment that changed her life, because she met her future husband that evening, the producer Bert Schneider.

Bert was tall and elegant and sleepy-eyed, like he'd just rolled out of bed. He moved like a snake. One of the handsomest men I'd ever seen, he was one of the "B"s in the title of the film company BBS Productions, which he shared with Bob Rafelson and Stephen Blauner. Bert was a producer on *Easy Rider* and *Five Easy Pieces* and one of Jack's dearest friends. He was a freethinker, a confirmed liberal with radical leanings, a comrade of Abbie Hoffman. He went to Nicaragua at the height of the Sandinista revolution to make a documentary on Daniel Ortega, and gave Huey Newton of the Black Panthers a safe house when he was running from the law.

When I first met him, Bert was seeing Candice Bergen. I think they had just come back from Nepal. Bert loved to travel to exotic places and take drugs and go native. He was, in his serpentine way, both lovable and a little scary, and always provocative.

Bert bought a lovely piece of land on Oak Pass overlooking

greater Los Angeles, and he built what looked like an enlarged Japanese teahouse, with sliding shoji doors and bamboo matting and a great big kitchen made of maplewood with a huge Wolf stove where Greta and I would cook delicious meals. They had interesting friends, went on amazing journeys. Bert and Greta took me on a wonderful twelve-day adventure with some friends of theirs down the Green River in Idaho.

I met Huey Newton up at Bert's on Oak Pass. He told me he liked me a lot and tried to kiss me. I thought he was gorgeous but more than a little dangerous. I asked him if it was true that he'd killed a woman in Oakland, but he said he'd prefer not to answer that question.

Aspen in the summertime was an explosion of green, red, yellow, orange, purple, and gold. The rivers ran fast and cold down from the mountains. Hiking on Hunter Creek, the air was fresh with the scent of pine. On the lower elevations, pale delicate ferns broke through the moss, and the silver-barked trees fluttered and whispered in the breeze. I loved climbing the narrow trails, often on horseback, when more often than not I would temporarily lose my way and have to circumnavigate streams and gulches on the descent. One day I almost lost my life on a thoroughbred racehorse that tried to back me over a ravine into the Roaring Fork River. But they were halcyon days, golden days.

The fields were rich with Indian paintbrush, crocus, and edelweiss, and the sun cast long golden shadows before the sky turned pink in the evening, then a cool translucent blue as the stars came out. The bears came into town to hulk around the garbage dump just north of Hallam Lake, where Jack and Lou had purchased a beautiful Victorian mansion, forest green with white trim, on the edge of town, "to hang my pictures and watch football on Sundays with the lads!" There was no thrill too fast nor risk too fearsome that didn't get serious consideration. Many of our dear friends from the mountains had the impermanence and fleeting quality of the drifting snow—locals, artists, athletes, drug dealers, and movie stars, a heady combination of interesting and good-looking people. Music was always playing in town—by resident musicians like the Eagles, Jimmy Buffett, and John Denver, who sometimes gave us rides back and forth to L.A. on his private plane.

Back in Los Angeles, on October 23, 1979, Jack and I went to a glamorous party that Sue Mengers threw for Princess Margaret, who, according to Suzy in her *Daily News* column,

> wound up her visit to Los Angeles with a smashing, probably because it was informal, buffet dinner given in her honor by Sue Mengers, the superstar agent, and her husband, Jean-Claude Tramont. Everyone out there was anxious to entertain the princess, but because Sue knows the star-studded world, and because that world seems to flock to her door, she was chosen. The party not only brought out the best of Hollywood, especially the young, but the best in everyone who was there.
>
> The security was extraordinary. Helicopters circled above Sue's house, searchlights filled the garden surrounding it, and the police were everywhere. Guests, of course, were carefully checked.
>
> Margaret never looked better. She wore a black-and-silver dress by Dior and a magnificent diamond necklace and earrings left to her by her grandmother, Queen Mary.

She spoke to and mingled with all the celebs, who found her totally charming. She insisted on standing in the buffet line herself, and when she did sit down, she had Gov. Jerry Brown on her right and Michael Caine on her left. That's some seat. Margaret arrived promptly at 8:30 and stayed until 12:30 when Prince Rupert Loewenstein, her friend and a reigning wit of the international set (he also manages The Rolling Stones), took her home.

Incidentally, Brown came to the party with Linda Ronstadt, who was wearing a white cotton dress up to her knees and dear little red boots. It would seem that there is still something going on between these two, whose hot romance I reported to a waiting world (first) what seems like quite a long time ago.

Farrah Fawcett and Ryan O'Neal, whose hot romance I reported to a waiting world (first—then everyone jumped on it) several weeks ago, arrived together. Farrah was fetching in silk pajamas. Barbra Streisand, in black pants and a long black chemise, was with Jon Peters, naturally. Robin Williams (Mork) and his wife, Valerie, Gore Vidal, handsome Sean Connery and his wife Michelle, Ken Tynan and his wife Kathleen (they had given a small lunch for Margaret that day), Sybil and Jordan Christopher, Nick Nolte and his wife Sharon, Sylvia and Danny Kaye, David Geffen with Joni Mitchell, Mary and Swifty Lazar, Ali MacGraw in a short gold-and-black dress, and Barry Manilow with Linda Allen all chatted with the guest of honor.

Also eating lasagna and chicken and looking gorgeous . . . were such luminaries as Shakira Caine (Michael's wife), Neil Diamond and his wife Marcia, Gene Hackman and his wife Faye, Peter Falk and his wife Shera, Gladyce and

David Begelman, Peter Asher, Danny Melnick with Kelly Lange, NBC's good-looking anchorwoman out there, Barry Diller and—get ready—the big sensation of the evening, Jack Nicholson with Anjelica Huston! My dear, everyone gasped. So unexpected. So whoever told you this one was over can go fly a kite.

Mengers had a staff of 25 to help with the party, one that will be talked about for a long time.

In January 1980 Helena started a Monday-night ritual at a roller-skating rink in Reseda, where a whole group of us glided mindlessly for hours under the colored lights reflected in a mirrored ball that hung from the ceiling. The music was mainly disco with some R&B thrown in. Helena named the club Skateaway but spelled it Skataway. She didn't allow alcohol, so these evenings had an athletic freshness to them, and attracted people as disparate as the football star Jim Brown and Robin Williams and even Cher, who showed up wearing one of those fake rubber bottoms in case she fell. Marlon's daughter Cheyenne appeared at Skataway one evening. At eleven, she was already tall and exquisite, with Tahitian features, blond hair, caramel skin, pale green eyes, and a high voice that tinkled with laughter. Ed Begley was there, and the Arquettes and Harry Dean. Broadway singer and dancer Charles Valentino became my dance partner. Valentino had performed some years before in New York in *The Wiz*. When we got out of our skates, we would keep on dancing. He'd pick me up and twirl me around as if I were a silk scarf. When we were at a party, I never sat down unless he was dancing with his other favorite girl, Joni Mitchell. The clothes designer Richard Tyler made up some custom satin jackets with the names of the founding members embroidered on the pocket, and on the back the image of an eagle on roller skates. After shutdown, we'd move on to Carlos'n Charlie's on the Strip, where Robin Williams would riff a blue streak and still be in a monologue when you returned from the dance floor.

Allegra had begun to help Helena with the memberships and the organization of Skataway. She often stayed with me up at Jack's, and suddenly the butterfly began to emerge from the chrysalis. That winter I had stayed in Aspen longer than I had said I would, and Allegra was hurt and let down, because I had promised I would come back to L.A. and help with her end-of-term exams. Helena had taken over in my absence, and now they were good friends. Helena had given Allegra a purpose, and it was great to see her involved in physical activity for the first time. But one night at Carlos'n Charlie's, I caught her kissing a boy and reprimanded her for "acting cheap." I was one to talk! It's an old story—you don't want the people you love to make the same mistakes you've made. I need not have worried; within a few years she was accepted to Hertford College, Oxford University, and graduated three years later with a First in English language and literature. Dad always used to say that Allegra was a lot smarter than any of the biological Hustons.

CHAPTER 12

Jack was starting work on *The Postman Always Rings Twice* up in Santa Barbara, and was being short-tempered with me—a pretty reliable sign that he was otherwise distracted. Jessica Lange was starring and she was at her most luscious. Jack described Jessica to me as the "It Blonde." I asked him what that meant, and he said, "One comes along every decade or so—it's a special thing." The love scenes between them in the movie were torrid.

Bob Rafelson and Jim Harrison were both smitten with Jessica, and I guessed Jack was, too. Rafelson was directing. He and Jack offered me the part of Madge, a lion tamer into whose caravan Jack's character is drawn to spend the evening.

I had done my homework on the part, researching the great touring circuses of the time, and the lion tamers, particularly Mabel Stark, who as early as 1910 did performances with unreliable cats like panthers and leopards and survived not only twelve maulings but five husbands. My mother's friend Dorothy Jeakins, the costume designer on the film, had chosen a beautiful wardrobe for me, with jodhpurs and a wide leather belt and riding boots, and I had found some tiger-claw cuff links in an antique shop in Montecito. I've always liked to wear something of my own when playing a character—it's like mixing sauces.

Because they needed photographs for the walls of my car-avan in the movie, I had gone out to have some pictures taken at a wild-animal sanctuary in Calabasas, California, working with a young tiger. It was great to spend time with him off-leash; we took him swimming in a river and fed him many chicken parts until he started to look at me like one, and then we called it a day.

My first scene in the movie required that I be topless, which was something I had done before for photographs, but I was nervous. We did a rehearsal and then showed it to camera. It was a fractious love scene in which I relentlessly instructed Jack's character on how to pleasure me. I could feel Jack's irritation when I accidentally moved in the opposite way to what we'd rehearsed, and I felt my own hair-trigger temper about to snap in self-defense. But ultimately, the scene went well enough.

As we walked away from the set, Jack pointed to my trailer. "See what Curly put on for you? Your own trailer. That's nice, isn't it?" I felt he was condescending. I remem-ber the resentment a small remark like that could conjure up, my teacup outrages at any suggestion of what was being done for me, and wasn't I a "lucky girl." And how hard it was for me to accept. I wanted desperately to be desired for my own worth, not to be the recipient of a consolation prize. It was a difficult balance.

I went back to Los Angeles and left Jack and his character and his cook, Kathleen, in Santa Barbara. She was a chilly girl with a blond Dutch-boy haircut who baked the best cookies I've ever eaten.

I was driving in my little Mercedes convertible down Coldwater Canyon, a winding road that leads from Mulholland Drive to the valley, when directly in front of me, a silver BMW crossed the line from the opposite lane, hitting the rear bumper of the car in front of mine. As I watched in horrified slow motion, the car turned and came straight at me. Later, they estimated that the BMW was traveling at sixty miles an hour. I was not wearing a seat belt; this was before it was compulsory. There was the image of his headlights, and bracing myself for the impact. I hit the windshield hard.

Everything blacked out but my brain, and it was saying, "Are you blind? Why can you not see?" I felt for the gears and pushed the stick shift forward to park. I was wearing flip-flops and left them on the pedals when I ran out of the car, feeling my way around to the side of the road. Some people came down from a hill with blankets and water, and then the police showed up and called an ambulance. The boy in the BMW was also hurt; he had broken a kneecap.

Sitting on the curb, I discovered that what I had ascribed to blindness was in fact the sheet of blood falling into my eyes from a gash in my forehead. When I put my hands up to my face, I could feel that my nose was flattened. A cop came over. I asked him if my face was badly cut.

"Your nose is broken," he said. "The ambulance is coming—they'll take you to Riverside Hospital."

"No, thank you," I replied. "The plastic surgery is better at Cedars-Sinai."

I got him to call Annie Marshall's number and asked her to come get me. My face looked awful in the rearview mirror. When we arrived at the emergency room, they took me upstairs for X-rays, and Annie set about calling her doctor, who was on the board of directors at Cedars. Just as soon as they had completed a full session of imaging, a diminutive woman appeared. She looked to be in her seventies, with brown hair, and was wearing a white coat. Her glasses hung lopsidedly from her neck by a chain. Annie greeted her with obvious affection. That was how I met the wonderful, compassionate, and renowned Dr. Elsie Giorgi.

Born in the Bronx on March 8, 1911, to Italian immigrants, Elsie was a doctor and friend both to celebrities in Hollywood and to underprivileged minorities in New York and the Watts section of L.A. The youngest of ten children, Elsie put herself through medical school, and after working at Bellevue Hospital and at clinics in East Harlem, she moved west in 1962.

Elsie came over to take a look at me and said sweetly in a heavy New York accent, "Don't worry, dearie, we'll fix you up." She proceeded to order a whole new set of X-rays and booked me into the hospital. It was just a matter of allowing the swelling to reduce for a couple of days before I would have my nose rebuilt. Elsie got me the best plastic surgeon in the hospital, Dr. Adrien Aiache. Because my nose was broken in eight places, it took a long time to extract the bone splinters from my nasal cavity.

Jack was still working on *Postman* but came to the hospital on the night of my surgery and stayed through the whole operation. Elsie and he were both at my bedside when I woke up. Jack had brought champagne and soup from the Beverly Hills Hotel. He told me he loved me, then headed back up the coast to Santa Barbara. A feeling of extraordinary joy washed over me. I felt renewed. I had never felt luckier or stronger before this moment.

After I broke my nose, something changed in me—I made up my mind to take greater advantage of my life. The memory of the headlights of the oncoming car lived in my mind, woke me up at night, reminded me that life is short. How things come and go. How people come and go. I felt powerful, but in order to prove myself, I needed to do my own thing, to have something that was mine alone. So I decided to go to work on that.

PART TWO

FAME

CHAPTER 13

In November 1980, I took Phyllis and Lizzie Spender down to Puerto Vallarta with me to see Dad. Blond-haired and blue-eyed, with Slavic cheekbones, Lizzie was the daughter of the poet Stephen Spender. She and I had been best friends since we first met in London as schoolgirls in the early sixties.

A woman called Joan Blake, who described herself as Gladys's secretary, met us at the airport and took us to Dad's house in town, a solid three-storied edifice on Gringo Gulch. From there we were to head out toward Xalapa from a small harbor called Boca de Tomatlán, in a little motorboat called a panga. Dad's compound was on the coast and reachable only by the sea. We were told by Joan that Gladys was at Dad's, waiting with him for us to arrive.

Dolphins danced rings in the ocean as the sun set blood orange along the coast, and after about thirty-five minutes, in from deep water, we pulled up on the little white beach of Las Caletas. Dad was watching our approach from the cliffs above. Maricela came out to say hello, then went back into hiding. The buildings were all *palapas*—little open-sided dwellings with palm roofs and concrete floors and some mosquito netting. Dad's living quarters were separated from the rest by a bridge that went over a small creek, with bright pink bougainvillea.

Dad was living in a jungle enclave. There was no electricity. Everything worked off a generator. He eventually had a satellite TV, but he was essentially living in the wilderness. There were no roads. He had the forest at his back and the sea in front of him.

Looking down from the cliffs at the beautiful beach below, one would see the ocean alive with fish, manta rays flying out of the water, and there were even whales sometimes. It was an extraordinary place, full of natural beauty. Unpredictable and exotic. Snakes, lizards, scorpions, big bugs.

Next door to Dad's along the coast, separated from his property by jungle, the Von Rohr property was also spectacular—a long, even stretch of virgin beach, with one extraordinary wooden structure in the midst of banana plants and birds of paradise. I would sometimes visit Von Rohr, his wife, Cathy, and their child, Quique, who ran in the jungle barefoot like a towheaded Mowgli.

One day at Las Caletas, a helicopter landed on the beach, blowing shoals of sardines out of the water. It was an awful sight until the pelicans came along and ate them all up. The visitor was Carlo Ponti, the venerable Italian producer. He was traveling with a companion, an entrepreneur, who was building his dream hotel on the coast of Mismaloya.

Dad loved our morning conferences, when we would give each other updates on the preceding night, including sleep or lack thereof, dreams, visitations by mosquitoes, sightings of scorpions, and plans for the morning—reading materials, exercise, snorkeling. We had to report to the commander. This brought me back directly to my childhood in Ireland, when my brother Tony and I would run upstairs to Dad's bedroom for breakfast and he would ask us, "What news?" even though we had seen him at dinner the night before.

In the natural calm of Las Caletas, the days began with dawn and ended with the last glimmer of sunset. Dad's attitude had changed in Mexico; he was warmer, kinder, less judgmental, even if he asked me once, at twenty-eight, if I wasn't "a little old for that, honey" when I braced myself and said, "Dad, I want to act again."

Maricela was a constant presence in the background. Dad told me he thought she was like a little animal, a coati. She tended to his needs, and they seemed to have made a pact to be together. Dad, in his mid-seventies, was obviously feeling his age. He told me that he had leased Las Caletas for only ten years.

"Then, if I'm still alive, I can rent it again from the indigenous people, or it can just fall back into the jungle." Dad told me about his last conversation with his dear friend Willy Wyler. Willy had opened his eyes for the first time in a long time and said, "Hold my hand, Johnny, I'm dying."

Dad said, "Wait six weeks. If you feel the same, I'll help you."

"But that's criminal, John."

"Shit, Willy, we'll get on a motorbike!"

Lee Grant was directing a film based on the Strindberg play *Playing with Fire* in February 1981. It had a lovely cast, including Carol Kane and Maximilian Schell; I was excited and flattered when Lee offered me the part of Adele, the maid. I had very little formal training at this point, and apart from *Hamlet*, no stage experience at all. I could see this grating away at Lee in rehearsal. I could also see that my choices of flimsy summer dresses and strappy sandals for rehearsal had started to irritate her. Maybe Lee thought I was too flirtatious. The objective was to mount the play in an empty Spanish house that Lee had rented, and shoot it all the way through as a movie. I was going slow and having some issues with Adele, a complicated character who spends a lot of time in tears, running between the two male characters. I felt that Adele was quite manipulative, and I was still working out her intentions. One morning Lee grabbed my script and proceeded to enact the part of Adele, reading from the text in a voice thick with tears. I was astonished. Unfortunately, later that afternoon Lee discovered that she had lost the financing for the movie.

Driving back to town from Lee's home in Malibu with Carol Kane, I was feeling very sorry for myself, still stinging from the humiliation. "How could Lee have done that?" I asked.

Carol looked at me. "Have you ever gone to class?"

"Not really," I said. "I've just been doing it by instinct—I have no technique."

"Why don't you try it? You might like it, and at least you'll be able to say you've done it, if anyone asks." I went home and digested this advice, reminding myself of my new determination to get moving.

So when Jack's friend Harry Gittes suggested that I might like going along with him to audit an acting class, I agreed. The teacher, someone Jack had studied with in previous years, had a big reputation. It was a lovely gesture on Harry's part; he recognized how paralyzed I was and wanted to help me out.

The class was in a room somewhere in the San Fernando Valley. The teacher had a large white standard poodle that sniffed up the girls' dresses as they did their relaxation exercises. There was some neck rolling, loud yawns and sighs, and stretching on the floor. A few improvisations followed, culminating in a passionate breakdown on the part of a well-known television actress I'd admired for years in a Western series. She was on her knees, hands outstretched, sobbing and pleading with the teacher to give her a dime.

On the way home in the car, I ranted to Harry about what a wanker I thought the teacher was, how I could never attend such a class, how embarrassing it had been. Harry finally got a word in edgewise and said, "I'm sorry if you didn't like it. I just thought it might give you some ideas."

One evening Toby Rafelson gave a dinner at her house for Tony Richardson, who had moved to Los Angeles. Tony was seated on a low divan and called to me across the room. "Come here," he said, "you poor, dear, little thing!"

Obligingly, I walked over to him. "What do you mean?" I said, smiling defensively.

"Poor little you," Tony continued. "So much talent and so little to show for it. You're never going to do anything with your life." He had a singsong voice, like one of his own parrots, and he spoke with a slight lisp, but there was no mistaking the edge.

"Perhaps you're right," I answered. Inside I was thinking, "Watch me."

Even though I must confess to loathing criticism, it has often been my catalyst for moving ahead. And it is the sheer effrontery of someone telling me what I cannot do, or never will do, that brings out my most primal defiance.

It was not that I was merely sitting around, waiting for

things to happen to me; it was that I hadn't found my way in. I needed a background for my craft.

I spoke with my new best friend, Greta Ronningen, about a teacher she'd worked with—Peggy Feury, of the Loft Studio. Greta felt that we would be a good match. Within a few days, I met Peggy and joined her class. It is not enough to say that Peggy was a great teacher. To me, she was a revelation. I was, at thirty, the oldest person in her novice class. For the next couple of years, five days a week, I drove from my house to her studio on La Brea, sometimes with bags of props in the back seat, always looking forward to the work. The Loft Studio became my second home.

The first exercise Peggy gave me was to acquire an object from another actor—almost the same situation I'd witnessed in the class I'd audited with Harry Gittes. But this time it was me begging for the dime. I worked hard throughout the scene. After it was over, Peggy said, "Anjelica, you're a tall and imposing girl, a big presence. When you ask for something, you don't need to extend your hand. You have our attention." It was a great piece of advice. It was the awakening in me to the illusion of confidence. I had not realized it until that moment, but I was pleading for things that I could have simply asked for.

Peggy was slight, fair, with pale wavy hair and China-blue eyes that would roll back dreamily whenever she made a momentary departure from the scene—she had narcolepsy. She could fall asleep sitting on a stool. Peggy had a short torso and long slender legs, and she always wore skirts and pale stockings. Peggy derived great pleasure from teaching, although she could be openly bored or irritated by a student's actions or performance. She had a vast knowledge of playwrights and gave us assignments that challenged us, characters that made us stretch, parts that led us into new, unexpected directions. Peggy had coached or taught class to people like Lily Tomlin, Sean and Chris Penn, Michelle Pfeiffer, Meg Tilly, Melissa Gilbert, and Eric Stoltz, and it was no coincidence that they were among the best actors of their generation.

Horton Foote, Jr., was working at the Loft Studio at the same time I was, and we had access sometimes to his father's new work. Bill Traylor, Peggy's husband, gave improv classes. He and I butted heads quite often. But Peggy rebuilt my confidence the most by making me her friend, and I adored her.

In my diary, I wrote that Peggy and I had an unspoken conversation; words, when they came, were often superfluous. She had an extraordinary gift for making one feel understood. I would look over at Peggy in class sometimes and almost see a halo; I thought that she was halfway to heaven.

Peggy died several years later in a car crash. It is possible she fell asleep at the wheel. Her loss was deeply mourned by her students. Her memorial took place at the Mark Taper Forum, and the theater was filled to capacity. Her beautiful daughters, Susan and Stephanie, spoke. It was evident that Peggy's light shone through them. The aria from *Madame Butterfly* played. Lily Tomlin made us laugh through our tears. I held hands with Joan Didion.

Nona and Martin came to Aspen in March 1981. Her apparel on the slopes was an instant inspiration, and soon all the women in town were wearing jackets and parkas with inflated shoulder pads. Not that I ever needed them—my shoulders are so broad, I looked like a linebacker. We were all done up in spandex jeans in lurid shades of shocking purple, pink, and puce; Marsia Holzer's dangling metallic fish purses; the custom cowboy boots from Smith's; the Rocky Raccoon hat. My uniform was Levi's, pearls, and a mink coat.

Annie Marshall began working at Smith's on Galena Street. They were selling knitted angora sweaters with patterns of clouds and hearts and horseshoes, long skirts, and cowboy gear. I met the jewelry designer Darlene de Sedle Vare, who lived in town with her twin children, Tai and Jessie. Jill St. John, the gorgeous redheaded actress and friend of Cici's, lived up at Snowmass. Jane and Jimmy Buffett had bought a house down-valley in Woody Creek. The Eagles, Leonard and Jane Holzer, Peter Beard, and Michael and Diandra Douglas were often seen in town.

I used to walk around in big black furry boots to the knee with my new puppies, Ray and Dolly, trotting at my feet. According to the whim of the day, if we were not skiing, we girls would start up either at the Aspen Club for a serious workout on the Nautilus machines or belly up to the bar at the Mother Lode with a pitcher of margaritas in front of us. Often we would congregate at the Buffetts' in the evening, cracking open stone crab shipped in from Miami. Jimmy cooked gumbo. Great music, cool guys, beautiful girls hanging loose at Margaritaville in the Rockies.

Jack, Bob Rafelson, Coulter Adams, and I once shared a harrowing if ultimately miraculous escape from injury when a roofless Land Rover that Bob was driving did a rollover in the Maroon Bells and tossed us out on the dirt. The combination of thin air, the elixir of the mountains, the age, the times, the substances, the rate of consumption—for the sheer elation of grabbing a cat by all four legs and dancing with it till dawn if necessary, Aspen reigned queen!

Everyone was getting high in my circle. Coke and grass were ubiquitous. Something about that particular place, at that particular time, had us engaged in improving and expanding the life experience through the use of drugs, a choice that took a lot of people up and many down.

It was hard to tell who was having more fun, the cheerful outlaws in our midst or the DEA agents, who seemed to be in legendary half-pursuit. There were always tales of narrow escapes and foiled arrests in the *Aspen Times*. On one occasion, a private plane carrying a number of inebriated FBI agents crashed on Highland Mountain; no one was hurt, but a vast number of beer cans were recovered at the scene. These kinds of stories were commonplace.

We thought we were pretty terrific until a guy came into town like the Lone Ranger and burned all the girls so bad, they were crying and squealing one night at a party at Annie's. We called him "Dracula." He had torn a swath through the hearts of several in our ranks and was visibly moving on to another romantic quest that same evening. By the end of the week, there was not a female left standing, including me, after a horse ride up Hunter Creek, oysters at Abetone's, and a nightcap at his condo.

The following day he left town as quietly as a stealth bomber. The girls were like stunned chickens, with their eyes blinking and their heads bobbing in the aftermath. Then we heard that he was decimating the female population of Los Angeles. We cursed him, made effigies, spat on them, stuffed them with pins, and wished him old before his time.

In the eighties, practically every face on the mountain was famous. Gary Hart was gearing up for his presidential run. Jack and I were invited to a fund-raiser at a house down-valley.

When we arrived, Senator Hart was chopping away at some fallen wood with a hatchet for a photo op in the back yard. Don Henley was there, alongside a few other celebrities. A very pretty young girl, blond and about twelve years old, came over to sit beside me. She introduced herself as Gwyneth Paltrow and pointed out her mother and father. Looking nervously across the room at Jack, she said, "That man scares me."

"With good reason," I replied. "He scares me, too."

Suddenly, everyone was wearing fur and movie stars were ubiquitous, flying in for Christmas holidays, building mansions better suited to the South of France or Beverly Hills. You'd see Diana Ross without makeup on her way to the deli, and Goldie Hawn and her kids at the supermarket. Big movie stars behaving like ordinary people. This was before there was a gossip columnist at the *Aspen Times*, when the locals were still running the few restaurants and operating the ski lifts. Then all at once, the early freedoms disappeared. Oil-rich Texans took over for a brief moment. There was the short tenure of Marvin Davis at Aspen Mountain, and the creation of a Four Seasons Hotel, replete with gift shops, at its foot. The restaurants multiplied; Chanel, Prada, and Louis Vuitton opened boutiques. The airport was filled to capacity with Learjets. After the Texans came the Arab oligarchs and then the Russians. The runway was a great platform from which to view the changing dynasties.

In the eighties, the locals could no longer sustain in Aspen, and they moved down-valley to Basalt and Carbondale and Glenwood Springs. Those who once owned the town became its working class, serving the mega-rich on and off the slopes, until a new working class was imported to serve in the new hotels. They came from Guatemala, Mexico, and El Salvador.

To undermine the jobs and create another round of problems, crime and gangs proliferated, hitherto unseen in the Rockies.

One New Year's Eve at Abetone's, everyone kissed dangerously at midnight. There were whole uneaten, naked Cornish game hens illuminated by the low-hanging lamps on each table. Hunter Thompson was taking potshots at the lightbulbs with quarters and a rubber band.

On a subsequent New Year's, there was a scene involving an arson fire that was set after Jack and I left a party at a Tuscan villa in Woody Creek, where some girls who had stayed over had to leap from the balcony, nude under their fur coats, into a snowdrift. Things could get hardcore quite swiftly. There were always various stories going on in Aspen—dramatic stuff, like James Bond combined with *Tales from the Vienna Woods*.

But still there was the country itself—the clarity of the light that burnished the mountains to red-gold at sunset, the high lakes, the little streams that babbled in the summertime, the slopes thick with ferns and berries, happy days at the summer music festival, partying till the wee hours. One July 4, I rode horseback through town in the Aspen parade. Aspen was simultaneously healthy and hedonistic. There was also a dark streak to the place, given that it was heaven on earth to prospectors and outlaws. There wasn't a lot of conversation about what people did for a living, and we never complained that we were bored—there was always something going on; life was lived on the edge.

In April 1981, a call came out of the blue, as they will. It was Dad. "I'd like for you to come to me in New York," he said.

"Gladys has died." He sounded terrible, like he had been kicked in the stomach. He had been working with her on the script of *Annie*.

When I went up to his suite at the Essex House, Maricela and Tony were with him. Dad just lay on the couch with his face to the wall and wept. I had never seen him so bereaved. It was not meant for Gladys to go before him. They'd had a date for dinner, and she mentioned she was a little tired and went to have a lie-down. When he called her room, she didn't answer the phone. Eventually the hotel staff opened her door, and found her in bed. She had died in her sleep.

Maricela and I went to the Frank Campbell Funeral Home on Madison Avenue to say our final farewell to Gladys. They showed us to a gray room with artificial flowers and a box of Kleenex on the table and an open coffin in which Gladys lay, looking very much unlike herself. Her pale hair swept back from her forehead onto the pillow in an unfamiliar cascading wave.

CHAPTER 14

I received a letter from Dad's agent, Paul Kohner, suggesting that I agree to be represented by his agency. I said I felt that it was probably best to be in a different stable. Dad offered to call Sue Mengers for me. I was quite intimidated by her, having gone with Jack on several occasions to parties at her house in Bel Air. She was a "broad" in the old sense, as round and pale as porcelain, with a mane of ash-blond hair that fell forward over one eye. She spoke slowly and deliberately, with an emphasis on consonants, and rich with heavy pauses to accentuate her often surprisingly candid thoughts about life, gossip, the British royal family, and the sex lives of her favorite movie stars.

Sue's houses—the first one, in Bel Air, which she shared with her husband, Jean-Claude Tramont; the second, at the base of Coldwater Canyon, on Lexington Road—had the same color scheme, pale pink and blue-gray. Sofas and chairs in pastel silk, the long regency windows looking out on an oval balustraded swimming pool. The rooms were filled with French antiques, a Chinese ceramic given to her by Lorne Michaels, a Japanese calligraphy scroll that batted on the wall behind her head in a soft breeze. Sue, wreathed in pot smoke, would hold court, her guests settled around her, to the right and left, as she introduced topics that ranged from provocative to saucy to borderline outrageous.

She loved getting a bunch of women together for lunch, wherein she would extol our husbands or boyfriends and tell us how lucky we were and what a miracle it was that we might have such wonderful men in our lives. Sue blamed women for most things. Men could do no wrong, particularly after the death of Jean-Claude, whom she worshipped.

When I ran off with her client Ryan O'Neal, Sue was embarrassed and subsequently was photographed out a few times on Jack's arm. I flattered her by saying I suspected they were having a love affair. I said this in full knowledge that as much as Jack adored her, she was not someone who could be remotely described physically as his "type." But Sue loved this idea, and whenever I'd go over to her house for lunch with the most powerful women in Hollywood, she would be sure to rehash the story of how I suspected her of having sex with Jack. At the same time, Sue always said to me, "Jack is the best there is. You are a fool not to close the deal."

Sue represented just about every actor of consequence in the Hollywood firmament, and Barbra Streisand was her star client. She turned down Dad's request on my behalf without a moment's hesitation, replying that I was too similar to another actress she already represented, Ali MacGraw, who had starred in *Love Story*.

Sue, however, remained a mentor to me always, and although it was sometimes hard to take, I could rely on her to tell me the truth—an invaluable commodity in Hollywood. Through the years, I overcame my natural fear of Sue, and toward the end of her life, she and I had become good friends.

Despite the fact that Sue did not take me on as a client, this was a time in my life when roles began to come my way.

* * *

Anjelica and Manolo Blahnik at a photo shoot for British *Vogue* at the Negresco Hotel, Nice, France, 1973, styled by Grace Coddington. Photographed by David Bailey.

Anjelica and Ara Gallant in Munich, 1973. Ara was
"an artist who worked with hair" and later a photographer.

Music producer Lou Adler, Anjelica, Ara Gallant,
Jack's assistant Annie Marshall, and Cher at the airport in Santa Monica,
California, on their way to Aspen, 1975.

John Huston as Noah Cross with Jack Nicholson as J. J. Gittes
on the set of *Chinatown*, directed by Roman Polanski in 1973.

Producer Andy Braunsberg, Jack Nicholson, Anjelica,
her childhood friend Joan Juliet Buck, and filmmaker Henry Jaglom
at the Cannes Film Festival, May 1974.

Photographed by Kenny Solms

Anjelica in the trunk of the Mercedes
Jack Nicholson gave her in the mid-seventies.

Photographed by Michael Childers

Anjelica with Big Boy, a Labrador mix,
at home on Mulholland Drive,
in the late seventies.

Jack Nicholson and Anjelica
at the Academy Awards
for *Chinatown*, April 8, 1975.

Anjelica and
Ryan O'Neal.

Anjelica giving Harry Dean Stanton a haircut at Jack's house
in Maroon Creek, Aspen, late seventies.

Jack Nicholson, Kathleen Turner, John Huston, and Anjelica, publicity still for *Prizzi's Honor*, 1984.

Anjelica and Jack Nicholson walking into the Dorothy Chandler Pavilion for the 58th Academy Awards for *Prizzi's Honor*, March 24, 1986.

Jack with Dolly and Ray, 1979.

Celebrating Anjelica's thirty-fifth birthday at Helena Kallianiotes's night club Helena's in Silver Lake, 1986.

Anjelica and Jack Nicholson at the 51st Annual New York Film Critics Circle Awards, 1985. He won best actor and she won best supporting actress for *Prizzi's Honor*.

Photographed by Joan Juliet Buck

Anjelica posing as the Marlboro Man
in Montana, July 1975, while Jack
was shooting *The Missouri Breaks*.

Photographed by Phyllis Somer

Anjelica visiting her father
at his house in Las Caletas,
Mexico, in 1980.

Danny's mother, Zoë; Allegra; Danny; John; and Anjelica celebrating John's
eighty-first birthday in the intensive care unit at Charlton Memorial Hospital
in Fall River, Massachusetts, in 1987 during the filming of *Mr. North*.

In December, Penny Marshall offered me a guest appearance on her show, *Laverne & Shirley*. I was to play a jealous wife who catches her husband cheating with Laverne over dinner in a seafood restaurant. The episode was shot in front of a live audience and culminated with Laverne diving into a lobster tank and getting attacked by a giant clam. It was a great lesson in comedy, watching Penny at work with eyes wide, holding her breath underwater, her thigh in the vise grip of the huge crustacean, scrawling the word "help" on the glass in red lipstick and at the same time winning hearts by just being herself. I was speechless with admiration. I was to work on the show again the following year, that time as a fashion model teetering down a runway with an Eiffel Tower on my head.

Penny Marshall and Carrie Fisher were best friends. Following Carrie's separation from Paul Simon and her return to California, she and Penny would team up and throw themselves an annual birthday party. Carrie had a regiment of fabulous black women cooking in her kitchen, and they always served soul food. Her houses were playground haciendas, full of whimsy and humor. Penny's collections of lamps, hook rugs, sports memorabilia, and antiques were extensive. The parties were always brimming with interest; everyone went—artists, musicians, directors, writers, actors, moguls.

This was a time before sponsored events, which, along with red-carpet madness, changed the face of celebrity in the eighties. Although I am grateful for the attention I have enjoyed throughout the years, I don't believe that the level of interest ever merits a personal invasion.

It was at one such interesting and well-attended party at Penny's that I first encountered the screenwriter Mitch Glazer. I had met his dearest friend and writing partner,

Michael O'Donoghue, some time before, and we had become good friends—never in a carnal way, although I thought he had a crush on me. I adored him, and he was an eternal source of sharp-witted black humor. Michael was an original writer on Lorne Michaels's *Saturday Night Live* and was responsible for the creation of the character Mr. Bill. He had told me about Mitch, but I was unprepared for how handsome he was.

At the time, Mitch was married to Wendie Malick, a tall, pretty, slender actress working in television. Once when I was in New York over Halloween, I got caught in a gay parade on my way to their house on Tenth Street and was almost run over by a giant latex penis. Mitch and I have remained close since those early days. After he and Wendy broke up, he married Kelly Lynch, the great-looking blonde whom we first saw shake up the screen in *Drugstore Cowboy*.

I was asked by a young director, Lyndon Chubbuck, to play the lead in a short film adaptation of a William Faulkner story, "A Rose for Emily." In its small way, it was a professional breakthrough, and I was flattered to have been chosen for no reason other than that he felt I was right for the part. The movie was low-budget—we shot at a group of preserved Victorian homes off the 10 Freeway. The traffic made it very difficult for sound, but it was a worthy effort.

John Randolph played my father, Mr. Grierson. John Carradine, Sr., played Colonel Sartoris, and although he was aged and delicate, he was still game and a marvelous actor. Jared Martin played the lover I poison in the film; he likewise was a pleasure to work with. It made all the difference to have had the security of years spent in Peggy Feury's class. For the first time in my life, I had acquired some authority, had developed an overview and a plan for my character. And I was the teacher's pet. This feeling of confidence was new for me. I was excited to have been given the chance to prove myself to people who were not personally invested, like my father or my boyfriend.

On March 3, 1983, the American Film Institute dedicated an evening to Dad and his work, a big televised event at the Beverly Hilton Hotel in Los Angeles. Lauren Bacall was the host, and I had been asked to do a segment introducing various luminaries who had worked with Dad through the years, each of whom would have an opportunity to speak about him. It was a most beautiful night. The room was filled to capacity with people in Dad's life, past and present.

Ava Gardner, in a rare appearance, had come in from London. I was bowled over by how radiant she was, even next to the lovely Nastassja Kinski. Ava's beauty just jumped out at you; her eyes glittered and her skin glowed. She was wrapped in white fur, seated next to Dad like a snow leopard in a diamond necklace.

When Dad walked in at the opening of the show, I could tell he was holding his breath, having to move fast to get to his seat beside Ava, where his oxygen tank was concealed under the table. People stopped him as he moved through the crowd to congratulate him and shake his hand, and when he arrived at the table, he was gasping for air.

Lauren Bacall, the widow of Dad's beloved Bogie, was onstage, greeting the room. When it was my turn to get up, I was so nervous that I bungled my assignment and sped through the roster of famous names without pausing to allow any of them to speak. Only when I came to Zsa Zsa Gabor and saw the astonished look on her face did I realize my mistake. Thank God it was not live television. I had to go back to the beginning, which was humiliating, but the staff pretended graciously that it was a technical difficulty, and although I was still red in the face, I asked Dad from the stage if he would ever consider working with me again. The film that we had made together when I was sixteen, *A Walk with Love and Death*, had been a personal, commercial, and professional disappointment and I wanted a second chance. John Foreman was in the audience, and he decided he would do something about that, as I learned several months later.

At the end of the evening, on our way out of the ballroom, Jack and I joined Ava for the walk down the red carpet. She had been living in Europe for a long time, and the local press was overjoyed to see her. The flashbulbs were popping and the paparazzi were shouting her name exuberantly. Ava just glided between us with that million-dollar smile, uttering a stream of profanities.

Rob Reiner was planning an improvisational movie, *This Is Spinal Tap*, with a handful of brilliant people like Harry Shearer and Christopher Guest. I was asked to read for the snobbish British girlfriend and, as I recall, gave a passable audition with an authentic Notting Hill accent. But the part went to June Chadwick. As a consolation, Rob gave me the part of Polly Deutsch, the production designer who delivers an eighteen-inch Stonehenge to the band for their concert. Even though it was a tiny role, I was very proud to be a part of the comedy, which became a cult classic.

I auditioned for a Tommy Tune musical in New York, and I guess they liked my reading. I was unaware that I would be expected to sing. The part was oratorical, and I did it with an English accent. The producers asked if I'd come back and sing a song titled "My Love Is a Married Man." It was one of those Broadway auditions in front of about twenty people. Although I had hired an accompanist who had attempted to teach me the song, it was daunting. In the audition I not only changed octaves, I changed voices. Even though I destroyed the song, they all burst into applause. However, I knew very definitely that I hadn't gotten the part. They obviously found it audacious of me to even try. As I walked out onto Broadway, confused about whether to laugh or cry, I thought maybe I should hook up with a voice coach.

When I got back to Los Angeles, I sought out David Craig, who was known for teaching actors how to sing—people like Cicely Tyson, Raquel Welch, and Lucille Ball. There were interesting people in the class, like Melanie Griffith and Candy Bergen's mother, Frances. Some of the people there had been singing for years and just liked going to the class so they could practice. The first song David Craig gave me to sing was "Where or When," and I spent close to the entire three-month term trying to get through it without leaving the stage in tears. For a long time I found it difficult to sing in public. My voice reminded me of my mother's when she used to sing to me when I was a child back in Ireland. I would tearfully run across Hollywood Boulevard to Musso and Frank's after class and drink whiskey sours with my friend Ray Underwood, just to recover. It was awful. When I finally got through the song, the room exploded, everyone was so relieved. It was a full-on triumph. David said, "Now you don't ever need to come back," and I never did.

*   *   *

The Ice Pirates was essentially a B movie that John Foreman, who had become my champion, was producing at MGM. I was playing the part of Maida, the greatest swordswoman in the universe; Robert Urich and Mary Crosby were starring. My love interest in the movie was an Oakland Raiders defensive lineman, football great John Matuszak, "the Tooz," a sweet man with the frame of a gorilla. In one scene he allowed me to climb onto his shoulders; it was like scaling an oak tree. I liked creating Maida's wardrobe—leather armor, tights, thigh-high stiletto-heeled boots—and wearing long braids with the skulls of small monkeys and rodents attached like lucky charms. All through filming, the Tooz was mild-mannered and easy to work with. Apart from one instance when I walked into a camera shutter and gashed my eyelid, the shoot was calm.

On the last day of work, the Tooz asked if I'd like to go to his dressing room to say goodbye before leaving set. When I knocked on his door, he filled the space as it swung open and I walked inside. Without much ado, he pulled off an oversized cowboy boot and produced from it a handgun, followed by a big white bag of cocaine, which he proceeded to overturn onto a Formica table. The firearm and the sheer amount of the drug were unnerving. When he proffered a rolled-up hundred-dollar bill, I murmured an excuse about having to drive home and left as soon as I could politely get out the door.

Later that week, Greta reported on going to a heavyweight fight in Vegas with Bert and Jack and, incidentally, the Tooz. They were aboard an MGM Grand Air charter plane, and during takeoff, the Tooz mixed all the miniature bottles of

Stolichnaya at hand with a carton of orange juice into a jumbo plastic container, the kind old ladies cradled on their laps in front of the slot machines. Everyone on the plane was sharing this concoction. A few years later, John Matuszak died at the age of thirty-eight of a prescription-drug overdose.

CHAPTER 15

It was during *Ice Pirates* that John Foreman gave me a book by Richard Condon called *Prizzi's Honor*. He said, "Read this and let me know what you think of it."

I read it overnight. It was a wonderful book, a Mob story full of wit and black humor. I went back to him the next day and said, "It's great."

"What do you think about playing Maerose Prizzi?" he asked.

I said, "What a great idea. Fantastic!"

He said, "Yeah. What do you think about Jack as the hit man, Charley Partanna, and your dad to direct?"

And I thought, "Oh, damn!" because I knew I was going to be sandwiched between these two big rocks.

When *The Ice Pirates* came to a close, I got a call from Foreman saying, "We've got to get Jack down to Vallarta to see your dad. Your dad can't come up here, he's too sick. You've gotta get Jack to go there."

I said, "I'll get Jack to go, but I'm not going there with him."

And he said, "You have to."

I said, "I'm scared of flying, and anyway, I know what's going to happen. Inevitably, I'm going to get down there and hear everyone's problems, because there are always problems connected to work. I'm going to hear Dad's problems about

145

Jack, Jack's problems about Dad. And I'm going to be on an island in the middle of nowhere, with no way out. With the sea in front and the jungle behind. Forget it."

Somehow I managed to get Jack to go. I said, "Dad is sick. This could be it. Who knows if he's even well enough to make this movie? He adores you. Please do this." Jack sweetly complied and went down to Puerto Vallarta. Of course, there was no telephone; it was all CB radio down there, and Foreman couldn't get a beep out of Jalisco. On the third day or so, he was starting to get a little consternated. So he called me up and said, "Okay. We're leaving for the airport at six A.M. tomorrow."

I replied, "No we're not."

John said, "Yes we are. I'm gonna come to your house and pick you up at six. We're going down to Puerto Vallarta."

And I said, "No. I'm not going."

Next morning at 6 A.M., my doorbell rang. I opened the door in my nightdress. There was John Foreman. He said, "You're not ready. Get ready." To which I replied, "No. I told you. I'm not gonna be in the middle of this." John spun on his heel, furious, and off he went down my hill and took the trip to Mexico. By chance, upon arrival in Puerto Vallarta, he saw Jack buying huaraches at the airport. Jack was on his way back to L.A. They'd had the most fabulous time, he and Dad. They had watched female Olympic gymnasts on the satellite feed. Jack hadn't hitherto understood that *Prizzi's Honor* was a comedy. He'd read it as a serious piece. Jack had missed the point until Dad suggested that perhaps he wear a toupee as the main character, which Jack confided he had no intention of doing. But now that he understood, now that my father had explained it to him, it was all hands on deck. And that was the inception of *Prizzi's Honor*.

* * *

It seemed that no talent agency wanted to take me on prior to *Prizzi's Honor.* Most didn't even bother to return my phone calls. Eventually, I joined the Yvette Bikoff Agency. It was a small agency, but Yvette seemed to have more confidence in me than the others. Feeling that I had been instrumental in bringing together the main elements for the film, with Jack and Dad signing on for *Prizzi's Honor*, I suggested that Yvette might make an attempt to raise my asking price above scale. "I've tried," Yvette replied. "They refuse to even discuss it."

"Why don't you call the production guy now and just ask once more?" I pressed her. As I was standing there, she put the phone on speaker and dialed the number.

An irritated voice came on the line. "You want more money for Anjelica Huston? You must be kidding . . . go ahead, ask me!" said the voice. "We'd like nothing better than to see her dropped from the film. She has no talent. Her boyfriend is the star and her father is the director, that's the only reason we are even having this conversation."

Standing in Yvette's office, listening to this man rant on, made my eyes prickle and my heart beat with indignation. But I also vowed silently that when the movie came out, he would eat his words.

We were in New York, about to start *Prizzi's Honor.* I went to visit Joan Buck, who lent me one of her mother's couture dresses and jewelry from the fifties for the part. We were working in a rehearsal space somewhere in midtown. Costume and hair tests were also going on in the building. I was introduced to a hairdresser with a wild Afro called Anthony Cortino, who took me to a wigmaker for a waist-length fall, and to a tall man with a touchy demeanor, the costume designer Donfeld. He actually spelled his name all in one word. I thought that was very fifties, and he must have sniffed out my disdain. When I suggested that the taffeta sash on the vintage dress I was trying on for him should perhaps be Schiaparelli pink, he said, "I totally disagree," shaking his head and flinging his arms in the air. Minutes later, when we showed the dress to Dad, he looked me over for a few silent moments. "What if the sash were Schiaparelli pink?" he asked. Donfeld looked shocked. I laughed hard on that one. When Dad and I were in sync, we thought alike.

Dad's theory was that if you were looking to cast a character, you'd better go straight to the source, even if the person wasn't necessarily an actor. It was thus that Dad's secretary from years past, longer ago yet than Gladys Hill, came to act the part of Aunt Amalia in *Prizzi's Honor*. Her name was Annie Selepegno. She was a sweet woman and no doubt physically perfect for the part, but very stiff, and not gifted in the least as an actress. She had agreed to do the role because in spite of her eighty-plus years, she had something of a gambling addiction and needed to pay some outstanding bills. In the wings stood Julie Bovasso, a great New York stage actress, but Dad had refused to give her the part.

A few days into preproduction, Dad had the cast come in for a table reading after wardrobe fittings. He listened with his eyes closed as we went through the script. I wondered at one point if he was taking a nap, but this was not the case, since he got up abruptly and left the room as soon as we finished. I could sense that something was troubling him.

Two days later, he called Jack and me to request that the three of us assemble in Jack's suite at the Carlyle. As the sun fell and the shadows grew long over Central Park, Dad put an arm around each of us and drew us close to gaze out the window across the tree line. "Look at that," he said. "Quite something, isn't it?" We agreed that it was. Then, with a note of triumph, like a little boy with a lizard in his pocket, he said, "I've got it!" He produced a tape recorder. "Listen to this," he said, pushing the play button. "It's the voice of the movie!" Julie Bovasso's Brooklyn accent was to be our guideline. I took to frequenting churches in Brooklyn, while Jack visited the gaming parlors.

Laila Nabulsi had split from Hunter Thompson and was living at Judy Belushi's apartment in New York when she met John Foreman and became his assistant on *Prizzi's*. Boaty Boatwright, a senior agent at ICM and a longtime friend of my family, introduced them. Foreman ordered that his assistants have breakfast together each morning and proceed to set, to be there before anyone else arrived. When Dad walked on set, everyone stood up. Foreman ran a tight ship, and everyone knew it was worth it. He was a fantastic producer and wonderfully loyal to Dad.

Jack and I had met Tommy Baratta in Aspen, and now we were all frequenting his restaurant in the Village, Marylou's, hanging out, eating pasta, and practicing our Brooklyn accents. Tommy Baratta had a great way with food and became Jack's personal chef. There were always incredible smells emanating from Jack's trailer and enveloping everything in a haze of tomato and garlic and olives and New Jersey peppers. Generally, we would have lunch in or around Jack's trailer—since Tommy had now basically sacrificed his restaurant in order to cook for Jack—and the counters and cooking surfaces were covered with olive oil, salamis, and cheeses.

Laila knocked on Jack's door one morning to tell him they were ready on the set. Indira Gandhi had been shot that day in India, and Laila asked Jack if he had heard the news. Jack looked out the window. He was in full character as Charley Partanna. "Broads!" was all he said.

My part, Maerose, had all the good elements working for it. She was the exiled daughter of the Prizzi family, who would do literally anything to recapture the heart of its top consigliere, Charley Partanna. The character was an outsider, complex and layered, a dark horse who knew exactly what she wanted and how to go after it. I made off-work dates with individual members of the *Prizzi's* cast to get a feeling about who they were and what their standing might be in the setup.

Robert Loggia played my uncle Eduardo, the Prizzis' lawyer. He was by birth a blond Sicilian. He observed, "One of the reasons you might want to talk low and out the corner of your mouth is so that people can't see what you are saying—in Brooklyn as in Sicily, not everyone needs to know your business." That piece of advice gave me good insight into the nature of Maerose Prizzi.

Bill Hickey played the don. He was extraordinary. He had worked in *Wise Blood* and was a favorite actor of Dad's. They had a shorthand. "How do you want me to do this, John?" Bill asked Dad about the part of the don.

"Like a reptile," Dad answered.

Bill taught an acting class that I audited when I was in New York. He would sit motionless in his chair, a perpetual cigarette hanging from his lips, dripping ashes on his shirtfront, eyelids at half-mast, offering the occasional slice of dry wit or a cackle of irony. Every day he came to set with a flask of coffee that looked like squid ink when he poured it, a sandwich in recycled tinfoil, and an enormous bad-tempered English sheepdog with dreadlocks and bad breath.

I soon developed a deep affection for my hairdresser, Anthony, whom I nicknamed "Mittoine." He was a wonderful, gentle, sweet, funny man. We used to laugh like hyenas together. Mittoine was gay, and mad about Barbra Streisand. But he was also devoted to me and went along with all my opinions, even if they were way off the mark. Once in a while, just for the hell of it, I would criticize Streisand. Any word against her was akin to treason, and it caused him a terrible riot of emotion to have to tolerate my comments about the goddess he idolized. Sometimes, if I was on set but not working in a scene, we would fool around with John Foreman and Laila while the camera was rolling, just to see whom we could make laugh out loud by tickling each other or stepping on each other's feet. I know of no other producers who would risk losing a take because of such silly behavior, but John Foreman instigated it, and what a joy it was to feel such liberty—he was setting me free, and we both knew it.

There was also a friend from the Halston days backstage—Bruce Weintraub, who was working in the art department as the set decorator. We had an excellent, handsome Polish director of photography, Andrzej Bartkowiak, who really knew how to light an actress. For one particular moment in the film, when Maerose dresses in black and paints herself up to look like an old spinster, Andrzej said to me, "Do you want to look bad-bad in this scene or good-bad?" Even the scenes where Maerose looked rough had a certain glamour. I looked forward to every day on set. The atmosphere was conspiratorial. Foreman had handpicked the crew, from Meta Wilde, who had been Dad's script girl on *Maltese Falcon*, to

Rudi Fehr, his editor from *Key Largo*. Rudi was now working with his daughter, Kaja, in the cutting room. It was a great cast of characters.

Our first day of work was in a wedding chapel in Brooklyn, and I remember sitting in the back of a company car that morning on the West Side Highway, with dawn coming up over the city and nude men displaying themselves in the windows of the lofts in the Meatpacking District. I was sharing my ride with the girl who was cast to play the bride, and the driver remarked to me as we got out of the car that she was beautiful. I remember feeling a stab of jealousy and thinking, "Yes, this is what Maerose is all about. And now she's going to turn the tables."

Kathleen Turner was playing the part of Irene Walker, a killer hired by the Prizzis. In a moving dolly shot, sitting in the front-row pew, the entire Prizzi family attends a wedding. In close-up, Bill blinks like a lizard. The other members of the clan are introduced, including Jack as Charley Partanna and me as Maerose, then a cutaway to Kathleen Turner in the balcony—we are already set up as rivals. Typical of my father's films, most of the information is imparted in the first few minutes.

On the second day of shooting, the set-design team divided the ballroom from the hall outside by a movable wall of white latticework with two ovals cut out of the crosshatching. As I was standing with a group of extras, about to pass through to the hall for my first scene with Jack, for a moment Dad was perfectly framed in one opening and Jack in the other, like a pair of cameos. For me, it was one of those instances when life and art merge, and it somehow pinpointed Maerose's dilemma.

* * *

That day, the script called for a moment of tearful vulnerability on Maerose's part, after a scene in which her father derides her for looking like a whore at the wedding. She is confronted with advice from Charley to "Practice your meatballs!"

Dad was having a lot of fun with all this, and the nature of the piece—the fact that it was so tongue in cheek—gave us all a kick. Dad decided over lunch one day that Tommy should play the opera singer who serenades the don at his son's retirement party. Although performing was not his forte, Tommy took this proposal very seriously, and for days to follow, he was never seen without his sheet music for "Figaro" in hand, his fingertips nervously tapping his Adam's apple. He would be dubbed in the movie, but he wanted to be sure his lip-synching would be perfect. He had memorized his libretto, and after several hours in hair and makeup he came onstage to do his turn. Wardrobe had dressed Tommy in a blue ruffled shirt with a big gold chain hung about his neck. Dad sent him straight back to have the costume changed. "I don't want a mockery made of this man," he said.

Finally, Tommy returned to the scene. He was visibly uptight, in white tie and tails. I was sitting behind Dad on the floor beneath the stage, alongside the camera. Dad cocked his head and winked at me. Tommy lip-synched the aria brilliantly, if somewhat nervously. But when he came to the end, the music continued.

"Cut," Dad called out. Then he inquired seriously, "Tommy, what about the rest of the song?"

Onstage, in the glare of the footlights, Tommy turned pale green. "What do you mean, John?" he asked dazedly. He began to loosen his tie. "This was all I was given to learn."

Dad shook his head, feigning dismay. "But, Tommy," he said, "we need the rest of the song."

By now, Tommy had jumped off the stage and was running for the exit door of the theater. He disappeared for the rest of the day, and from then on he stayed in Jack's kitchen. I don't think we ever saw him walk on set again.

Another day, Dad and Kathleen were having a difference of opinion as to how a scene should be played. "Just go to the suitcase, close it, carry it out of the room, and shut the door," said Dad.

"But, John," said Kathleen, "I think I'd prefer to go to the wardrobe and take something to put in the case before I walk out and close the door."

"No, honey, just go to the suitcase, close it, carry it out, and shut the door."

"But, John!"

"Okay, honey, you do just what you want, and we'll cut it out later."

On a rare visit to a restaurant in Brooklyn one lunchtime, an elderly gentleman at the bar took stock of Dad as we walked in. "That's Walter's kid!" he exclaimed. After that we had a cashmere bathrobe made for Dad, navy blue like a boxer's, with the words WALTER'S KID embroidered on the back. We gave it to him as a wrap present.

The design of the movie was somewhat mysterious; undoubtedly, it had a timeless quality and seemed oddly rooted in the thirties, despite some modern notes. After the company had moved to Los Angeles, Kathleen Turner was wearing a very modern Kieselstein-Cord belt and Nikes when she looked out her trailer window at a long row of antique cars lining up for a shot. She called Laila over and asked, "Is this a period movie?"

"I don't know," Laila replied. "We should ask John Huston."

They made their way across the street to where Dad and John Foreman were sitting. "John," said Laila, "Kathleen wants to know if this is a period movie."

Dad tossed back his head and laughed. "We'll see if it matters, honey."

It was a wonderful thing to be given a part like Maerose Prizzi, ironclad, and I am forever grateful to John Foreman, Dad, and Jack for making it possible. For Dad and me, it was proof that if you believe in each other, are willing to risk humiliation, and put your heart on the line, miracles can happen.

About a month after I finished *Prizzi's Honor*, I received a call to audition as the replacement for Denise Crosby, who had the title role in a play called *Tamara* at the American Legion Hall on Highland Boulevard in Hollywood. It was a beautifully mounted experimental play, written by John Krizanc and directed by Richard Rose, about a visit the young Polish artist Tamara de Lempicka pays to the villa of the fascist poet Count Gabriele D'Annunzio circa 1927. It was one of the very few auditions that I had ever done well, most of all because I had seen Denise's performance and it had given me courage. Sometimes another actor's interpretation can give you ideas. I started rehearsals a few weeks later.

It was an elegant production, with the Legion post transformed into a 1920s Italian villa. The costumes were by Gianfranco Ferré and the luggage by Louis Vuitton. The scenes were acted out simultaneously in different rooms, and members of the audience followed the characters of their choice as they moved around the house, opting sometimes to

155

change direction or to follow another character. There were ten of us, five upstairs and five below in the servants' quarters. Karen Black, Jack's co-star from *Five Easy Pieces*, played D'Annunzio's mistress, and she was a pleasure, if surprising, to work with. She was very spontaneous and never repeated the same performance. One matinee, Karen got locked in her wardrobe and couldn't get out until the second act. Often we would walk into a room to find the audience playing with our props or in our beds and have to go blithely on with the show, so it helped to be good at improv.

For no apparent reason that I could fathom, the actor playing D'Annunzio insisted on French-kissing me in the oratorio scene. I was getting irritated with this, and my performance began to suffer, but he persisted despite my complaints to the stage manager. Sometimes if you moved too fast, you'd lose the audience, and I was giving less time overall to the kissing scene. Consequently, on more than one occasion, I would find myself all alone, having fled to Tamara's bedroom too early and performing only for myself. But then the audience would trickle in and I'd snap back into character.

Outside the building, we had several vintage cars parked— one a Bugatti for Tamara's departure from the house at intermission. Invariably, at the beginning of the run, I'd get stuck and let out the clutch too abruptly and the vehicle would shudder to a halt. Eventually, in an attempt to improve on this maneuver, I pressed my foot hard on the accelerator, so that the car leaped forward under the porte cochere, into the traffic on Highland Avenue. I did this night after night. It's a miracle no one was killed.

From what I later came to understand, through an article in *The New Yorker*, my former lover Bob Richardson was now homeless and living on the beach in Santa Monica. In the years I had been living in Los Angeles, he had lost everything in New York and drifted west. When I was working on *Tamara*, he was camped out on the boulevard below the American Legion Hall, watching me come and go in the Bugatti.

It was at this time that I signed with Toni Howard, of William Morris. Although Yvette Bikoff had done very well by me, it had become apparent that I needed stronger representation. Toni was a brilliant agent, and became a dear friend, and we worked together for the following twenty-four years.

On June 14, 1985, *Prizzi's Honor* opened nationwide, and on the twenty-sixth of the same month, Dad was rushed to Cedars-Sinai to spend several weeks in the respiratory intensive care ward. In September, I went to the Venice Film Festival to pick up a Golden Lion for him, then returned to New York, where, in November, the Museum of Modern Art put on an evening with screenings of two documentaries Dad had directed for the War Department during World War II, *The Battle of San Pietro* and *Let There Be Light*. Dad flew in to attend that event.

A year or so later, Ted Turner, a dedicated supporter of the colorization of black-and-white film, caused a public outcry when he proposed to color-tint Orson Welles's masterpiece, *Citizen Kane*, for television. Almost simultaneously, the Turner Entertainment Company's colorized version of my father's classic film *The Asphalt Jungle* appeared on the French television channel Le Cinq, which led to a landmark three-year legal case in France. Using French copyright law, the Huston family set a binding precedent in 1991 preventing the distribution or broadcasting in France of any colorized version of a film against the wishes of the original creators or their heirs.

Major legislative reaction in the U.S. was the National Film Preservation Act of 1988, which created the National Film Registry and prohibited any person from knowingly distributing or exhibiting to the public any film in the registry that has been materially altered (including by colorization) unless the film bears a label stating that it has been modified without the participation of its creators.

In the aftermath of this legislation, under the aegis of the Directors Guild of America, a group of Hollywood heavyweights, including Martin Scorsese, Francis Coppola, Mike Ovitz, Steven Spielberg, and George Lucas, joined to launch the Artists Rights Foundation, an organization devoted to protecting film authorship. With a $100,000 contribution from J. Paul Getty, and spearheaded by the director Elliot Silverstein, the John Huston Award for Artists Rights was established in 1994.

CHAPTER 16

I had a dream that I wrote down:

> I am having an extraordinary and blissful love affair with
> Michael Jackson in a glittering penthouse. He is wearing a
> red satin suit with sequined lapels. His voice is deep until
> I remember it's Michael Jackson, and then it gets breathy
> and high. We are levitated four feet above the ground. Then
> suddenly we are in long shot; we are in a sparkling desert.
> A herd of elephants thunders behind us. I travel in and out
> of my body, watching the herd advance. The elephants raise
> their trunks, forming a bridge over us, which becomes a
> tunnel. Michael and I float in the vortex, ecstatic.

I had not thought too much about the dream, nor had
I met Francis Coppola, before he asked me to come up to
his offices at Zoetrope. He was planning something entirely
new with George Lucas—a 3D short that would be introduced as an attraction at Disneyland, starring Michael Jackson. He offered me the role of the Supreme Leader. I was
to play the evil sorceress of a wretchedly grim planet, from
which I would be delivered by Michael, transforming all that
was shadowy and dark to cheerful and radiant in one transcendent song.

The piece was titled *Captain EO*, and the shoot was scheduled to take only three weeks. Of course, I was reminded of the dream I'd had about Michael and the herd of elephants. It was amusing to see that in the cast of supporting players, one member of Captain EO's posse was a small green elephant called Hooter.

When Michael and I started to rehearse, I was impressed not only by his extraordinary androgynous beauty but also by his exertions to keep it all in place. It was evident at short distance that he had undergone a lot of bleaching and surgery; his facial skin was several degrees whiter than his hands, his eyebrows were tweezed, his mouth and eyelids tattooed. Every morning he showed up with his face covered in thick makeup. When Francis asked us to improvise a scene, I was struck by how obviously hard it was for Michael to display anger. He seemed incapable of it.

Michael had a friend, a blond boy about twelve years of age, who kept him company on the set. They often spoke on walkie-talkies, and sometimes the kid would sit on Michael's lap. At lunch, they would retire to his complex of mobile trailers to watch Disney movies and eat vegetarian lunches provided by Michael's cook, who was a Sikh. Michael's manager was often present, a short, older, glossy-looking man who wore shades and signet rings and smoked a fat cigar.

Every other day, a big movie star would come to visit Michael on set and write her name in lipstick on his dressing room mirror, sealed with a kiss—Sophia Loren, Elizabeth Taylor. There was usually a sighting at lunchtime.

Once, on a break, Michael disappeared, then returned with his arm in plaster from a children's ward that he'd dedicated at a hospital nearby in Culver City. No one had seen him hurt himself. It was as if he had invented the injury over the course of the morning. I felt that Michael, like a child pleading for recognition from his parents, was probably hooked on getting attention from the world at large.

One morning, production called to ask that I come in early to get into full costume and makeup for Michael's side of the scene. I was not to be on camera that day but had to undergo hours of preparation and then get strung up to the rafters in my uncomfortable costume so that he might react to my character. I was slightly put out—until the music started and he rose dancing on an elevated hydraulic platform opposite. Instantly, my annoyance was dispelled as I witnessed the heart-stopping brilliance of Michael Jackson, live and up close, singing just for me.

From the shy, reclusive boy with whom I had rehearsed, this new entity, given a song with which to express himself, was fiercely urgent and commanding. It was as if the voice, which had not been able to defend itself above a whisper in rehearsal, now commanded each phrase, every note, and I felt my heart beating hard and high in my chest as I watched the power of his astonishing transformation.

One morning in February 1986, asleep in my house in the canyons, I was awakened and told by Toni Howard that I had been nominated for Best Supporting Actress for *Prizzi's Honor*. I remember being very excited and nervous over the next few weeks, but the time leading up to the Academy Awards was not as fraught, it seems to me, as in the present day, when there are so many awards shows presaging the main event. I had no publicist, no manager, no stylist. Through Mum's friend the designer Dorothy Jeakins, I had met Tzetzi Ganev, who worked at Western Costume and was known for cutting the best pattern in Hollywood.

"Would you make me a dress for the Oscars?" I asked Tzetzi.

"Sure," she said in her round Hungarian accent. "But you have to bring me the fabric."

This was a mystifying challenge, and when I walked into International Silks and Woolens, a riot of color met my eye, but one color sang louder than the rest. I went back to Tzetzi with a bolt of kelly-green silk jersey under my arm. She threw it over my shoulder as I stood in front of a mirror at Western Costume, and the fabric floated to the ground on the bias like a stroke of luck. That was the birth of my Oscar dress.

Laila was going to the Oscars as Tommy Baratta's date. She and Greta helped me get ready at my house. In addition to the green dress, I wore the fabulous jewels that Jack had given me for my birthday—the diamond-and-ruby clips and a matching ring and earrings, from the estate of Tamara de Lempicka, and a white fox stole I rented from Somper Furs.

Dad was very sick; the oxygen tank followed him everywhere. At the Oscars, he sat in the audience with Maricela across the aisle from where I was sitting with Jack. We had eight nominations, including one for John Randolph for Best Supporting Actor, one for Jack, one for Dad, and one for me. We were also nominated for Best Picture. Directly in front of me, the bald head of John Foreman shone under the arc lights.

The Best Supporting Actress category came up very early in the program. My name was called out by Marsha Mason and Richard Dreyfuss. From far, far away, the announcement trickled down from the stage and into my consciousness. Everything went into slow motion. After I waded up there through the limelight, I accepted the Oscar in memory of Bruce Weintraub, who had become sick during the making of the film, and in honor of my teacher Peggy Feury. But in my delirium, I forgot to thank Jack and John Foreman. I managed to thank Dad, then spontaneously ran off the front of the stage back into the audience. I didn't go backstage with the minders to the press room but dashed back up the aisle toward my seat like a homing pigeon. I turned to see my father in the middle of the center row, tears coursing down his cheeks, and when I looked to the left, there was Jack, looking emotional. John Foreman was crying, too. I was electrified. I couldn't believe it. They were all awash in tears, and I was dry as a bone. Someone came and got me from my seat beside Jack and brought me backstage to the press room, where a hundred cameras flashed and the reporters yelled and gradually I returned to consciousness. But out of eight nominations for *Prizzi's Honor*—including Best Picture, Director, and Actor—mine was the only win.

As we pulled away from the Dorothy Chandler Pavilion in the limousine, my cheeks were twitching from smiling so long in front of the cameras. I held the Oscar on my lap as we drove over to the Mondrian Hotel on the Sunset Strip, where Dad was staying. He had left right after the awards. Jack, John, Laila, Tommy, and I had gone briefly to the Governors Ball.

The atmosphere was charged from my coup, but we were all a little rueful that Dad and Jack had not won as well. If that had happened, it would have echoed the dual win Dad shared with his own father for *The Treasure of the Sierra Madre*, when he had won for Best Director and Walter for Best Supporting Actor.

When we arrived at his hotel room, Dad was sitting in

his wheelchair, wearing his customary white Sulka pajamas, breathing oxygen through a plastic tube attached to a scratched-up green canister in a corner. It looked like a bomb, and the oxygen made a sound like gas escaping a balloon, until we realized that Tommy had been accidentally standing on the conduit.

"I'd hoped they might have let us share that one," Dad said to me, "but I am so proud of you."

We stayed only a short while. Below the third-story window overlooking Sunset Boulevard, colored lights and flashbulbs filtered through the drapes and reflected on the walls. A cry arose from the crowd outside. Swifty Lazar's party was heating up across the street at Spago, and a line of pedestrians and photographers were calling out to the movie stars as they walked into the restaurant.

Dad glanced out the window. "I wonder if this town realizes how much it will miss Swifty when he's gone," he said quietly.

Swifty Lazar's parties were almost as important as the Oscars themselves. No favors, no compromises, no additional guests, no cancellations. He ruled with an iron fist. Swifty was beloved to us all. He was a gnomish figure, with his egg-bald head and a large pair of tortoiseshell spectacles perched on his refined little owl's beak; he stood no more than five feet two, but he was a dynamo and a very powerful figure in Hollywood. You wouldn't want to laugh at him or criticize his bearing or his distinctly British choice of tailoring or how he stressed the "A"s pronouncing the word "caviar." Or his challenging expectations of his dinner guests. Having sold the rights to many autobiographies of famous people at record prices (both Dad and Henry Kissinger were clients of the moment), he himself was a celebrity. He was a stickler for decorum and fetishistic about order and cleanliness; stories abounded about how Swifty always brought his own sheets and pillows to hotels and laid down a track of towels on the floor from bedroom to bathroom so his feet would never touch the carpet.

Swifty's wife, Mary, was pretty and sweetly obedient. Up at their house on Carla Ridge, the parties were sleek and smart. Billy and Audrey Wilder were always in attendance; Billy was gruff and brilliantly fast-witted, and she was a dark, glittering presence in a Clara Bow haircut, dripping black jet and diamonds. By contrast, Willy Wyler and his wife, Talli, were understated. Often the guest of honor would be a writer or a politician. Swifty was from my father's generation—there was a grandeur about him, scornful if things were not up to par. He was one of the grown-ups.

Back then most of the action took place at people's homes. Roddy McDowall was another dedicated host; he brought together stars as brilliant and diverse as Elizabeth Taylor, Maureen O'Hara, Vincent Price, and Gene Autry and matched them with up-and-comers like Winona Ryder and Johnny Depp. Roddy's Tudor house was right down the hill from Mulholland, in the Valley. It always felt like Christmas at his place—lots of dark wood and low-beamed ceilings and an extraordinary collection of items, awards, objects, photographs, and memorabilia, and a beautiful garden that he tended himself. But above all, Roddy collected famous and talented friends.

One evening at Sammy and Altovise Davis's estate, four armed bodyguards ran back and forth on the tennis court under floodlights while Sammy stood before a tank of flesh-eating piranhas behind the bar, displaying his collection of handguns to a small group of dinner guests, including Jack and me.

There were cocktail parties at Fran and Ray Stark's house, which had previously belonged to the Bogarts. Fran was the daughter of Fanny Brice; her best friends were Nancy Reagan and Betsy Bloomingdale. Her daughter Wendy's friends were Helmut Newton and David Hockney, local artists, social New Yorkers, lots of visiting Europeans, and the usual movie people.

Almost everybody had a screening room and you saw all the new movies before they came out. David Begelman's room had a cash register on the bar, and Bob Evans's was red tartan on a background of mahogany. Dinners at Evans's house were always great. His chef invariably served the same meal: consommé madrilène with sour cream and caviar, duck à l'orange, and crème brûlée for dessert.

I remember an evening when Bob and his houseguest Alain Delon, looking oddly alike with their black hair and bronzed skin, wore matching cashmere sweaters and socks in contrasting colors, each with a silk foulard at the throat. Every work of art in Bob's house was lit by a small spotlight, which made the objects look museum-quality precious. French doors opened to an oval swimming pool, a fountain, and a rose garden; a well-behaved fire warmed the living room. I thought Bob was like a latter-day Jay Gatsby—cynical and romantic and eccentric at the same time. He had a vast number of beautiful girl-friends and was prone to marriage, although he always spoke of Ali MacGraw as the love of his life.

A few days after I received the Academy Award, I did a screen test for the Australian director George Miller for his new movie, *The Witches of Eastwick*, based on the novel by John Updike. I had already met with him a couple of times for the part of one of the three witches, and I felt the meetings had gone well. The part of Alexandra Medford seemed like a good fit. Bill Murray was going to play Daryl Van Horne, essentially the devil, but then had suddenly dropped out. Upon hearing this news, Jack, who had no reservations about going after something he wanted, had asked that I put in the word to George Miller that he was available.

I called the director. "Mr. Miller," I said, "you are in luck. Jack Nicholson wants the part. He's perfect for it." Within hours, Jack was signed. Later that week Amy Madigan and I were screen-tested with the already-cast Michelle Pfeiffer. When Amy and I drove up to the Warner Bros. lot in our cars, Michelle, looking like the breath of spring, was already installed in a camper. She had been signed for the role of Sukie Ridgemont but had come to read with us. The screen test was set up on a garishly lit set with a lot of green sidelighting, which I was all too aware did not enhance my features. The dialogue was tough to deliver, and in all the Oscar excitement, I hadn't the time nor the concentration to learn the lines as well as I should have. Needless to say, I was terrible.

As we walked away from the set after saying goodbye to Michelle, Amy said, "Well, I don't think we're in any danger of getting cast!" It was humiliating. Ultimately, I think it was probably best that they didn't cast me. I had temporarily lost my confidence. On one hand, I was mad at Jack for not calling George Miller and standing up for me, and on the other I'd probably have resented him if he'd called in the favor. Cher was great in the role.

CHAPTER 17

I hadn't really been aware of Jack's reputation at first. It kind of grew over time, I think, that idea of Jack: He's so baaad! Even though Warren Beatty was one of his best friends, I wasn't recognizing Jack as a world-class philanderer at the time. For as prolific as he seems to have been, and as I have heard reported, he was actually quite discreet. Occasionally, I'd find a piece of female apparel—once a jacket of mine turned up on a girl in the street—or I'd find some hand cream, or a trinket might get left behind in the soap dish. Sometimes I'd take to wearing the jewelry to see if anybody would come up and claim it, but that never happened. It could have been left there by Helena or Annie or any number of the women who came through his life. So there was no way of pinning him on something like that, or ever truly wanting to. I left him more than a few times, and I have such vivid memories of getting into my car and driving to Kenny Solms's house with my bags all packed, intending never to go back to Mulholland Drive. Kenny would take pictures of me on his Polaroid camera, sitting in the trunk of my little Mercedes, crying over my suitcases like spilled milk.

But Jack and I had a very good rapport. He could really turn up the corners of a day. I loved him. I wanted to be with him and have his children. I thought that having a child might create an intimacy between us, and eventually I began tak-

169

ing hormones for in vitro therapy, although I was unsure that having a baby would dispel the issues of Jack's chronic unfaithfulness or my own past indiscretions.

When it became evident to me that Jack was not a faithful man, I didn't know what I could do about that. There's only so much that you *can* do. Then at a certain point, other people start to look good to you, too. This dilemma is something I would very much have wanted to talk to my mother about, but I never had the chance. I don't know whether her affairs were designed to spite my father or to comfort herself. She had neither explained my father's dalliances to me nor openly displayed her pain. She had held so much within, and I was following her construct.

The subject of marriage arose at various points in my relationship with Jack, but neither of us ever seemed to feel the urge at the same time. Jack's business manager and his lawyer encouraged us to get married over the years, possibly because they saw it as a way to save Jack a lot of money in taxes. I found this idea strictly unromantic. Also, I was a child of the sixties and, to a degree, regarded marriage as a form of bondage. Sometimes I liked the idea, but more often I feared it. To correct the confusion and doubt, to address the lack of intimacy, or simply to surrender was a challenge neither of us volunteered to undertake.

One afternoon I went out with some girlfriends to El Cholo down on Western Avenue, and several margaritas later, they persuaded me that this was the moment—that we should go back to the house after lunch, and I should tell Jack that I was going to marry him. Everything went according to plan until Jack came downstairs and Phyllis said, "Go on, Tootie, tell him."

So I told him what we had discussed, and he said, "Are you serious about this?"

I burst into tears, turned on my heel, and left the house, sobbing. It was humiliating for Jack and me. I guess we needed to break up, but we couldn't let go.

The next morning I was crying in my kitchen. The relationship was strained to the breaking point; I was convinced that he was seeing someone else. The phone rang. It was Dad. He was in Malibu, holed up at Burgess Meredith's. I explained my state of mind.

"Come down here and see me, honey," he said. "Just get down here now!"

I took a shower and answered the phone, which was ringing off the hook. It was Carol Kane; she talked me off the wall for about an hour, and then Dad called again. "Where are you?" he asked. "I've been waiting for you."

Finally, I got myself down to Malibu, to his bedroom overlooking the sea, where I found him propped up among the pillows in a state of irritation.

"What is it, dear?" asked Dad with a measure of impatience.

I began to cry. "It's Jack," I said. "He's unfaithful. It really hurts me. I can't live with it."

Dad threw me a look of exasperation, as if dealing with a difficult four-year-old who won't let go of an idea. "Stop crying!" he said with an incredulous shake of the head. "This is nonsense. Meaningless, honey. Men do this—it means nothing. Why do you care?"

Suddenly enraged, I turned on him. "Dad," I said, "how meaningless does it feel to be despised? Because that is what every woman feels in her heart when she's betrayed."

* * *

On April 12, 1986, Dad was again at Cedars in the respiratory ICU, and I was having lab tests done at St. John's. Two days later, I had a hysteroscopy. Dr. Ross Donald was the surgeon. At this time, I began to visit a group in the San Fernando Valley who belonged to the Church of Healing Light, for the laying on of hands by some elderly white witches. I had finally proved myself professionally, and now I was hoping very much to become pregnant in the near future.

Ten days later, Dad was at the Jules Stein clinic at UCLA having a cataract operation on both eyes. When I went upstairs to see him, he was in a darkened room and had big Ray Charles shades covering half his face. My brother Tony greeted me, said goodbye to Dad, and left us alone. Tony was by now separated from Margot and the children and living in Los Angeles.

Dad asked me if I saw a script on the bedside table. I said that I did and picked it up. It was titled *The Dead*, based on the story by James Joyce. In smaller letters, it read "Screenplay by Tony Huston." I was surprised. I had heard nothing of this project and was unaware that Tony had been collaborating with Dad. I will confess, now that I am out of Dad's immediate earshot, that I hadn't even read what is considered as arguably the best short story ever written.

Dad said, "Read it to me, honey." And for the next ninety minutes, I did just that. I was amazed at the beauty and simplicity of the script. *The Dead* was the observation of an evening of music, food, and dance, an actual epiphany set at a dinner party in Dublin on the eve of the Epiphany, 1904. The Morkan sisters, Julia and Kate, host this annual dinner for lovers of the arts, young and old. Over the course of the evening, we learn more about the guests—Gabriel Conroy and his wife, Gretta, are regulars, and Gabriel worries about the speech he has prepared for the occasion. Poems are recited, songs are sung. Gabriel and Gretta leave after he watches her listening to a tenor sing "The Lass of Aughrim," a song that seems to affect her deeply.

They make their way to their hotel in a carriage; snow is falling. Once they are in their room, Gretta confesses a love from the past that she has kept secret. Gabriel realizes that although they have been married for many years, he has never really known his wife, and contemplates the mysteries of life and death.

"What do you think?" asked Dad. "Shall we do it?"

"Of course," I said.

I was on my way to Washington two weeks later to work again for Francis Coppola.

Arlington Cemetery was the main protagonist in Francis's *Gardens of Stone*, based on a novel by Nicholas Proffitt with a screenplay by Ronald Bass, about the devastating sacrifices of war made on the home front during the Vietnam conflict. The action focused on the elite ranks of the Honor Guard, the company charged with the task of burying dead soldiers returning from the fields of battle. I was playing Samantha Davis, a conscientious objector who finds herself falling in love with a sergeant in the Honor Guard at Arlington Cemetery.

Overall, the novel took a sympathetic view of the armed forces. *Gardens of Stone* was all about losing a child, a son, a soldier, a favorite boy. It was something of a surprise to me that Francis had chosen to direct the movie, given that *Apocalypse Now*, a film he had made seven years prior, seemed almost its antithesis. Possibly it was his way of weighing in for the other side, a documentary choice rather than a political one.

I was very excited to come to Washington, D.C., for our first read-through at the Kennedy Center. I have a pleasant memory of working with Jimmy Caan in those early days, in the glamorous, high-ceilinged, white-walled rehearsal hall with honey-colored wooden floors, and Francis's dark-eyed, raven-haired son, Gio, recording the scenes on video. Those moments were the best for me, more real and direct than anything later committed to film.

A week or so before shooting, we had a big table read. It was a strong supporting cast—James Earl Jones, Lonette McKee, Laurence Fishburne, and Mary Stuart Masterson. Jimmy Caan was starring as the conflicted sergeant Clell Hazard, who raises a young soldier in the ranks of the Honor Guard only to lose him later in battle. Jimmy was among Francis's alumni from the *Godfather* movies, and I recognized Larry Fishburne and Sam Bottoms from *Apocalypse Now*.

I was immediately drawn to Sam; he was blond and handsome and quiet and shy and had a sweet, sly sense of humor. In those first few weeks of May and June, in the golden light of early summer, Washington, D.C., was spectacular and romantic. A group of us often went to see the memorials in the evenings. The Lincoln and Washington monuments were quite astounding, but we were most emotionally drawn to Maya Lin's Vietnam Memorial—a black granite wall etched with the names of the dead. We were far from alone. Hundreds of people clustered there, searching for the names of their loved ones, leaving flowers, lighting candles, shedding tears of loss. I felt that we were in the very heart of the nobility and sorrow of human sacrifice.

Ryan's son, Griffin O'Neal, had joined the cast. I hadn't seen him in close to ten years, and was glad that Francis was giving him an opportunity to be part of the team. One night, as a bunch of us were crossing a high bridge over the Potomac River, Griffin suddenly jumped up onto the balustrade and started to walk along it; the drop looked to be almost a hundred feet. I pleaded with him to get down, which eventually he did, after scaring me silly. It reminded me of Ryan's friend Joe Amsler, and of the time I thought Joe had died when he fell off the boulder and down the ravine in Malibu.

A few weeks later, I got a call from Laila in New York. She was working at Broadway Video as one of Lorne Michaels's associate producers. "Is there any chance you can come here this weekend to do *Saturday Night Live*?" she asked. "We'd like you to cohost with Billy Martin." Billy was the manager of the New York Yankees.

Production gave me the okay, and I flew to New York for two days of manic intensity in rehearsal with the *SNL* cast. On Sunday morning a call came from Sam Bottoms: "Gio Coppola died in a boating accident yesterday."

That evening I returned to Washington. For the next few days, we walked around like zombies, until Gio was buried in a hero's funeral at Arlington. Griffin had been driving the boat. Francis sat in front of the monitors like a ghost for the following days, until he was admitted to a hospital for rest. Gio's mother, Ellie, was quiet and contained. Gio's little sister, Sofia, and his fiancée, Jacqui de la Fontaine, seemed as though they were literally holding each other up. The grief surrounding Gio's death was part of the collective grief of Arlington Cemetery, with all of its pomp and circumstance, pain and loss.

Francis valiantly stayed on to finish the film, but one felt suddenly bogus, like a pretender in the face of what had happened. Griffin was replaced in the film and later charged with accidental manslaughter but pleaded guilty to the lesser charge of negligent operation of a boat. He received a fine, was sentenced to probation, and eventually served a short jail sentence for failing to perform his four hundred hours of community service.

But the ending to this sad story was nothing short of miraculous. Jacqui revealed that she was pregnant, and a little more than seven months later, baby Gia was born.

CHAPTER 18

Dad called and asked if I would go with him to look at the stuff he still had in storage from Ireland. His old friend and sidekick Billy Pearson would be meeting us at the facility and was interested in taking some of the pieces. Billy was now living in Holland with his latest wife.

The cases were opened. The narwhal tusks that had occupied the hall in the Big House at St. Clerans were exposed. Billy said, "I really want those, John."

Dad replied, "Take them, kid. I no longer have a use for them."

Later that night, Dad was looking through some of the items he had taken out of storage. He came upon a small brown leather box with the initials J.H. inscribed in gold. Inside was his ID from the War Department adjutant general's office in Washington, with the fingerprint of his right hand—first lieutenant in the Signal Corps, issued 4/29/42. Also in the box were his medals from the Asiatic Pacific, European, African, and Eastern campaigns, a small enamel Maltese cross, and the Medal of Freedom, mounted on a silver bar. He made as if to throw it all in a wastepaper basket. When I stopped him, he asked why on earth I would want to keep it. The war was over. So was the dream of St. Clerans. That chapter was closed. Dad used to say, "Remember, you can always put your hands in your pockets and walk away." But I think it broke his heart when he left Ireland.

Dad told me the sad story of the death of Derek Trench, who had introduced him to County Galway and who, in the years after we left St. Clerans, didn't have a horse left to hunt. He had sold all of them. At the opening meet of the fox-hunting season in 1978, Derek was there, his van stocked with oysters and champagne, and he followed the hunt in the van all day. That evening, Derek said to his wife, Pat, that he was taking his Labrador and going out to shoot a pheasant. Pat heard one report from the gun. Shortly afterward, the Labrador returned to the house without Derek.

That summer, Dad was too frail to travel to Ireland, so his producer, Wieland Schulz-Keil, brought the mountain to Mohammed. A top casting director, Nuala Moiselle, recorded the best working actors in Dublin on tape, and Dad made his casting decisions for *The Dead* in Beverly Hills. One day a movie camera and some lighting equipment was brought into his living room at a rented house on Laurel Canyon, and Donal McCann and I did a screen test together, in the roles of Gretta and Gabriel. Donal, who had just flown in from Dublin, was a remarkable actor, with brooding dark eyes and a troubled soul. Initially, I found him dour, but I grew to like him very much.

It was also a clever stroke for Schulz-Keil to have secured a warehouse in Valencia, California, a suburb of Los Angeles best known for the dubious distinction of being home to the Magic Mountain theme park. Apart from the lack of sound-proofing, the warehouse proved to be an ideal setup, a totally contained environment in which Dad would be afforded the ease to make the film. Because of an insurance clause, Dad also had to agree that should anything befall him health-wise, there would be an alternative director standing in the wings ready to take over. Dad and the producers had agreed on Karel Reisz, who became a gentle presence on the set day to day as we were shooting. It was a kind and thoughtful personal gesture, as well as a professional one; it cannot have been an easy position for him.

The cast members, many of whom came straight off the stage from the Abbey Theatre, were assembled at a motel a few miles short of Valencia on the freeway. There was a running game of cards on set at all times, and after work most of them were taking Western two-step classes in the motel lounge. Peter O'Toole's daughter, Kate, was playing the role of Miss Furlong, and having her with us made it feel all the more like extended family.

Stephen Grimes, Dad's production designer since *Moby Dick*, was working with his set decorator, Josie MacAvin, downstairs in the basement prop room. His beautiful watercolors and sketches lined the walls. On the ground floor, carpenters had partitioned off a section and erected plywood cubicles for the actors. I put up an Ed Ruscha poster in mine—BRAVE MEN RUN IN MY FAMILY in stark print, over a tall-masted ship forging through a stormy sea.

Dad's first assistant was Tommy Shaw, who had terrified me long ago on the set of *Freud*, always bellowing for quiet before the cameras rolled. His daughter, Molly, a cherubic twenty-year-old, was filling in as my driver during her summer holiday. After *The Dead*, Molly came to work for me as my first personal assistant. Our beloved Dorothy Jeakins was designing the costumes; one of Dorothy's favorite colors was something she termed "goose-turd green," and she used this shade for my one and only dress in the movie.

Roberto Silvi, Dad's editor, was in a cutting room on the second floor. Dad and he were always in contact. One morning Donal and I did a scene in the back of a carriage, filmed inside the dark warehouse; we were supposed to be riding around Dublin at night. Dad placed the camera strategically through the window of the cab, and we acted out the scene in a two-shot. After it was completed, Tommy asked Dad, "John, do you want to move in for close-ups?"

"I don't think so," said Dad, "but ask Roberto. He might need it."

Roberto Silvi came downstairs.

"Do you need close-ups on this scene, Roberto?" Dad asked.

Roberto shrugged. "I don't think so, John, not if you don't want it."

"I'll never use close-ups here," said Dad. "You've got to see the distance between the characters; that only happens in a two-shot."

Tommy had plotted that this scene would go on all day. But there was nothing else scheduled, so we were sent home at lunchtime. This was typical of Dad's economical approach. Nothing excessive, just the important stuff, the footage he needed.

I became very tired when we were shooting *The Dead*; sometimes it was painful for me to get up in the morning. I asked for a bed in my cubicle. I went to Dr. Giorgi and tested positive for mononucleosis. I felt that, imagined or not, my body was ailing in sympathy with Dad's.

There was a documentary crew on set, and I asked that they not film me while the movie camera was rolling. By its mere presence, the documentary camera breaks the code of imagination by recording the actor as himself, and whenever confronted by it I have always found it intrusive during scenes. There is a moment in *The Dead* when my character, Gretta Conroy, is riveted by a piece of music. A scaffolding had been rigged above a flight of stairs, and when I reached the top, I was to stop in my tracks and listen to the song. On the first take, I climbed the stairs and looked down at Dad sitting in his wheelchair. This vision gave me the feeling I needed for the scene. But suddenly the lens of the documentary camera loomed from behind his head, pointed straight in my direction. It cut my emotion like a knife. I had to ask to shoot the scene again. I also could not help but feel that the documentary was pointing a fatalistic finger at my father, as if this picture had been pegged to be his last, and I dreaded the possibility of that.

I believe it was as proud a moment for Tony as it was for me to be working with Dad's team. It felt like we were new instruments playing in his well-tuned orchestra.

Because the movie was shot in almost perfect sequence, I had a lot of time to think about the last scene. Initially, when we meet the characters in *The Dead*, they are seen full-bodied, all containing their own spirit and history, but it's Gretta's speech at the end of the evening that provides Gabriel with his personal epiphany. I asked Dad and Dorothy Jeakins if I might wear a nightdress in the scene, so as to emphasize the distance between the social interaction of that evening's party and the confessional night that follows, when Gretta and Gabriel are alone in their hotel room and her vulnerability surfaces as she tells him of a long-lost love.

When I arrived that morning, I was raring to go. Dad and

Donal and I went upstairs to the set to rehearse. As we walked through the scene, everything I had held pent-up for weeks erupted and flowed. Afterward, as we walked downstairs to get ready in hair and makeup, and the grips went in to light the set, Dad said, "That's good, honey, now put it in the past." When we went back, he shot the scene in one long take.

Because Dad couldn't travel to Ireland, he instructed a second-unit crew on what to shoot for the last images in the movie. The famous line "Snow is general over Ireland" was a surprising premonition for that year, as the country was blanketed in white for the first time in more than a decade.

After *The Dead* was completed, Dad wondered to me privately if an audience would have the patience for a movie "whose most animated moment is the breaking of a wishbone," but I knew that he was excited about it. "It's not quite like any film I've seen," he said. I heard the underlying pride in his voice.

Later that summer, Dorothy Jeakins, in accepting the Crystal Award from Women in Film, said in her speech, "Most important to me is John Huston and his remarkable family and the years of work and friendship we have known. Each of these people is here. Here they exist, where I see everyone in the inner crystal chamber of my mind."

When I was working on *A Walk with Love and Death*, I found a poem in a book of anonymous Irish verse that I loved. It went like this, in part:

> *You promised me a thing that is not possible,*
> *that you would give me gloves of the skin of a fish;*
> *that you would give me shoes of the skin of a bird;*
> *and a suit of the dearest silk in Ireland.*

*My mother has said to me not to be talking with you
   today,*
or tomorrow, or on Sunday;
it was a bad time she took for telling me that;
it was locking the door after the house was robbed.

*You have taken the East from me; you have taken the
   West from me;*
*you have taken what is before me and what is behind
   me;*
*you have taken the moon, you have taken the sun
   from me;*
*and my fear is great that you have taken God from
   me.*

When we made *The Dead*, Tony included the poem in his screenplay.

In the spring of 1987, Jack was making *Ironweed* in New Jersey with Meryl Streep. When I arrived on set, she was in his trailer, and they were speaking the lingo of their characters, alcoholic lovers. There was no doubt they were very comfortable in each other's presence, because neither one broke character to greet me.

It was to be Jack's fiftieth birthday. I had called an assortment of his friends, from Michael Douglas to Art Garfunkel and Helena to Suze Forristal and Carol Kane, and hid them in an indoor swimming pool in the basement of the house he had rented. They all arrived before he awakened in the morning. As soon as he had the coffee mug in his hand, I dragged him downstairs, where there were at least eight of his best friends swimming laps and singing "Happy Birthday." He remained in a bad mood all day.

Back in California, Jeremy Railton took me up to a little town in the foothills of the Sierra Nevadas, situated near the Kaweah River, to look at some land to buy. At first I was skeptical—the tule fog was thick on the highway until the ascent to higher ground. The terrain was rocky. The sun broke through in patches; the pastures were wet with frosty dew. I said to Jeremy, "This is coyote country."

Jeremy went ahead and bought some land there anyway. In the spring I returned with him to the property and this time I noticed a small house with a bunkhouse on a hill close by. Jeremy explained that it was constructed from adobe brick pulled from the bed of an old lake that was now a tangle of briars and weeds. The house was the color of mud. I bought it and three acres for $107,000. It was the first land I had ever owned, with the first real money I'd ever made, and I was so selfishly satisfied with this acquisition that I didn't tell anyone about it, not even Jack, for a full year.

Jeremy, Tim, and I started to spend a lot of time up in the Sierras, riding in the back country, going up to Mineral King and Crystal Cave, and swimming in the rivers. For me, it was like a little taste of St. Clerans in the American West, a place where I could commune with nature. Jeremy and Tim occupied the bunkhouse next to the adobe house, while Jeremy built a house of his own design on his property next door. We accumulated animals rapidly. Soon I had eight horses, and Jeremy acquired a pair of ostriches and a small army of emus. When a property next door came up for sale, I bought it as well, and Tim moved in. Jeremy, Tim, and I formed the three sides of the triangular map that together we had sketched out on paper when we were still at Beachwood. We felt that the farm was the manifestation of our hopes and dreams for a small utopia.

A couple of years later, Tim agreed to move there permanently to supervise the property, and more animals followed. He adopted a spaniel-Labrador mix he called Jake, and a female whippet called Whippet, who ate all the chickens and became pregnant. Eventually we kept one of her progeny, and she was shipped off to a friend of Jeremy's in Oregon. The puppy's name was alternately Francis and Whippet II. Laila became a frequent visitor to the farm and adopted a miniature Shetland pony she called William Valentino Blake.

Soon Yolanda Araiza came to work for me. She had come to California by way of Texas and had worked as a fruit picker and in the Tulare County Fire Department as well as at the Sequoia National Park. Yoli was a descendant of the Zapotec tribe from the Isthmus of Tehuantepec in Mexico; although not too tall, she was very strong and could do anything a man could. I have seen Yoli in many situations—digging ditches and skinning rattlesnakes, making bonfires, raising children, and facing off with wild boars, all in the course of a day. She has as much knowledge of nature and the seasons as any almanac. Tim swore she wasn't really human and was, in fact, a Sasquatch. He was only partly kidding. If I ever had to go into hiding in the wilderness, Yoli would be the first person I'd take with me.

One morning as we were sitting around at breakfast time, a little brown dog came by. His coat was tangled, and it looked like he'd been running hard. Later we learned that Barney was his name and that he lived up the road, but after that, he never left us, and his owner didn't seem to care. Jake, Whippet, and Barney had some wonderful times up in the hills, chasing rabbits and coyotes and mule deer and bears. They would go missing sometimes for several days and then come limping back to camp and sleep for several more.

Tim was like St. Francis in the spring, when the fledgling birds would often fall from their nests. He would rescue them from the jaws of the dogs and raise them on cat food. They were so tame, they would fly from the trees and alight on your shoulder. Tim and I were great riding companions and had fine times herding cattle with our cowboy friends at a nearby ranch and exploring the pristine back country on our beautiful little fleet of Arab quarter horses.

After the death of Jeremy's parents, his younger brother, Joce, came over from Zimbabwe to live in California. Joce was helping to build Jeremy's house, a few acres above my property in a grove of oak trees. He had married and was the father of little Jack, who, as a toddler, was as intrepid as his uncle Jeremy, going barefoot in the winter wilderness. I furnished my house with objects found at the local swap meet. Through the years, the farm became a refuge for all of us, family and friends—every Thanksgiving, every Christmas, every Easter, most birthdays. Allegra, who had graduated from Oxford University and was working for a publishing house in London, and Tony and Margot's children, Matt, Laura, and Jack, often came to visit from England.

CHAPTER 19

In the summer of 1987, Dad was intent on going to Rhode Island to be with Danny, who was about to direct *Mr. North*, an adaptation of the novel *Theophilus North*, by Thornton Wilder. After Danny graduated from film school in London, he had made a short film starring Buzz Meredith called *Mr. Corbett's Ghost*. *Mr. North* was to be Danny's second outing as a director. Dad had written the screenplay and was going to play the part of Mr. Bosworth. I was set to play the part of Mr. Bosworth's daughter, Persis. I think it was more important than anything to Dad that he was making this choice because he could—to continue to travel and work. In true Dad style, no one was going to tell him what to do, at the risk of going under themselves.

Before we left for Rhode Island, Dad was saying that he needed some shoes. This seemed to me so poignant from a man who'd had the closet of a king just a decade before. I went out and bought him some midnight-blue suede loafers, as soft as rabbit ears. "Do you like them, Dad?" I asked.

"I love them so much, honey. I'll never take them off."

The trip from L.A. to our stopover in New York was difficult, as Dad was wheezing and frail from lack of sleep. He hadn't really recovered from his last stay in the hospital. Nonetheless, the day after our arrival, he was eager to visit Picasso's

Guernica at the Museum of Modern Art with his dear friend Lillian Ross, the author of *Picture*, a book about the making of Dad's film *The Red Badge of Courage*. He invited me to go along with them, but I was determined to enjoy a rewarding lie-in, having reached New York, a milestone toward our final destination. When I phoned his room to beg off, Dad reacted to me with scorn. "Tired? From what exactly, honey?"

The following day, we made the final leg of the journey, to Newport, Rhode Island. For the first few days, Dad's health was touch and go. His doctors at Cedars-Sinai in Los Angeles were dismayed that he had made the trip; the chances of infection were very high for his compromised immune system, and the idea that he would be so far from their care should he go into crisis was, in their words, dangerous.

In Newport, Dad was soon installed in a pretty house among the sand dunes that the producer, Steven Haft, had rented for him; it had a beautiful view of the sea. For the first days that we were there, Dad was making an attempt to go with Danny to look at locations and generally supervise the plan of action. According to the script, a large portrait of my character, to which Mr. North finds himself attracted, would hang above a fireplace in a grand home. I had been obediently, or so I thought, posing every day for several hours for a local artist to paint my picture, as directed by the art department. When Dad had stopped by on his tour of locations, he happened to see it, half finished, on an easel in the room where I had been posing.

That evening I received a call from him. "How could you let this happen?" he said. Clearly, he was appalled by something.

"What's wrong, Dad?" I asked. "What have I done?"

"It's the portrait," he said. "It's terrible."

"But that's not my fault," I said. "I was just sitting for the thing. I didn't paint it."

"It is your fault," he replied. "I taught you what was good art. This is your responsibility, how you are portrayed. The smart ones look after themselves."

I realized after I thought it over that he was right. My participation had made me responsible.

I don't know whose idea it was for Dad to start giving dinner parties in Rhode Island, because he was seriously ill. About ten of us, including Danny; his mother, Zoë; Allegra, who had flown in from London; and Tony, Roberto Silvi, Steven Haft, Lauren Bacall, Harry Dean Stanton, and several other cast and crew members were seated at the dinner table when Dad started to talk about old times, about *The African Queen* and Bogart and Katie Hepburn. He went on and on about Katie Hepburn, how wonderful she was! A man's woman, a woman's woman, a superb actress, an inimitable character. She was the best female friend he ever had! Betty Bacall was listening to this shower of praise for Hepburn. Dad had all but ignored her—she who had cooked for the crew of *The African Queen* and kept spirits aloft during their dangerous sojourn in the Congo.

The night before, I had witnessed Betty correct a fan who made the mistake of complimenting her on *Casablanca*, a movie in which Bogart starred with Ingrid Bergman, so I was amazed when a small voice from Betty asked sweetly, "But John, what about me? Wasn't I your friend, too?"

The question hung in the air for a moment. Dad replied in a consoling tone, looking at her fondly down the length of the dinner table. "Oh, honey, you didn't count," he said. "You were married to Bogie."

Betty Bacall told me later that when Bogie became terribly sick with cancer, she called Dad in Paris to tell him the news. Dad said, "I'll be right there, but don't tell him I'm coming." When Dad arrived in Los Angeles, he went straight to the hospital. The doctors had taken Bogie from his room to perform some tests. As Dad waited for him to return, he climbed into Bogie's bed, and when his dearest friend was brought back to the room, Dad cheerfully flung open the covers and invited him in.

Dad was at Charlton Hospital in Fall River, Massachusetts, near the end of his life. During our second week in Newport, it had become apparent that he needed to go into intensive care. Before we left L.A., Dad had asked if Bob Mitchum would replace him in the film should anything go wrong. After hearing the news of Dad's failing health, Mitchum came in overnight, worked the next day, and drove up to Fall River that evening. He took one look at Dad, who was very thin and very weak, and knew the situation was grave. He summoned a young, pretty nurse. She came into the room, and he said, "Miss, would you please stand over there? In front of Mr. Huston's bed."

"Okay," said the nurse.

"And if you don't mind," said Mitchum, "would you tuck your skirt up just a little bit?"

The nurse was in this hospital room with these two old geezers and she was game; she rolled up her skirt just a little bit.

Mitchum said, "Maybe a little more, honey," and the nurse rolled it up one more turn.

Dad broke out laughing. "You're right, Bob," he said. "I haven't been eating enough."

The great beauty and socialite Marietta Tree came from New York to visit Dad in Fall River. The first day, she came into the hospital wearing a black and white polka-dot dress, with a big white picture hat and elbow-length white gloves. Whenever she came into his hospital room, his heart monitor would peak. They would read poetry to each other. It was a big love affair with Marietta. Zoë, always devoted to Dad, nursed him through several nights at the hospital. If they visited, Maricela would disappear. She told me that there were a few women with whom Dad remained very much involved. On his last visit to London, he had said to Maricela, "I need eight hours of oxygen for tomorrow and a limousine," and she asked, "Why? Where are you going?" And he said, "Don't ask." She ordered the oxygen and showed him how to change the canisters and spin the valves, and off he went. Later she found out from the limousine driver that Dad took the car to Heathrow Airport, where the actress Suzanne Flon got off an Air France plane. He took her to Prunier's, and they had a lovely dinner: champagne and caviar. Afterward, they got back into the car, and Mr. Huston took Mademoiselle Flon to the airport and put her back on the plane to Paris. That was the last time he ever saw Suzanne.

On one occasion when Dad was in the hospital, one of us tried to broach the subject of where he might like to be buried. He was outraged and disgusted that such a subject would even come up. There were people who plan their funerals and think about these things, but not Dad.

His stay at the hospital in Fall River had lasted more than three weeks. He had spent his eighty-first birthday, August 5, anxiously awaiting our arrival from the set in Newport, a couple of hours away. When eventually we arrived, he had been upset, and scolded me for being late. Now he had returned to the house in Newport. He was as weak and transparent as lace. Zoë had come to the house with Danny for dinner; Allegra had gone back to work in London; Tony had been staying in a room downstairs. Dad had not slept in a couple of days.

It was after ten o'clock. I was ready to drive back to my apartment on the harbor.

"Must you go?" Dad asked. "Can't you stay a little longer, honey?"

"It's late, Dad," I said. "I'm working in the morning. I'll come and see you tomorrow." I kissed him good night on the crown of his head.

The call came at dawn. It was Maricela. "Your father has passed away," she said.

I was shocked that I did not have a premonition, some foreknowledge of what might happen in the night.

I got into the rental car and drove to the house. When I walked into his room, he was lying on his side, facing the bed-side table, and under his outstretched arm was a dictionary. I sat down on the bed in the curve of his body. His hand was soft but growing cold. I stroked his back. Maricela stood by.

"What happened?" I asked.

"It was after you left. He became very restless. I asked him if he wanted the doctor, and he said no. I told him I was call-ing the ambulance, but he said no. Not to do it. He said he was tired. He lay back down, and then he said, 'Have you got the express rifles?' And I said, 'Yes, John, we have lots of guns.' And then he said, 'Do we have ammunition?' And I said, 'Yes, John, we have tons of ammunition.' Then he said, 'Let's give 'em hell.' Those were his last words." It was August 28, 1987. He was hunting big game or out there on the fields of battle.

When Dad died, everything went silent. There was an empty chasm where he had been, the sound of his voice stilled. Like a whale that breaches and dives into the deep. All that character, emptied of expression. I longed for him—his burst of laughter, his head thrown back, his monkey grin—and I cursed his disease, and time, for taking him. Zoë told me she had known, and had told Danny, that Dad would die that night.

We called Allegra to tell her the news. Then Tony and Maricela left to take Dad's body back to California.

That evening I sat in my little rented bungalow on the harbor, and Harry Dean came over from his place a few doors down on the wharf in Jockey shorts and cowboy boots and sang Mexican love songs with a sob in his voice.

The following morning I got a call from Tony, who was making arrangements for the funeral. "I know that we had decided to keep it limited to family," he said, "but Dad's lawyers are coming out from New York."

I had come to resent my father's lawyers and business managers throughout the years. Dad was never much interested in how his lawyers dealt with his dependents. "No," I said. "No way do I want to see them at Dad's funeral." Tony didn't reply.

Then all at once, I heard Dad's voice everywhere, in every corner of the room. It was in direct contradiction to what I was feeling—as ghostly an experience as I've ever had. "Don't be ridiculous, honey," he said. "Of course they should be there."

Dad was buried at Hollywood Forever Cemetery, beside his mother and his grandmother, Rhea and Adelia Gore. Jack brought me to the funeral. It was in the chapel on the grounds.

I don't know who decided that Dad should be embalmed, but they gave him a rather florid paint job. He looked benign, if a little pink and waxy. Billy Pearson, his old friend, stood up in the church and said, "I'm not gonna speak for long, John, because I know you want to get the hell out of here and get that makeup off your face." Later, at the grave site, the funeral director handed me a lead box. And I said, "Oh, it's heavy!" And he said, "Your father was a very big man." You want to weep, but you also want to cry with laughter. Sometimes that's all you can do.

A small monetary inheritance was eventually distributed among Zoë and the four siblings. Two houses and the greater part of Dad's estate went to Maricela, who came up to my farm a few months after the funeral, bringing me a set of exquisite Mexican serving dishes and a painting by Dad entitled *Spirit of St. Clerans*, a portrait of a pale-faced Gothic knight vanquishing a red dragon. It was the last time I ever saw Maricela.

There was news from Jeremy that Tim was sick. His feet hurt. He was getting thin. Tim came down to L.A. and made the decision to take a blood test. I was with him when he went to the doctor's office in Santa Monica. It was a harsh sunny day, and we came out of the elevator and past the tinted-glass windows of the medical building through the automatic doors and into the flat light outside. "This is what the end of the world looks like to Tim," I thought. A week later, when the tests came back, they confirmed our worst fear.

In the late eighties, there was a growing awareness of AIDS, although facts were shrouded in mystery; there was much speculation and no clear plan of treatment. People were dying in their homes. Although a lot of money was being raised, and there were important charities working to save people, it was a plague—stigmatized, mysterious, and terrifying.

So many friends from that time—as fate would have it, so many people in the arts—were struck down. It was devastating; the end of an era. I, and many others I knew, stopped wearing color in the eighties.

CHAPTER 20

Under the auspices of MGM, the producer Ileen Maisel offered me a development deal. On my first day, I was sitting in an empty office in a charming older building on the lot in Culver City, wondering what exactly to do with myself. Through the glass-topped door to the outer office, I could see the temporary assistant they had assigned to me as she played with paper clips at her desk. The phone rang, making both of us jump. The assistant spoke a few words and put the caller on hold.

"It's Marlon Brando," she said.

At first I thought it was a joke. Though it was true that I had recently won an Academy Award, this was a little much to hope for. But indeed it was Marlon. He told me he'd loved my performance in *Prizzi's Honor.*

"You are a queen," he said. "Remember that."

Whenever I feel down or underappreciated in my work, I try to remember his words. I felt that I had some good ideas for Ileen, but MGM did not respond to my suggestions. It became evident that what they really wanted was to have me play the part of "Miss Ernst" in Roald Dahl's terrifying children's story *The Witches*, about the leader of a coven who is determined to turn small boys into mice. Nicolas Roeg, the director of the spellbinding *Don't Look Now*, was set to direct the film—a prospect I found both daunting and thrilling.

Soon I found myself in London at Jim Henson's Creature Shop, getting fitted for my part. The prosthetics for Miss Ernst's transformation to the Grand High Witch were extensive. The various features—contact lenses, full facial mask, hump, withered collarbone and hands—took over six hours to apply and almost as much time to remove at the end of the day. I had asked Laila to be my assistant on *The Witches*, and she assured me that she would meet me in London after a short trip to India. Weeks later, she was marooned in Bhutan. When at last she arrived, I had set myself up in Cadogan Square in Chelsea, in a generous apartment nicely furnished with antiques and within easy access to the Kings Road. In spite of the constant car alarms that rang out all day and all night on the square, it was a pleasant spot.

As shooting progressed, I became increasingly dependent on Laila's help in all things—namely, feeding me, blowing my nose, and pulling up my tights. The brilliant minds at Henson's lab in Hampstead had created a wonderfully intricate pair of mechanical hands for me, but it took a full hour to reattach them once they had been removed, so Laila assumed the responsibility of coping for me in various ways. This went on for a relentless three weeks. The contact lenses came in different sizes and in colors ranging from yellow and orange through varying degrees of mauve and purple. Some had tiny apertures that obscured my vision, and because special effects had a fondness for a particularly greasy and lurid acid-green smoke they had perfected, the lenses would get fogged up with oil-based junk that had to be flushed out of my eyes by an "eye expert." I would venture to say there is no such thing, having endured contact lenses for work on several occasions.

Early on, before we started filming, the costume designer Marit Allen came to my flat, and I tried on some clothes for her. We were looking for a good dress for the character of Miss Ernst that could plausibly become the costume for the Grand High Witch. We settled on a black crepe dress, high at the neck and cut below the shins on the bias. We thought Nic would love that idea. The following evening, he came by to look at our choice. I twirled around in the dress, but Nic's face darkened and he said nothing. Finally, Marit broke the silence. "What is it, Nic?" she asked. "What's wrong?"

There was an exasperated sigh from Nic. "It's just not sexy," he said. That was the first time I'd imagined that this horrible creature in a children's movie should have sex appeal. It simply had not occurred to me. But of course Nic was absolutely right. His vision was diabolical and dark and brilliantly funny. If a witch was to be at the center of this plot, she needed to be sexy to hold the eye.

Nic and I had a good rapport, and it is my honor to be the recipient of his steady-cam award, a silver charm that he makes for his favorites. I won't forget how he helped me with a difficult monologue when I was so uncomfortable and tired of being encased in rubber under hot lights for hours that the lines had ceased to make sense to me and all I wanted to do was cry. But he coached me through it. Later that night we all went to dinner at Marit Allen's house; Theresa Russell, whom Nic was living with, was also there. She was very patient with both Nic and me as all evening he just beamed in my direction, exclaiming over and over, "By God, we did it! We broke the spine of the bastard!"

The following night, when I left the apartment to go to a party in Notting Hill Gate, I accidentally left open the ground-floor window. When I returned at 3 A.M. the place was ransacked. My father's little gold-and-alligator Tiffany travel clock, the gray baroque pearl Jack had given to me from Darlene de Sedle's collection—I still search for those pieces in every antique jewelry store I pass when I am in London.

Before I reported for work on *The Witches*, I'd already signed for my next role. Suzanne de Passe had offered me the part of Clara, a frontierswoman, in the TV miniseries *Lonesome Dove*. I considered myself incredibly lucky to work on such a great endeavor, because I had loved the novel and was impressed with how the scale of the American West was depicted by Larry McMurtry, as something vast but also as a human microcosm. It reminded me of the qualities that I associated with the movies of the great John Ford—wild, beautiful landscapes, horses, cowboys, and women whose emotions run strong. The movie tells the story of an ex–Texas Ranger, Augustus McCrae, played by Robert Duvall, who joins up with his old friend and partner, Woodrow Call, played by Tommy Lee Jones, to embark on a cattle drive from a dusty town in Texas across the country to Montana. Along the way, they encounter fearsome weather, sodbusters, outlaws, whores, Indians, grizzly bears, and water moccasins. My character, Clara Allen, is the long-lost love from Gus's youth whom he reencounters at the end of the trail.

By the time I started shooting, Robert Duvall, Tommy Lee Jones, and most of the cast had worked on the series for several months out in Texas and at the beautifully named location of Angel Fire, in northeast New Mexico.

When I joined up, the crew had made its final move to the red-clay town of Santa Fe for the last three weeks of filming. A week or so prior to my departure, I received a call from Robert Duvall, whom I had never met. Over the course of the conversation, he asked me a few loose questions—the month of my birth, my favorite song, my favorite food. It was only when I arrived in Santa Fe that I realized why, when he threw me a beautiful party with crab cakes for dinner, and a mariachi band playing "Galway Bay."

Bobby Duvall was a prince to work with, as was Tommy Lee Jones, albeit a more silent one. Bobby was verbal and communicative and always took it upon himself to help his fellow actors with their jobs. Being in a scene with Bobby was like having a pillow to lean against. Since all my work had been scheduled in a block, the shooting days were often long and arduous. But Bobby took the pressure off the scenes, one time playing "Galway Bay" on his tape recorder to induce my tears as his character rode off into the sunset.

It was also on *Lonesome Dove* that I met an actress I love and admire, Glenne Headly, who was originally with the Steppenwolf Theatre Company in Chicago. I had met Diane Lane when, as a sixteen-year-old, she was doing a movie for Lou Adler called *The Fabulous Stains*. She had grown up into a beautiful actress. Chris Cooper, Freddie Forrest, Robert Urich, Danny Glover, and Rick Schroder rounded out the spectacular cast. Suzanne de Passe was our executive producer, and our line producer was Dyson Lovell, who was Franco Zeffirelli's casting director when I tried out for *Romeo and Juliet* at the age of fifteen. Santa Fe was a fabulous location. We filmed some twenty-five miles outside of town, in Galasteo, at the Cook Ranch, a magnificent spread, which years later was owned by Tom Ford and his partner, Richard Buckley.

Before I had left for London and *The Witches*, I'd had a conference with the *Lonesome Dove* costume designer, Van Broughton Ramsey, about the wardrobe for my character, Clara. I had agreed on a number of sketches, Victorian silhouettes with bonnets and petticoats, and then gone off to work with Nic Roeg and totally forgotten about the next task at hand. When I came back to the U.S. to do *Lonesome Dove*, it was evident that I had not thought through the passage of my character—Clara's husband had suffered an accident that had left him paralyzed and Clara in charge of the ranch. As soon as I took on the role, I realized that I would need a more functional costume. So my first morning on set, I knocked on the door of the wardrobe truck and raided the clothing racks for work boots, men's shirts, a duster, and a beat-up cowboy hat. It was this last-minute decision that led to the truth of my character. Van understood perfectly, or he had the grace to pretend to.

Later, in 1994, when Suzanne de Passe again gave me a great part, as Calamity Jane in *Buffalo Girls*, Van did wonderful, authentic costumes. I loved the Santa Fe aesthetic and adopted it for the little adobe house that I had bought on the Kaweah River, going so far as to purchase corny howling coyotes and applying the very particular palette of turquoise and red clay that you see in New Mexico.

I flew back to London for my next role, as Mrs. Rattery, a huntress and aviatrix with a dash of the Duchess of Windsor, based partly on Beryl Markham, who flew her own plane solo over the Serengeti and shared Denys Finch Hatton with Isak Dinesen. The movie was *A Handful of Dust*, based on the novel by Evelyn Waugh, to be directed by Charles Sturridge, an Englishman. Kristin Scott Thomas was the young star of the film. She had a very beautiful, striking, chiseled face and large, deep-set eyes above high cheekbones. She barely said a word to me, and I didn't spend much time in her company.

I loved the character of Mrs. Rattery; it was not a large part, but she was very game—a throwback to the women I remembered from growing up in Ireland, who were so intrepid on the hunting field. I had only three scenes—alighting from a biplane, a hunt meet, and a game of cards. I enjoyed the company of the two male co-stars, Rupert Graves and James Wilby, and we filmed in some spectacular locations, like Carlton Towers, a Victorian Gothic country house belonging to the Duke of Norfolk; and a fifteenth-century castle armory in Cheshire, which contained the stuffed remains of various extinct birds and waterfowl I had no idea ever existed— mad-looking speckled brown creatures, with duck bills and long legs and bodies like swans, that had waded in European waters in the olden days.

It is extraordinary how many species went extinct in the nineteenth century. And in the last one hundred years, such damage has been done to the planet like never before, as with the taxidermied, prehistoric-looking avians in their glass domes, in that gloomy moated castle. The songbirds of the world are also fast disappearing.

The duke was more often than not on set, observing the crew at work. I was impressed one evening when he revealed a secret drinks bar, hidden behind a mahogany panel in the library. Consequently, we met for gin and tonics every day at wrap. He was a most charming gentleman with an excellent sense of humor.

CHAPTER 21

Woody Allen wrote me a letter in October 1989. He didn't tell me the name of the movie he was going to be making, but suggested that I might respond to the character of Dolores, the needy flight attendant whose constant demands force Marty Landau's character, Judah Rosenthal, a happily married and successful ophthalmologist, to murder her. I agreed immediately.

I thought it might be a good idea to meet Woody, as I happened to be in New York. I called his office and asked if I could speak with him. They said they would give him the message. A few hours later, the phone rang. It was Woody.

"I heard you wanted to speak with me?" he asked haltingly.

"Yes," I said. "I thought that perhaps since we have never met, and since I'll be working with you in a few weeks, that maybe we could have a drink, or tea, or something."

There was a long pause. I wondered, was it boredom or anxiety? "Why?" he asked.

"Well, I thought it might be a good idea," I said.

"I'm sick," he said. "I've got a cold. When did you want to have this tea—this drink?"

"Well, perhaps on Thursday," I suggested, casting it out like a fly on a dry river.

"Okay," he said. "We'll have a drink on Thursday." There followed a long pause and an intake of breath. "What if I'm sick on Thursday, too?" he asked.

"Well, I guess we won't get to have the drink," I replied.

Needless to say, the drink never happened.

When I returned to New York two weeks later, I went straight into fittings with the costume designer, Jeffrey Kurland, for *Crimes and Misdemeanors*. Among other options, he had chosen a seriously ugly argyle sweater for Dolores, and although I felt it was a deeply unflattering shape and pattern, I kept my mouth shut. I had heard that Woody had fired a famous actress when she refused to wear a jacket of his choice, so I was determined to love my wardrobe. But in truth, Jeffrey's choices were perfect for the cloying, overbearing woman I was playing, argyle included.

Woody's hair-and-makeup department was run by two wonderful women, Fern Buchner and Romaine Greene. Woody called them the "Salad Sisters." Both ladies of a certain age, they were adorable and comforting to be around, as well as professionally trained in the old-fashioned sense. Fern became my makeup artist for many years, inventing, among other looks, my makeup for Morticia Addams, which was considerably more complex than it seemed.

It was not necessarily Woody's habit to give the entire script to the supporting actors—just the scenes they would be shooting. So I had still not read the script and didn't get to meet Woody until the first scene, in "Del's apartment." It was a humid, rainy day, and we were shooting in a nondescript glass high-rise in the East Thirties in Manhattan, as Dolores threatens and cajoles Judah and tosses down tranquilizers with alcohol. I had walked upstairs from my trailer into the bright hot lights and the bodies crowded into a small apartment, through cables and standing arcs and equipment—you had to duck under to get inside. Sven Nykvist was the cameraman. Sven and Woody were wearing identical blue wool caps and neutral-colored parkas, like climbers on the Matterhorn. It was 150 degrees when Marty and I started into the scene. Woody indicated that I should stalk from room to room, and I did my best, swallowing pills while desperately trying to remember my lines as I stumbled into doorways and lurched over cables and standing arc lights. Woody kept on shooting. He asked if I could pronounce the word "been" as "bin," which for some reason I found harder than speaking Russian.

After his initial direction, he never said another word, but we shot quite a few takes, and soon there was a deep frustration between Marty's character and mine, and I believe that was what Woody was looking for.

There was one scene that Woody was never happy with. It moved from a diner to a car wash to a Chinese restaurant, and every time we reshot it, I tried harder to make it good. I think that's probably what was wrong with it—you could see the effort. Working for Woody was another sort of challenge as well: often there was quite a lot of dialogue, and one didn't want to fail him as a screenwriter any more than as a director.

Moviemaking on the streets of New York was not a glamorous affair. One day at lunchtime I was sitting in my slip on the grim chocolate-brown banquette of my double-banger trailer, parked on Third or Lexington somewhere in the Fifties, outside an Irish bar. I'd been persuaded to share the trailer with Marty, even though I could hear his toilet flush and his side of telephone conversations behind a thin compartment, so I wasn't in a great mood. The air conditioner had broken down, and the teamsters had gone to eat lunch. Outside, it was pouring rain. Suddenly, without warning, the familiar blue cap and beige anorak backed in through my door. Slightly embarrassed, I grabbed a robe and inquired gently, "Is that you, Woody?"

The figure wheeled around. It was neither Woody nor Sven but a toothless vagrant clutching a bottle in a brown paper bag. "Wow!" he exclaimed, looking around at the shag carpet and the colorless walls. "Is this Hollywood? It sure don't look like it!"

"I couldn't agree with you more!" I said.

We were entirely alone as he sat on the leatherette La-Z-Boy, polishing off his bottle and eyeing the refrigerator. "Got anything interesting in there?" he asked. Mercifully, the accountant dropped in and my new friend was persuaded to leave. At the same time, at the opposite end of the trailer, Marty's briefcase was lifted, script and all. There was some serious tension when the theft was reported to Woody, who liked to keep his scripts under wraps until release.

Early the next year, I read a script from Paul Mazursky, an adaptation of the great tragicomic novel by Isaac Bashevis Singer, *Enemies, A Love Story*, about a concentration-camp survivor with three wives. Ron Silver was set to star as Herman Broder. The part I was offered was beautiful—that of Tamara, the Polish mother of the survivor's two deceased children, who tracks down her husband in Brooklyn after the war.

When I went to see Paul, I realized that it was in the same office on Beverly Drive where Elia Kazan had rejected me for the lead in *The Last Tycoon* some fourteen years before. But this was a very different experience. Even though no deal had been made for my services, when I walked in, I was delighted to see a photograph of myself prominently displayed on a bulletin board, next to a picture of Ron Silver, and one of the wonderful actresses from *The Unbearable Lightness of Being*, Lena Olin.

Before I start any movie, I amass whatever information I can about my character, piece it together, and usually arrive at some conclusion. There are the obvious questions, like the character's social position, her auspices, and her age. But also the less evident ones—her health, her choices, her hopes and dreams and disappointments, her secrets. Is she still a sexual being? Or has she given up the ghost? Much of who we are is reflected in the way we dress. So these choices are very important.

If I am working on a period movie, I do my best to research the day-to-day life of an actual person living under circumstances similar to my character's. When I made *Enemies, A Love Story*, I read Primo Levi and watched Alain Resnais's *Night and Fog* and documentaries on the Nazi atrocities from the BBC. I spoke to survivors of the war and spent days in the Hasidic neighborhood of Williamsburg, Brooklyn, observing the behavior of the residents and going to synagogue. But then there is the moment when you must trust your preparation and allow your imagination to take over in order for a character to exist. In a way, it's like conjuring up ghosts; but with a character like Tamara, who had been through so much, I had to accept the heavy burden of responsibility for what had happened in her past in order to represent her.

Paul Mazursky was a man of powerful emotions, knowing and compassionate, funny and wise. He would literally jump up and down if he liked something you were doing. I've never seen a man happier in his work than Paul on *Enemies*. He worked closely with Pato Guzman, his production designer, and Fred Murphy, our cinematographer from *The Dead*. We had the luxury of rehearsing for several weeks in New York before we started shooting. Albert Wolsky was the costume designer, and between him and David Forrest, my makeup artist, we came up with a look for Tamara's first meeting with Herman Broder that was both sad and vulgar—in a pale pink dress, hollow-cheeked, with dark circles under my eyes and a bright red mouth.

In April 1989, before we left for New York, Paul had arranged for those of us who lived in L.A. to go to a seder at a house in the Fairfax district that belonged to a woman called Magda Simon. Her story was surreal, full of terror and extraordinary courage. Captured as a young girl, she had been incarcerated and tortured at Auschwitz. Paul told me that Magda had lost her hearing, having contracted diphtheria in the camp.

When the door to her house opened, I was surprised. Instead of the person I'd expected—a broken soul or someone physically demolished—there appeared a good-looking, healthy blonde in her late sixties or early seventies, dressed in white and turquoise. She introduced us to her "self-portraits"—big imposing oil paintings of cats imprisoned behind bars, on fire, or both—hanging on her walls. That night our group joined six survivors at her dinner table; Magda welcomed us and led us in a short prayer. As we ate, they each laid out their personal histories for us to hear, one more stilling than the next—tales of love and fortitude and courage, all told with a lack of tears, as if they had gone too deep to cry for what was lost, including themselves.

A balding man in a cable-knit sweater told of being shot at by a Nazi firing squad as a child, lined up with his family against the wall of their barn. He had lain among their lifeless bodies until night came, when he escaped into the countryside just days before the liberation. The survivors all wore bold patterns and bright colors, like Magda. When the meal ended, each dish was polished clean.

For the first few weeks, we shot the big exterior scenes on the Lower East Side in New York, then flew to Montreal for studio work. It was summer, a season of celebration for all Canadians. They were out in force, in the cafés, by the lakes. The city was on vacation. Joan Buck had given me Leonard Cohen's telephone number and had told him to expect my call; he was lovely to me, taking me out to play pool and to dine on corned-beef sandwiches. Laila came to Montreal as my assistant and introduced me to Tom Schiller, an *SNL* alumnus. Tom contrived to visit our set in the full costume of a rabbi, complete with *payot* and top hat. Mazursky was at first honored to receive the guest, then shocked, then vastly amused when Schiller's disguise evaporated and he flung himself into an energetic mazurka before the crew at lunchtime.

There was a comedy festival playing the length of one of the popular walk streets, and one afternoon Schiller proposed to Laila and me that we take a stroll. A number of pedestrians were ambling around—there were a few jugglers, a scattering of people telling jokes here and there. Schiller turned to me. "Let's have a fight," he whispered, and suddenly, with a loud groan, he smacked his hands together and careened, as if he'd been hit, into the front wall of an apartment building. I charged after him furiously and aimed several fake swipes about his head and cheeks as he continued to clap his hands together, whimpering and simulating sounds of attack.

All at once we had an audience. An outraged woman started shouting at me, "Leave that poor man alone!" as I chased Schiller in and out of shops, comedy stores, restaurants, and discos, all the way up to the top of the street. When we were finished, we had a crowd of about fifty people. I honestly can't remember having more fun, which I guess says something about my childish nature. But it was brilliantly unrestrained.

Ron Silver told me stories that he worked for the CIA and spoke Chinese. I was never up to checking either claim, but he was full of contradictions, and we got along quite well. None of the wives worked in scenes together until the climax of the movie, when we all find out about each other, so I rarely saw Lena off set. Her infant son was with her at the hotel, and the third wife, Margaret Sophie Stein, a lovely young Russian actress, was working when Lena and I were not on call.

The comedian Alan King, who plays the rabbi in the movie, decided that he had a crush on me and left a red rose outside my hotel room door each night. On a break from filming, Laila and I drove up to Sydenham, Ontario, to stay at our friend Dan Aykroyd's lakeside compound. Dan had told us that he would meet us at the local gas station so that he could ferry us the last leg, a few miles, to his home. When we pulled up, he was seated on a big black Harley-Davidson, and as he led us down the leafy roads, we put Leonard Cohen's "I'm Your Man" on the tape machine and watched Dan bump along in front of us. A moment frozen in time.

Down several more country lanes, we found ourselves in

the clearing of a heavily wooded forest where a vast log cabin, worthy of Papa Bear, was under construction. That evening, when we went down to the lake, the water was like swimming in liquid oxygen. For some reason, Dan's wife, Donna, was not there, but Dan was a great host. He took us in his motor-boat to a funny little island way out in the deep, calm lake, where he had erected a tent. Inside were a couple of arm-chairs, a charming little red stuffed couch from the fifties, and a television set from the same era that had a rabbit-ear antenna and operated off a generator. There was a hefty ex-cop com-panion of Dan's who fed us dinner and stayed behind to clear the debris while Dan, happy as a child, having shown us his toys, then ferried us back over the dark water to his giant's lair in the woods.

CHAPTER 22

Jack and I had been seeing less of each other. I had been going out with him to public events for years, and somehow we still clung to that old habit, but we were undoubtedly drifting apart. I did not often spend the night at his house. He was directing *The Two Jakes*, the sequel to *Chinatown*. On the occasions when I would go up to Mulholland Drive to see him, there was now an array of creams and perfumes by the master bathroom sink. Evidently, they did not belong to Helena or Annie. I didn't ask whom they belonged to. It was like being a child again—don't ask questions, you won't get answers. I didn't think I could handle the truth.

Not long after the wrap of *Enemies*, Stephen Frears spent the better part of an evening in New York telling me why I was all wrong for the movie he and Marty Scorsese were planning, based on a Jim Thompson novella called *The Grifters*. I had met Stephen that night at Boaty Boatwright's dinner table in her apartment at the Apthorp. She was representing writers and directors at ICM. Stephen had wanted Melanie Griffith for the role of the icy con woman, Lilly Dillon, but she had passed.

I thought no more of it until a month or so later, when I was back in L.A. and received a call from Toni Howard.

"Scorsese and Frears want you to read for the part of Lilly Dillon," she said. "I'm sending you the script."

When I read the screenplay, I was transfixed. It was a hard, dark thriller full of twists and turns. There was a scene, however, that gave me pause, in which Lilly's boss, Bobo, beats her so savagely with a sack of oranges that she defecates on the floor.

"I don't want to be that woman," I said to Toni. "It's too explicit."

Half an hour later, she called back. "Sue Mengers is thinking of coming back to work at William Morris. We want you to come in and talk to us."

"Okay," I replied, wondering what Mengers might say to me.

When I walked into the office that afternoon, Sue fixed me with a firm eye and declared matter-of-factly, "Anjelica, if Stephen Frears tells you he wants you to shit in the corner, then that's what you must do."

The next day I put on a red silk Missoni dress with no bra underneath. I was tempted to find a blond wig for the character, but thought they might think that was a bit over the top. I drove over to the Chateau Marmont, where Stephen was staying, and went up to his suite. It was the same room where Helmut and June Newton usually stayed when they came to town, which I took as a good omen. Marty and Stephen were sitting on the couch. After the reading, Marty left, and it was just one-on-one with Stephen. He expressed the idea that I might play Lilly in a platinum-blond wig. That was when I knew I'd gotten the part.

At our first read-through of *The Grifters*, it became very evident that I should pull up my socks and get on board—

John Cusack was playing the part of my son, Roy, and Annette Bening, a newcomer, was playing the part of his girlfriend, Myra Langtry, and she was fantastic. As for my role, Lilly was spare and neurotic and cunning and totally selfish. In the last scene of the movie, she risks all to save herself and, having committed a final, unthinkable deed, flees Roy's apartment under cover of night.

John Cusack was great to work with, and we had a strange, slightly perplexing attraction to each other, made all the more intense because I was playing his mother. Stephen Frears was a master storyteller, and I learned a lot from working with him. He always upped my game.

I never enjoyed playing a part more—that is, actually delivering lines—than on *The Grifters*. I was nominated for a Best Actress award by the Academy. Kathy Bates won that year for a role in *Misery* that I turned down in order to do *The Grifters*, but I've never regretted my decision to portray Lilly Dillon. It was arguably the best role of my life.

During rehearsals for *The Grifters*, I received a call from Jack. "Tootie, could you come to dinner tonight?" The request had a sweet, unusual formality, and I said yes. I had a feeling something was up. We had a lovely dinner that evening, cooked by Jack's chef. Jack was friendly, and for the first time in a long time, we had a few laughs.

"I have something to tell you," he announced over dessert. The words came smoothly, deliberately. "Someone is gonna have a baby."

There was a top note of pride in his voice and an odd sense of déjà vu to this moment. It reminded me of the day Dad told Tony and me about the existence of our baby brother,

Danny, when he was a toddler and we were teenagers summoned to Rome to meet him.

"Is it Rebecca Broussard?" I asked. When I said her name, Jack looked surprised. This was a girl—blond, sexy, full-lipped, and drowsy-eyed—whom I'd seen working at Helena's new dance club in Silver Lake. Jack had been spending time there after his basketball games. She'd shown up in Aspen the winter before, as his daughter Jennifer's friend. When I had gone to see a rough cut of *The Two Jakes* at Paramount a few days before, she had appeared in a scene playing his secretary, with a rose between her teeth. He hadn't mentioned to me that she was in the movie, and I had experienced a mild wave of dread—the little premonition that says, "Not all is well."

I asked Jack what he was going to do about it.

"What do you mean?" he said.

"Is she going to have the baby?" I asked.

"Yes, she's going to have the baby. But I don't want nothin' to change." I asked if he was going to stand by Rebecca, and he said, "Yes. I am the father of this child."

"There's only room for one of us women in this picture, and I am going to retire from it," I said. Something like that. And then we hugged, and I wept, and felt the floor dropping out from under me, and some wave of forgiveness, and, finally, the hopelessness of a relationship that's done, flopped, croaked, and over. I went home and cried and drank vodka all night and did the crosswords in the *Los Angeles Times* that were stacked up by the fireplace. The next day I announced the news to one of my chattier friends with the idea that everyone would be in the know by lunchtime.

* * *

I received a call from Bob Colbert, Jack's business manager. "Jack's lawyer thought that we should sit down with you sometime soon to discuss the future." We met a few days later at Ma Maison. They sat opposite me at an outdoor table in view of the new Sofitel going up across the street.

"Anjelica," Jack's lawyer began the conversation loudly, above the noise of the drilling at the building site, "imagine you are a parking lot attendant and you charge two dollars an hour for parking. Well, imagine that I come in with a really expensive car—say, a Rolls-Royce. You're gonna think maybe I owe you more than two dollars to park my car, right?" Maybe this was an analogy they'd cooked up on the way to the restaurant, but it had not occurred to me to ask Jack for money. I looked at the man and wept.

The next morning I awoke and lay in bed, blinking at the ceiling. Life was irretrievably altered, the way it feels around a death—the irony being that this was about an impending birth. I wondered what Jack was eating for breakfast. Would he have coffee? Eggs? Would he go for a swim in the late morning? Would he dive or jump into the pool? All patterns, all routines and habits, had changed forever. I called him on the telephone. "Jack," I said, "your lawyer is a real prick."

"Well, you know lawyers," he said sleepily.

I wondered if Rebecca was lying beside him. I was overwhelmed with jealousy.

"How could you allow him to talk to me like that?" I demanded tearfully.

"I'll have a word with him," said Jack, as if he had no part in any of it.

When Jack and I split up, what was the most shocking, in a way, was the collateral damage. People don't mean for it to

219

happen, but sometimes it is so hard to be stuck in the middle that they feel forced to choose, and sometimes it's not even a decision. I lost several people whom I considered dear friends when Jack and I split. All of them were men, guys I had cooked for. No matter what they do to each other, it seems to me the guys generally stand together.

At first some of the women seemed to feel forced to take sides. Jack's daughter Jennifer, caught up by happenstance in this divisive scenario, was a friend of Rebecca's but remained close to me. Although they were in the eye of the storm, Annie and Helena remained two of my dearest friends. We had been in the trenches together, and they both helped me to grow up.

I got a call from Susan Forristal a few days later. "I've got some bad news for you," she said. She went on to tell me about an article in *Playboy* magazine in which a young woman made claims in an interview that Jack playfully spanked her with a Ping-Pong paddle in one particularly romantic encounter. I called Annie Marshall and said, "It's too much! How can he dare to do this as well as the bomb he dropped on me just a few days ago?"

Later that morning I was in a dressing room at Western Costume, being fitted for *The Grifters*, when a telephone call came in from Annie. She said, "I have Jack for you."

"Toots," he said when he came on the phone, "that *Playboy* article is meaningless! It's a reprint of an article that came out in England last year!"

"Where are you?" I asked.

"At home, but I'm leaving for work at Paramount."

"It's just up the street from Western," I said. "I'll see you there." A half hour later, when I drove onto the lot, I saw Jennifer walking toward me. I parked the car. "I've come to see your father," I said.

"Good," she said, and gave me a hug. I was shaking.

When I got to his bungalow, an assistant behind a desk in the reception room asked if she could announce me. I told her that would not be necessary and walked straight into Jack's office. He was coming out of the bathroom when I attacked him. I don't think I kicked him, but I beat him savagely about the head and shoulders. He was ducking and bending, and I was going at him like a prizefighter, raining a vast array of direct punches.

Finally, I was exhausted. We sat down, and I cried. Then, with renewed effort, I attacked him again. And all the while I felt a strange underlying gratitude to him for allowing me to beat the living hell out of him. Later, in the days that followed, I talked to him on the phone and he said, "Goddamn, Toots, you sure landed some blows on me. I'm bruised all over my body." And I said, "You're welcome, Jack, you deserved it." And we laughed. It was tragic, really.

Jack and Rebecca's baby, Lorraine, was born on April 16, 1990. I was very lonely at this period of my life. But I realized that it had been Jack's life, for the most part; I had existed in it. That was over now. And I'd turned the tables on him, too, in my way. I had thought of him as grumpy Jack. In keeping with my early experience, I had turned him into an often irritated and forbearing parent instead of a husband, a lover. The truth was that we had lost interest in each other.

After Jack and I split, I asked him to avoid talking about it, which he was able to do for some time. I tried to imagine Rebecca in a domestic scenario with him, following the floor plan, moving through the rooms at Mulholland Drive as I had done before her. Around this time there appeared an article in *Life* magazine with soft-focus portraits of Jack and a moonfaced Rebecca Broussard in a large picture hat, alongside quotes from old pals like Bob Rafelson and Henry Jaglom, saying how great it was that Jack had finally found true love. When asked how he felt about his baby daughter, Jack was quoted as saying that the sight of her fragile skull reduced him to gibberish.

The fact that Rebecca Broussard had become pregnant where I had failed made me feel inadequate and bitter. The path to discovering what was wrong with me, and why my reproductive organs were not functioning, was a long and arduous one. The fertility doctors had discovered that I had endometriosis, and had probably had it since my teens. I had undergone a laparoscopy, followed by a hysteroscopy, but a child was not to be. As hard as I might try to visualize it, I found the idea of having a baby frightening, and could never truly imagine such a thing as pregnancy happening to me. I think much of what a woman is has to do with procreation. And to find oneself infertile somehow renders one useless as a woman, in the grimmest set of the mind's eye, so I was very conflicted.

I was never completely sure until my late thirties that a baby was what I really wanted, or if it was more about pleasing my mate. I still felt like a child myself, maybe because I'd lost my mother so early. Selfishly, I didn't want to grow up to be someone else's mother. Jack had been enthusiastic about trying in vitro, but we agreed that having intercourse by the numbers was a turnoff.

It rained heavily that month. A mudslide came down the

cliff and washed away a portion of the Japanese garden behind my house. There was a loud scratching in the ceiling above my bed, which upon further investigation turned out to be a nocturnal army of rats. As I lay on my bed unable to sleep at night, I held my dog, Minnie, in my arms. It felt as if she had literally absorbed my pain and anxiety when, just a few weeks later, she suddenly went blind from the effects of diabetes.

In the short time since Jack and I parted, I realized how many of our friends had not told me the truth about Jack's involvement with Rebecca. I probably would have resented them if they had. I went up to Oak Pass to see Bert Schneider. He and Greta had recently divorced, and I was surprised when he told me that Rebecca Broussard had been staying in his guesthouse. I heard from Jack's decorator, Jarrett Hedborg, who had helped me with my house also, that he was shopping and designing for Rebecca's new home.

I was feeling a lot like Lilly Dillon in my personal life— that I was having to sever a very vital part of me and let it go. No matter how good the image of us looked on the outside, it had been a long time since I had been really connected to Jack. We'd fallen out of step even before Rebecca Broussard came along. And shortly after she did, I heard she tossed a plate of spaghetti in Jack's face and I thought, "I bet that will keep him interested." I was right; he had another child with her—a son, named Raymond. Which was odd, because we'd once owned a dog by that name.

Although in many ways it was not logical, the sense of betrayal was overwhelming; I felt abandoned and dejected and humiliated. I was not yet forty, but in magazine articles, I was described as the older woman. We were now living separate lives, but I had always thought of Jack as family.

One morning I opened the door to the FedEx man, who handed me a package. It was from my mother's half brother, Fraser. I took it inside and sat down with it at the kitchen table. A note said that he had found a poem written by Mum in a corner of his attic in Long Island and thought that maybe I would like to have it.

The poem was written in spidery italics and set in a dark wood frame.

THE CEDAR TREE

The cedar tree
is very strong
it sways and rocks in the wind
and when the wind goes howling by
I think of the bird with the broken wing
who found the shelter the cedar would bring

Enrica Soma 1938, age 9

I was feeling very blue and went for a walk on the hill behind my house. A van had stalled on the side of the road, and a well-built older man was walking up and down, shaking his head. He told me that he was a boxer's manager and that he had his fighter in the van, but they'd broken down on the way to their gig. He asked if he might give me his card to call a towing company to help him out. Then he looked at me closer and said, "I know you—you're John Huston's daughter. I can tell you've been crying, but you're a strong girl. You are your father's daughter, and you must never forget that."

Mum and Dad are like that, angels in the woodwork.

That Christmas holiday, another package for me was dropped off, from Mulholland Drive. I took it up to the farm and waited until Christmas day was over before opening it alone in my bedroom. It was an extraordinary pearl-and-diamond bracelet that Frank Sinatra had once given to Ava Gardner. The card said he hoped I would not find it overbearing. "These pearls from your swine. With happiest wishes for the holidays—Enjoy—Yr Jack." I was devastated.

Bernardo Bertolucci was the president of the Cannes jury in 1990 and invited me to come join him as a member. Since Bernardo was a dear friend of Jack's, I was flattered that he had included me, although I suspect that his longtime girlfriend, Clare Peploe, proposed the idea.

I immediately set about finding a wardrobe that would sustain me for fourteen days and nights in the glamorous South of France. Evening gowns were required for each night at the screenings at the Grand Palais, and unless you got up early—usually after a busy night of partying—to watch the first jury screening of a selected film, attendance at the evening galas was a requirement.

I had traveled to New York and stayed at Joan Buck's new apartment for a few days. Now we were flying together to Cannes on the Concorde. In the airport lounge, we ran into Paloma Picasso and her husband, and I wondered why Joan turned green. It was only when we landed in Nice that she told me she had experienced a nightmare that we were in a plane crash and that Paloma and her husband were also in the dream. I, too, had been trying to come to terms with a growing fear that the flight to Nice might possibly go down, as I had been embarrassed about tipping the scales with my four overstuffed suitcases at the Air France transfer desk in Paris en route to Nice.

But when Elizabeth Taylor's luggage sailed by with her sitting in the front of a flatbed minivan at Orly, I estimated some fourteen pieces of Louis Vuitton in all. As we took off, there sat Liz in the first row of the plane with a Pomeranian in her lap. She smiled and waved happily at me. She was an ambassador for the Foundation for AIDS Research and had always been one of my heroines. I figured if we were going down, she'd get the headlines.

As Joan and I made our way down the aisle to the back of the plane, Prince Albert of Monaco said hello and asked where I would be staying. We exchanged phone numbers, and Joan said, "He's going to ask you out for dinner."

I was staying at the Majestic Hotel on the Croisette, in a beautiful room overlooking the festival. This was before the movie stars began hiding out at l'Hôtel du Cap, some twelve kilometers down a coast of hairpin turns. At one time they were happy to be seen, and that was what Cannes was all about—starlets on the beach, lunch in tents along the sand, paparazzi a presence but not swarming. After l'Hôtel du Cap, everything got decentralized.

The jury met in seclusion at least every other day, then daily toward the end of the festival. The jurors included the Japanese producer Hayao Shibata, whose mother started buying movie theaters in Japan in the thirties; Aleksei Gurman, a large brooding Russian director; the lyrical French beauty Fanny Ardant; Sven Nykvist, Bergman and Woody Allen's cameraman; the brilliant young Indian director Mira Nair, who had made *Salaam Bombay!* the previous year; Françoise Giroud, the journalist and screenwriter who had coined the term *"nouvelle vague"* in 1958; Bertrand Blier, the French writer and director; and Christopher Hampton, the celebrated British playwright and film director known for his recent adaptation of Stephen Frears's movie *Dangerous Liaisons*—all presided over by Bernardo. Even though some of the jurors did not speak English, it was great to feel in the thick of it with these very smart people.

The first week was something of a disappointment, but in the second week the films improved radically. There was an exquisite Chinese film, Zhang Yimou's *Ju Dou*, about a young woman married to the owner of a dye factory who is having an affair with a man employed there. There was a complicated film by Jean-Luc Godard, *Nouvelle Vague.* Clint Eastwood had come to the festival with his film *White Hunter Black Heart*, based on Peter Viertel's book about my father. It was actually a strange experience to watch Clint as Dad. At long distance, the similarity was often quite close. But whenever the camera moved in, the illusion dissolved. Bernardo left me out of the voting on that one.

Then there was the American tour de force by David Lynch, *Wild at Heart.* The movie was fast and violent and proved very controversial, with extraordinary performances by Nic Cage and Laura Dern. At the screening, the audience booed, but some gave it a standing ovation. At the beginning of week two, there was a powerful movie from Russia and I mentioned to Aleksei that I liked it. Every time I liked something else, he took the opportunity to playfully tell me that I had liked the Russian film best.

Often, after the evening screenings some jury members would have dinner together and wind up at the Carlton Hotel in the suite the producer Jeremy Thomas, his wife, Eski, and his business partner, Hercules Bellville, shared with Bernardo and Clare, and talk freely about the films in competition. Hercules wore black velvet Chinese slippers and sometimes a little wooden bow tie. Herky was now working with Jeremy Thomas at the Recorded Picture Company. Jeremy's suite was the hub of the party, the heart of the festival. All the cool people congregated there in the after hours.

At our closing deliberations, there was a full-on lunch buffet and a bank of seafood, including a large poached salmon on the bone. As we were eating, Bernardo rose fretfully from the table and backed toward the window, waving his napkin. "There's a bone in my throat," he gasped. Soon all the women in the jury were staring down Bernardo's throat. As I ran past him to go upstairs and get my tweezers, Aleksei stopped me and said, "I wish I had a bone in *my* throat."

Bernardo was taken to a nearby hospital and attended to. That afternoon we were whisked away from the Majestic in a fleet of Citroëns and taken to a castle in the hills above Cannes, where we were to cast our final votes, then change into our evening dress—in my case, a sleeveless black velvet, lace, and yellow taffeta confection designed by the Emanuels. Mira Nair was in full sari with pendant earrings and a bindi on her forehead. Fanny Ardant was a vision in black Dior tulle and diamonds. We made the descent from the hills surrounded by gendarmes, traveling rapidly with sirens wailing, in a full motorcade to the Grand Palais du Festival to announce the winners. The Palme d'Or was awarded to *Wild at Heart*.

The night after the festival, I went with Prince Albert to dinner at a delicious and proper restaurant in Èze, a drive out from Cannes in his sports car. I had worn high heels, which was gauche, because the little medieval streets of Èze are made of cobblestone. On our drive, his bodyguards accompanied us in two cars, front and rear.

Dinner was a bit stiff. Prince Albert was very nice, but I wasn't sure we had too much in common. After dinner, I clattered down the steep cobblestone incline to his car. As we made a wide turn, the bay of Nice shimmered before us in the sunset. He pulled over to the side of the road, opened the passenger door for me, and gave me a surprisingly ardent kiss with the bodyguards looking on, which I found quite disconcerting.

PART THREE

FORTUNE

Photographed by Brigitte Lacombe

CHAPTER 23

Although I may have wished for the obvious in my relationships—mutuality, sharing, caring, and fidelity—the hard reality was that these were qualities that did not necessarily turn me on. I've always been attracted to cowboys and rock stars, artists and wild men. Men you can't depend on. Guys who have you waiting by the telephone—not, for the most part, the kind and easy ones you can relax around.

And then I met Robert Graham. Bob was Mexican but took his name from his Scottish grandfather. Bob was a famous sculptor, known for his massive bronze works. A mutual friend, Earl McGrath, who happened to be both an art dealer and the manager of the Rolling Stones, had told me that Bob was crazy about me and told Bob that I was crazy about him. Neither of us had any idea.

On June 23, 1990, Bob and his driver, Nick, picked me up in his long gunmetal-gray limousine on the way to Earl McGrath's for a dinner one Gay Pride weekend in West Hollywood. Bob didn't like to drive, he said; he got distracted. Tall and handsome, Bob had a steel-and-silver mane of thick shoulder-length hair that he wore either in a Japanese sumo twist at the nape of his neck or in a ponytail, and a small goatee. His skin was more café than lait. His eyes were dark as teak. He watched me over the rims of his blue-tinted shades.

Bob was ultra-cool. He moved with ease and grace. After dinner, we climbed the stairs to Earl's rooftop to watch the fireworks. I looked over at Bob and thought, "Hmm, I wonder." It was a strange feeling, being around him. There was a strong attraction but also a feeling of destiny.

When we drove back to my house that June night, I was nervous and didn't ask Bob in. I could tell he was a little surprised. "I'll call you tomorrow," he said. Thirty minutes later, he called me from the car on his way home. "Will you come to my studio on Sunday?" he asked. "I'd like to show you my work."

On Sunday I put on a dress I'd bought years before on a trip to Hawaii, black and white and flimsy, made of silk scarves stitched together, and drove myself and my dog, Minnie, down to Venice. It was a beautiful, fresh, windy day, the sun glinting off the ocean. There was a chill in the air. We had lunch and walked on the beach. Bob told me he wasn't taking off his shoes; he didn't like to walk barefoot.

We came to a stop and sat down. When I rolled over to lie on my stomach on the sand, the wind came up and blew the skirt of my dress over my head, exposing my underwear. With the hint of a smile, Bob simply reached over and caught the hem of the dress and pulled it back down without a word. I thought that was very courtly of him. Then we went back to his studio and made love.

I was amazed by Bob's work. My friend Greta and I had first seen his bronze gateway, standing twenty-five feet, a colossal sculpture of two headless naked athletes, at the Los Angeles Memorial Coliseum on the opening day of the 1984 Summer Olympics. During those high bright days of July, inside the Coliseum, the physiques of the women runners had never looked so strong or so muscular. And the sight of those beautiful superwomen, with their red USA uniforms and their gleaming black skin, their dreads and their gold jewelry glittering in the sun, proved that the Graham sculpture was no exaggeration.

When I asked Bob about the pieces, he said, "I sculpted what I saw."

As I came to know him and to understand his process, I saw that it was the relentless and irresistible challenge to perfect his craft that drove him. I saw him destroy work that failed to be faithful in some way to its subject. Bob never cheated, never took the easy way. The work was everything. His hands were the means by which he expressed himself; they were his voice.

Bob told me about growing up in Mexico with his three mothers—his actual mother, his aunt, and his grandmother. Bob grew up under the impression that his father had died; that was what his mother had always claimed. But then, on his twelfth birthday, a strange man had come to his house and taken him out to lunch. During the meal, he told Bob that he was his father. As far as I know, Bob never saw him again. Bob said his father had another family living in Sonora.

Bob remembered fondly the evenings when, as a small boy, he would choose among the three women whose bed to sleep in. His grandmother warned him that if he dropped their hands while walking on the Paseo de la Reforma, he would be stolen by gypsies, have his eyes gouged out, and be put out on the street to sell Chiclets. So he held on for dear life.

Bob's predominant memories of childhood were riding his bicycle around the adjoining interior balconies of their apartment building, and craving sugary pastries from the bakery down the street. When they went to visit his uncle's house in Sonora, the women never allowed him to touch the earthen floor, so as a result, he never moved but stayed on his bed all day, making figures from Plasticine and drawings of his three mothers.

Bob had amazing dexterity. Sometimes in restaurants he would fashion animals or figures or make constructions out of bread dough or mashed potatoes. He threw knives with chilling expertise, usually in public after a few tequilas, which had its charm but made me a little nervous. But his friends seemed unfazed by it. He had an eclectic collection of knives, pistols, and various firearms. Bob was great on harmonica and enjoyed playing along with Van Morrison on *Astral Weeks*. At times he was dead serious, but he could be ludicrously funny. He had all the best parts of Dad and Jack but not the temper, or the women. Early on in our relationship, he amused me by walking fully clothed into a swimming pool at a fund-raiser at Paul Mazursky's. I don't think he even asked for a towel afterward. Bob was also pyrotechnically inclined and liked to mess around with gas and lard and flame, frying up a whole turkey sitting on a can of beer, New Orleans–style, at Christmastime.

He loved jazz. He was elegant and wise and devil-may-care. He smelled of mint soap and clay and fresh cigar ash. He liked to wear a uniform of crisp cotton trousers, a starched white shirt ironed by his devoted housekeeper, Dora, and black Nikes. When I came into the picture, Dora had been working for Bob since 1987. She had a round pretty face and a steady gaze. I think it took a while for her to like me. Bob had been married twice before and had a grown son, Steven, by his first wife, Joey.

It was quite surprising how alike his and Dad's and Jack's

experiences had been as kids: single male children raised like little pashas by doting, often suffocating women. Jack, whose grandmother curled his hair in the beauty parlor as his aunt and mother lied about their relationship to him, claiming instead to be his sisters; and my father, who was confined to his bedroom as a child and taught himself to draw and paint and invent stories. Perhaps it was a common thread that also made them so comfortable and attentive in the presence of women but particularly responsive to the opinions of men.

Bob's mother, Adelina, was a Rosicrucian and a charismatic. He told me that she could move a glass across a table with sheer willpower, that she loved to sing and dance; she was, in his words, a ham. His uncle ran a radio station in Mexico City that played jazz. His aunt Mercedes had been the inspiration for the Mexican singer and songwriter Agustín Lara when he wrote "Maria Bonita" and "Solamente Una Vez."

Bob had an unusual living space a block from the beach, comprising three trailer units that had once been joined together to form an outlet for Bank of America. His studio, a tall Victorian brick building, was next door on Windward Avenue, the gateway to Venice. When I first began staying over, we were awakened one night by the sound of someone walking on the roof above the sliding-glass doors that led to the bedroom. As I watched in silence, Bob slipped out of bed with the stealth of a puma, gripping a snub-nosed .45 between his fingers. As he pointed the gun aloft, I heard him say, "You've got exactly ten seconds to get down from there." The guy was whimpering as Bob began the countdown. It was impressive.

Bob cooked me perfect breakfasts and took me salsa dancing. He owned two Rottweilers, Duke and Natasha; Minnie made the mistake of considering Duke's dinner one day, and he went for her. He didn't hurt her, but she was scared. I was, too. After that, Bob rented an apartment for his dogs across the street; appropriately, it bore a mural with the words ANIMAL HOUSE above its windows.

I was always worried about Minnie's diabetes, and I hoped that my assistant, Molly, would remember to give her insulin shots when I was away or working or staying at Bob's. One evening Bob and I went to see *Schindler's List*, and when we got back to my house, I couldn't find Minnie. Eventually, after some panic on my part, we discovered that she had somehow gotten out of the back yard and was shivering on the first step of the swimming pool, waterlogged but mercifully still alive.

Soon Bob and I were seeing each other regularly. He often made the commute to my house, and sometimes the journey from the sea to the hills of Benedict Canyon felt endless. I decided to show Bob the farm. "Don't dress up," I told him. "It's very rustic."

On the appointed day in July, he appeared in a white ten-gallon hat with a mink hatband, ostrich cowboy boots, and a huge turquoise-inlaid belt. He looked like he'd walked straight off the set of *Dynasty*. I was momentarily horrified but determined not to show it. When our eyes met, he laughed. "It's okay, don't worry," he reassured me. "It's a joke."

Bob was thin with long legs. Like Dad, he was born under the sign of Leo. He was a tenderfoot and, as it turned out, he hated to get his paws wet. Unaware of this phobia, in the heat of summer, I took Bob up into the Sequoia National Forest above my farm, where the river was fast-running, and the water flowed down fresh from the mountains, full of golden and rainbow trout. Bob had borrowed some banana-yellow Bermuda shorts from Steven's collection of surf-wear, and as we waded across the shallow water by the bank, over the slippery rocks, I laughed out loud at his incongruous appearance. Not until we were midway and entering the deeper water in the middle of the stream did I notice that his eyes were wide with fear. I could tell by the expression on his face that this was his idea of hell, like putting a cat in a bath. The rocks were very slippery and he was crouched over, visibly panicked.

When we reached the opposite bank of the river, he sank down to his knees in a cave and said, "That's it, I'm staying here." It took a good hour for me to convince him that he would not drown on the way back and that it would be a good thing to leave before dark, when the bears and rattlesnakes would come out.

Back on dry land at the farm, Bob said that he wanted to learn to ride a horse, so I put him up on my best and eldest mare, Kahlua. She was reliable and safe. When he rode her in the dressage ring, I could tell he was a natural. A few days later, I took him to a ranch next door to my property, and we made a long ride up through cattle pastures toward the top of a mountain overlooking the valley. At one point, the dirt road became steep, and the land beside the mountain trail fell away to a sheer drop on either side. Bob had an attack of vertigo and insisted on dismounting. The terrain was rugged and rocky. I could tell that he was unhappy, although he was very quiet. And so, with little space to turn around, I dismounted with him and we headed back down the mountain, the horses' feet clip-clopping on the dry shale behind us.

After that misjudgment on my part, Bob was reluctant to ride again. He said that what he wanted was a two-year-old, so they could learn at the same time. We went to a local horse farm in Woodlake, and he picked out a beautiful bay filly he christened Isis.

Bob never rode her, but I did, and I loved her. I could take her anywhere—she was always willing. I used to sing a song in her ear when we were out together, "Isis is nicest," and I knew she understood. Isis was the smartest, fastest, and prettiest of my horses.

That Thanksgiving Bob presented me with a delightful pet, a "miniature" black potbellied pig we christened Giorgio. He arrived in a little cage and was, quite astonishingly, house-trained. His breeders had told Bob that Giorgio had a fondness for grapes. Within the first couple of weeks, he had doubled his original size and was soon growing tusks. Laila gave him pedicures and rubbed him with body cream, but it soon became evident that he was not a city pig. Giorgio went up to stay with Yolanda at the farm, where he went on to lead a fine life, strolling the grounds, eating acorns, and sleeping under the moon in great piles of oak leaves.

It was around this time that Toni Howard called one morning to say that Scott Rudin and the director Barry Sonnenfeld wanted to meet with me to discuss the possibility of my playing Morticia in *The Addams Family*, which, like the 1960s TV series, was based on Charles Addams's *New Yorker* cartoons. I had been obsessed with Morticia since I was a child. "What do you think?" I asked Toni. "Why haven't they asked Cher?"

I met Scott and Barry seated at a round table in the bar at the Beverly Hills Hotel. As I remember, I asked them the same question. I was delighted and incredulous when they offered me the part.

I was looking for a template on which to base Morticia Addams, a key to giving this potentially cartoon character some humanity. I decided on my friend Jerry Hall, the beautiful Texan model, feeling that her kind and gentle disposition and utter devotion to her children might lend some warmth to Morticia's chilly, unflappable nature.

Before long, I was in costume fittings. There were to be several variations on Morticia's ubiquitous black dress, some with subtle additions of lace and beading. Ruth Myers was the costume designer, and she was a zealot when it came to foundation garments. In keeping with my theory that a witch is a witch because all witches are in torture, the corset was so tight that for the first few days of filming, until the boning broke in to some degree and became more pliable, I literally could not sit down and had to be transported to set from my dressing room recumbent in the back of a station wagon. Fern Buchner contrived to make my eyes slant by gluing tabs of fabric to my temples and securing them firmly behind my head with a sturdy elastic band. The only problem with this was that in the screen test, the lower part of my face appeared to be sagging, so she attached two more tabs behind my jawline.

We agreed that the look worked, but it was like being in traction. I was in constant discomfort, unable to turn my head without resistance, so unless I released the tension at lunchtime, I had intense headaches in the afternoon, and my neck began to blister. To cap this off, there was the question of the wig. The hair and makeup took almost as long to remove as to apply in the first place, and if one of the tabs snapped, the wig would have to come off in order to reattach the elastic bands, then be replaced on my head.

After I broke all the acrylic fingernails that had been laboriously applied, by painfully snapping them off while trying to hold open an elevator door, I resorted to wearing blood-red stick-on nails. Thereafter, I left a trail of sticky nails wherever I went—in pockets, in cars, on the street, in the carpet. Once I found one glued to Minnie's bottom.

The days on *The Addams Family* were long and arduous, because I couldn't move. Every time I turned my head and the hair split or the tabs snapped, Scott and Barry would call, "Cut!" Finally it occurred to me just to turn my body from the feet up.

There were several cast members who had a worse time of it than I, including Judith Malina, a wonderfully eccentric actress and one of the founders of the Living Theatre, who was playing Granny, and whose solution to the discomfort of being embedded in latex for over twelve hours a day was to smoke an endless series of joints in her trailer throughout filming. At least she was in a perennially good mood.

Christopher Lloyd, as Fester Addams, was likewise encased in prosthetics but also managed to stay upbeat. I don't think we ever really had a conversational exchange—he was monosyllabic, which I put down to his being a really good character actor.

The children, Pugsley and Wednesday, were as different as night and day. Jimmy Workman was a contented, plump little soul but not what I would call a deep searcher in life. Christina Ricci was just the opposite. At eleven years old, she had a haunting dark-eyed gaze, level and unblinking; one withering look could render you speechless. Her line readings for Wednesday were deadpan, always impeccably delivered.

I had been a smoker since the age of sixteen, and Jimmy and Christina liked to visit my motor home at lunchtime and lecture me on why cigarettes were bad for you. One day Christina showed up alone at my trailer and asked if she could come in. "I'd like to try a cigarette," she said, eyeing me coolly. "Can you give me one?" I resisted, although she was very persuasive.

Raúl Juliá—who played Gomez, the patriarch of the family—was the heart and soul of *The Addams Family*; he held us together with his sweet nature and ebullient joie de vivre. He was kind to everyone, sang opera, and played with the children all day long. Bob and he got along very well and shared interests in Latin music and Cuban cigars.

Nothing seemed to faze Raúl. One morning he walked on set with an extremely bloodshot eye.

"What's that?" I asked him. "How did that happen?"

"My eye just fell out," he replied.

He went on to tell a very unusual story of how he'd been at the bar of the Sunset Marquis the night before, having a chat with a friend—I believe it was the singer and musician Robert Palmer—when, alarmingly, he realized that his eye had come loose from its socket. "It was dangling in front of me!" he said.

"What did you do?" I asked, horrified.

"I just grabbed it and put it right back in," said Raúl. "Then I went to the emergency room at Cedars. The doctor said it was the right thing to do."

That afternoon I phoned a joke shop and ordered dozens of those glasses with the drop eyeballs on springs, and the next morning the entire crew wore them for Raúl's arrival on set. We all made light of what had happened, but he must have been scared beyond belief.

CHAPTER 24

From the time we first met, I wanted to take Bob to Ireland. I was convinced that he would love it almost as much as I do. We flew to London on the Concorde. In the hot, crowded cabin, as the flight attendants served breakfast, Bob got an entire serving platter of smoked salmon and scrambled eggs dumped on his head. It dripped off his hair and onto the shoulders of his maroon cashmere jacket. By the time we arrived, and despite our best efforts to rinse him off, Bob smelled rank, and even after sending it to the dry cleaner when we got to the hotel, the jacket had to be disposed of. Bob was cold but refused to buy another. Later in the week, we flew into Dublin with Sabrina Guinness, whom I had met originally when Jack was making *The Shining* in London. My plan with Bob was to stay a few days in Dublin and then drive down to the West Country, where I grew up.

No sooner had we installed ourselves at the Shelbourne Hotel than our suite was filled with a host of welcoming friends, excited that their prodigal daughter had returned. Some friends had brought others along with them, and most were displaying great interest in the minibar. At one point Bob took me aside with his eyes wide and asked who the hell were all these people. Soon the party crawled downstairs to the Horseshoe bar, where the Guinness runs on tap.

That night we went to dinner at a restaurant with my old friend Garech Browne and a countryman who sang songs in ancient Gaelic with his eyes closed, holding your hand and moving your arm to his rhythms. The following morning we went out to the Cliffs above Howth, where William Butler Yeats and Maud Gonne had roamed together in their youth. The wind was so high, it almost blew us off the mountainside. Bob assured me that he loved Ireland but said that he was not used to the temperature.

On our way down west, we stopped off in Killarney and walked through the ruins of a twelfth-century fort at Dingle. Eventually, we came to the Burren, where Sabrina's sister Miranda lived out on a sea of limestone rocks with barely another cottage in sight. From there we split off temporarily from Sabrina, with Bob and I continuing our road trip on to Galway.

By the time we reached Oranmore Castle that evening, Bob had come down with a bad case of the flu. I ate fattened sheep on a spit at the fireplace downstairs in the baronial hall at a party thrown in our honor by my childhood friend Leonie King, now married to the musician Alec Finn of the group De Dannan, whom I had met years before at Tony and Margot's wedding.

Bob lay shivering under an enormous pile of blankets upstairs in the tower, where the wind and sea foam blew in through the open fortress windows with the cries of the cormorants. When I joined him after dinner, he declared quite seriously through chattering teeth that he thought he might die from the cold.

I think Bob was ultimately shocked back to health by the volatility of his surroundings. I was determined to show him the places where I had grown up, and decided to take him to St. Clerans just a few days later, on a Sunday morning, when I presumed everyone would be at mass.

I had a memory of Mrs. Cole, from whom my father bought the estate and who used to come to visit the old castle on the grounds, and how we as children had thought of her as an oddity, a displaced outsider. Now I was in her position. When our car drew up on the driveway outside the Little House, we climbed out to peer through some tall black cast-iron gates at the entrance to the courtyard. There had been gateposts but never gates when we were growing up. A young man, maybe seventeen years old, came walking toward us across the gravel. As he opened the gate, he stared long and deep into my eyes. "I always dreamed of the day Anjelica Huston would come home to St. Clerans," he said simply.

He welcomed us into the courtyard, and we followed him to the front door of the Little House. I looked up in the eaves as we passed the back door; there was always a nest there in the spring when Tony and I were growing up. The boy explained that the name of the family in residence was Corbett.

A couple, whom I assumed to be the parents of the boy, kindly asked us to come in. They offered us Irish coffee and biscuits. But I was crying and couldn't stop. I asked if Bob and I could wander through the garden. My mother's garden. Although the ancient crawling boughs of the old yew tree still yielded their invitation to climb, the place was very different. No tall delphiniums or snapdragons here, no hydrangeas fed with copper sulfate to stain them blue, no wall of sweet peas begging to be picked, no pious fuchsia in skirts of papal violet and blood red. Just as the rooks on the property seemed to have crowded out the songbirds, so had the perennials fought for their place among the weeds resting against the high rock walls, the annuals of my mother's day all but forgotten.

At the top edge of the vegetable garden was Betty O'Kelly's forlorn tennis court, now mossy and gray. After a full walk-about of the grounds, we arrived at the tack room, and Mr. Corbett reached up and gently brought a photograph down from the wall. The image was of an African-American jockey, very dark-skinned, astride a racehorse. Mr. Corbett pointed to the jockey. "Isn't that John Huston?" he asked eagerly. I agreed that the jockey looked very much like Dad, although perhaps of a different ethnic background. We left soon after without going up to the Big House. I didn't have the heart for it.

That night we were booked to stay at Dromoland Castle before returning to Dublin on our way home. When we reached the hotel, I walked with Bob on the golf course and told him the stories of when Tony and I were kids and loved to chase around the corridors of Dromoland while Dad's assistant Gladys and the owner, Mr. McDonough, held hands on the front lawn on a rare visit. And how the suits of armor were all imported from Scotland and England by rich entre-preneurs like Mr. McDonough, wishing to rewrite Irish history, of which there was little known since the burning of the national archives during the Irish civil war.

We were shown to our room upstairs; our suite had a full Jacuzzi bathtub, no doubt a blessed relief for all those cold golfers at the end of a day on the links. When I got out, pink and covered with bubbles, Bob handed me a glass of cham-pagne, went down on one knee, and proposed marriage. He tossed two small boxes on the bed. One contained a ring with a rare turquoise-blue stone, a Paraíba, and the other a ceremo-

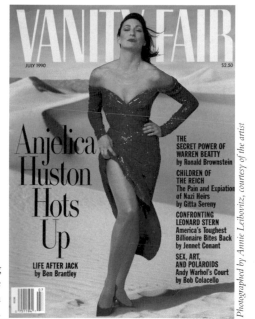

In 1990, after shooting *The Grifters*, Anjelica gave an interview to Ben Brantley for *Vanity Fair*.

Anjelica as Gretta Conroy with Donal McCann as Gabriel Conroy in the adaptation of James Joyce's *The Dead*, the last film directed by her father, January 1987.

Anjelica as Miss Ernst in the adaptation
of Roald Dahl's *The Witches*,
directed by Nic Roeg, spring 1988.

Anjelica as the Grand High Witch
in *The Witches*.

Anjelica and Robert Duvall as Clara and Gus on the set
of the television miniseries adaptation of Larry McMurtry's
Lonesome Dove, photographed by Bill Wittliff.

John Cusack as Roy Dillon with Anjelica as Lilly Dillon
in *The Grifters*, directed by Stephen Frears.

Snap/REX USA

Anjelica as
Morticia Addams
in *The Addams Family*,
directed by Barry
Sonnenfeld.

Anjelica directing her first film, an adaptation
of Dorothy Allison's *Bastard Out of Carolina*, in 1995.

Anjelica playing
the Supreme Leader
and Michael Jackson
in the title role in Francis
Ford Coppola's *Captain
EO*, August 1985.

Bob Graham and Anjelica's engagement at Dromoland Castle
in County Clare, Ireland, in 1991.

Bob Graham with Anjelica
at their wedding ceremony
at Hotel Bel-Air, May 23, 1992.

Anjelica with Bob Graham at Earl
and Camilla McGrath's Villa Marlia
in Lucca, Italy, 1990s.

Photographed for the Vanity Fair Hollywood Issue by Annie Leibovitz,

The Huston family posing in a 2003 photograph by Annie Leibovitz at Ahmanson Ranch in Calabasas, California, for *Vanity Fair*. Anjelica is with her nephews Jack and Matthew; her siblings, Danny, Allegra, and Tony; and Tony's dog Frankie.

Photographed by Ari Michelson

Anjelica's brother Danny and her niece Stella at home in Hollywood, California.

Anjelica's nephew Jack
and his daughter, Sage.

Anjelica's sister, Allegra, and nephew
Rafa at the top of Italianos Canyon
in Taos, New Mexico, where Allegra
has lived since 1999.

Mercedes "Mecha" is a purebred
Xoloitzcuintli. Pootie was a gift
from Bob Graham in June 2007.
She is a mystery—probably Lhasa
Apso or Havanese.

Anjelica's nieces and nephew, Shannan, Sage, Noah,
Mathilda with Laura, and Matthew and Jack's mother,
Margot, at Houghton, Norfolk, England, 2013.

Anjelica's nephew
Jasper and niece
Stella in Central
Park, NYC, 2012.

Anjelica on an Irish thoroughbred at Luggala,
friend Garech Browne's estate in the Wicklow Mountains, Ireland.
Photographed by David Bailey © June 1988.

nial ring with the enameled heads of two spotted dogs, inlaid with emeralds, their mouths open with little teeth bared, as if barking at each other.

We ate a very formal dinner that night in the hotel dining room with several toasts, but nonetheless, we were surprised the next morning when everyone from the chambermaids to the doormen at reception wished us a wonderful life together. When we got into the car, the driver congratulated us and then turned on the radio, which was reporting on-air that I had become engaged the night before in the west of Ireland at Dromoland Castle.

When we got back to New York, Joan threw an engagement party for us and invited just about everyone. The rooms in her apartment were packed with friends. She presented us with a cake with two little figures on horseback on top, which she claimed were Bob and me riding off into the sunset.

Back in California, Bob introduced me to his artist friends, many of whom, like him, lived in Venice. I took Bob up to Santa Barbara to introduce him to Dorothy Jeakins and to take her on a picnic to the gardens of a Japanese monastery. We ultimately didn't get too far—only to her back yard. But even though Dorothy was frail now and using a wheelchair, she flirted sweetly with Bob.

Gordon Davidson, the founding artistic director of the Center Theater Group, suggested that I do a presentation at UCLA. At this time I was working to produce a screenplay of Nancy Cardozo's book *Lucky Eyes and a High Heart*, about the spiritual and political connection between the Irish poet William Butler Yeats and his muse, the great beauty and patriot Maud

Gonne MacBride. I decided to talk about their passions, namely Yeats's for MacBride, and MacBride's hopes for a free Ireland, reading from their letters and his poems. For the second part of the program, I would read Molly Bloom's soliloquy from James Joyce's *Ulysses*. Afterward, when Bob and I walked out into the starry night, my heart was still pounding in my chest from adrenaline. Nick was standing by the limo, a small portable television in his hands. "L.A. is on fire," he announced in disbelief.

The city had erupted in the aftermath of the acquittal of four Los Angeles police officers accused of beating Rodney King. On television, downtown looked like a war zone, with looters scrambling over each other to get into Samy's Camera and people being pulled out of their vehicles and getting beaten up. That afternoon I went to a nearby market in Beverly Hills, where everyone was queuing for bread and stockpiling cans of beans; they seemed to be in it for the long run.

The next day I drove through Beverly Hills down to Hollywood to see what was going on, which at that point wasn't much. But it was obvious that there was a big disconnect between those who lived the affluent life tucked away in gated communities in Beverly Hills and those who confronted real life on the streets downtown. There was no doubt that Venice would provide excitement. I decided to sell my house and look for a place nearer the beach, where Bob and I could live together.

I had loved veils throughout my life but decided to wear a white crepe Armani suit and a picture hat for my wedding. I wanted to look the way women do on their second marriage. It felt more like the truth and more dignified than skipping down the aisle at forty, trying to look like a girl. There was not a moment after Bob asked me to marry him that I doubted it would happen. Now I was shopping with Sabrina Guinness at Bullocks on Wilshire Boulevard, trying on and buying beautiful Manolo Blahniks two sizes too small, and wearing an emerald engagement ring on my finger. I wondered if it would make any difference to Jack when he heard the news.

I had decided that we should get married in the garden at the Hotel Bel Air; it would be traditional, grown up, and sophisticated, and Bob would take care of the party. He planned to set up a big tent on an empty lot he owned next door to his studio on Windward Avenue.

My assistant, Molly Shaw, was going through lists of food and people and flowers; my bridesmaids were multiplying by the hour, all of them concerned about what they should wear. Joan Buck had been appointed matron of honor and was instructing all the girls to wear beige, and Wanda McDaniel at Giorgio Armani was helping with a discount. My niece Laura was our flower girl, and her brothers, Matt and Jack, were ring-bearers. Bob had commissioned hand-forged flick-knives from Germany for his battalion of groomsmen, including my brother Danny; his best man was Earl McGrath.

The wedding took place on the bright and beautiful morning of May 23, 1992. Swans were floating in the stream; the pergola was decorated with gardenias, tuberose, and pink and white roses. As music sang on the bows of three violinists led by Henri Temianka, old, dear friends like Dorothy Jeakins and Lillian Ross, Swifty and Mary Lazar, Lauren Bacall, Mick Jagger and Jerry Hall, and my doctor Elsie Giorgi took their seats. Cici was there, as was Bob's aunt Mercedes, a vision in pink.

Margot and the kids had come from London for the wedding, and my brother Tony had come down from Taos. I was in the hotel manager's private office at the top of the garden steps when Tony came to get me. "It's time," he said, and tucked my arm under his, and we processed happily down the aisle as the trio played "Here Comes the Bride." My cheeks were twitching uncontrollably as my eyes locked gently with the eyes of my friends. I carried a bouquet of freesia, gardenias, and lilies of the valley. Bob was standing in a pale suit under the trellis, between Earl and Steven. The walk seemed endless, and there was a murmur of what I assumed to be appreciation for my hat. I moved forward beside Bob to face our judge, Mariana Pfaelzer, and take our vows. She made a beautiful speech, funny and smart and serious and heartfelt, and then, as we exchanged rings, pronounced us man and wife.

I don't know how I had remained oblivious during the entire ceremony. I had missed the sight of Swifty Lazar's chair unexpectedly tipping over onto the grass and the flurry of activity that attended it. After a brief difference of opinion between Betty Bacall and Dr. Giorgi about which hospital he should be taken to, Dr. Giorgi won, and Swifty was spirited away like a doll in the arms of my friend Joey Burke to have his pacemaker replaced. No one mentioned the incident to me until well after speeches and cake, when Bob and I retired to our suite for a few romantic hours before our big evening blowout party in Venice.

Mittoine had done my hair in a beehive for the party, like he used to do for his mother in the sixties. It was a style I'd never have dreamed of wearing if not to please him. It was a real updo; he had tucked red roses and gardenias behind my ears and puffed out my bangs. My makeup artist, Carol Shaw, did me proud all day and most of the night. The inside of the marquee was decorated with colored lights, seashells, and flowers, and Bob had invested in several great bands, blues and Brazilian, with feathered showgirls from Bahia. My nephews, little Matt and Jack, were fascinated by the girls and followed them around, mesmerized.

I wore a Richard Tyler white silk taffeta dress that we designed, with a ruffled Spanish dancing skirt tight to the knees, a blood-red sash, and a little bolero hand-embroidered with seed pearls in the shape of a winged heart. Seal was there with Olivia d'Abo. He and Harry Dean Stanton sang "Proud Mary," and Helena belly-danced. There were a few faces from the old life with Jack. Bob and I cut into at least twenty separate cakes, one for each table, with two ceremonial knives that he had ordered from his favorite jeweler, in Germany. My feet were still sore from the tiny Manolos, so I just kicked them off and danced like a dervish until three in the morning with my handsome husband.

When I look at the pictures of the wedding, everyone looks young and beautiful: Paula Yates in yellow polka dots, grinning in an Easter hat with a baby in her arms; Susan Forristal catching the bouquet I threw to her, payback for my snatching hers at her wedding; Jerry Hall looking stunning and slightly more bridal than I in cream lace Alexander McQueen; Mick in a little straw boater; Allegra with gardenias in her hair; my nephews Matt and Jack consuming champagne under the buffet table; Tony smiling broadly as he gives me away; Toby Rafelson looking very pretty with a rose in her hair; Lauren Hutton's golden skin; Dorothy Jeakins in a wheelchair, pressing a box into my hands (inside was a necklace of Mum's that Gladys had given Dorothy when Mum died—rows of carved intaglio portraits in lava rock with a Maltese cross pendant);

a long shot of Bob and me leaving the reception to go to our room, my Manolos in hand.

When we had become engaged in Ireland, Bob had told me he wanted to take me to Oaxaca, a beautiful little town in south-western Mexico, for our honeymoon. Friends of ours had given us the telephone number for a Mr. Guillermo Olguín, who was the son of a previous mayor of Oaxaca, as someone we should call when we got there, a friend and guide in the locality. Without our having made any previous arrangement, Guillermo was at the airport when we arrived, and walked up and introduced himself. He understood magical thinking and usually happened to be in the right place at the right time.

Guillermo offered to drive us to our hotel, El Presidente, located on a quiet street away from the *zócalo*, the main square. The building was set back behind a heavy stone wall. It had existed through the decades as a monastery, a barracks, and a convent, and at its center was a most beautiful tropical gar-den, with fountains and palm fronds, where one could take drinks or dine. After several tequilas, I had a brainstorm, or so I thought, that if Bob could build me a place like it in Ven-ice, we could live as if it were an oasis on Windward Avenue, one of the busiest streets in America. He was ecstatic when I shared these thoughts with him.

It was romantic to be with Bob in his home country. That night, mariachis serenaded us and played "Noche de Ronda." We were very happy, and I was very much in love. Bob called me his Honita and I called him Honito.

The union felt different, almost preordained. I was Bob's wife, but I also felt like his student. He was very informed, an art historian who could tell you pretty much anything you wanted to know about Mexican culture, from pre-Columbian art through Diego Rivera, so it was fascinating to go to museums and galleries with him. Guillermo took us to some beautiful old pueblos where the local artists made ceramics from black clay, distilled tequila, and wove blankets. Bob and I drew a design that they would make for us—a wedding blanket, with the image of us on a background of coccinella red surrounded by a border of squash blossoms.

Guillermo introduced us to his wife, Marie, who told us about her work with indigenous women in remote areas of Mexico and El Salvador. We went to an outdoor restaurant by a lake that served red ants and iguana, which tasted reptilian.

We visited Monte Albán in the scorching sun, thirteen hundred feet above the valley floor of Oaxaca, built in 500 B.C. by the Zapotec Indians, who actually practiced dentistry, as evidenced by some impressive stone carvings of primitive warriors having their teeth extracted. On our last night, Guillermo took us to a little bar on the outskirts of town to listen to a girl sing. Her name was Lila Downs. She had black braided hair, gardenias and red roses woven like a crown around her head, an embroidered blouse of dark green satin, carmine lips, many rings on her fingers, and huaraches on her feet. She looked a lot like Frida Kahlo and sang jazz and sad love songs. She came to L.A. not long afterward, signed a record contract, and became famous.

On our way back to L.A., Guillermo accompanied us to Mexico City, where we hung out with him for a few days, looking at fierce Aztec gods in the National Museum of History, checking out the Orozco and Rivera murals, and savoring *huitlacoche* enchiladas in some fine restaurants. I asked

Bob to take me to the building where he grew up, and as we made our way in a taxi, Bob and Guillermo discovered to their mutual astonishment that they had occupied apartments at the same address when they were children, and even had a vague memory of each other from that time. This was almost unbelievable in a city of more than eight million people, but somehow I was not too surprised. It was part of the magical thinking. The apartment building, from the forties, was across the street from a little park; the bakery was still just a block down the street, with the same sugary cakes in the window that Bob had loved as a child.

We went on to Polanco to see Frida Kahlo's little house, with its vivid walls and the tiny bed to which she had been confined for most of her life. I remembered a story about Frida—that before the bus in which she had been traveling as a teenager had crashed, leaving her crippled for life, she had been seated close to someone who was carrying art supplies. When they unearthed her from the wreckage, Frida was covered in gold leaf.

Bob and I loved to stay in Mexico City at the Camino Real Hotel, with its massive concrete walls painted by the architect Barragán. When we returned there in 1997, it was to celebrate a retrospective of Bob's work in the Museo del Palacio de Bellas Artes, formerly a very grand opera house. Under an extraordinary ceiling of Tiffany glass, Bob's work never looked more beautiful.

When we returned to Venice, Bob set about making preliminary blueprints for the house we had conceived, often asking me for input when it came to questions of style and concept. He had designed only one house before, one that I very much admired—a very simple oblong shape with a huge living room window that opened out onto the bay of the Pacific in Marina del Rey.

It had been Bob's idea that his artist friends participate in the design and decor of that interior, so there were floors and kitchen cabinets designed by Billy Al Bengston and doors by Tony Berlant. Bob always liked the idea of an artists' co-op, contributing to achieve a master plan. He took this idea directly from the Renaissance, a time when the Vatican sponsored sculpture and painting in cathedrals and churches. And Bob was always happy to work for the church, albeit his subject matter was generally the female nude.

Bob and Steven acquired all of the necessary permits, and Bob proceeded to build a house that was a graceful combination of all the forms I love—modern, art deco, Moorish, and Venetian, with arches and domes in white plaster.

On November 19, 1992, John Foreman died of a heart attack at sixty-seven. He was a marvelous, kind, smart, funny man, and I loved him. He adored Paul Newman and Dad—two people he could look up to, because there were few who met his requirements or merited his attention. He was attracted to the best, because that's what he was.

John produced such films as *Butch Cassidy and the Sundance Kid* for Paul Newman and *The Man Who Would Be King* for Dad. It was John's belief in me, and his determined efforts to launch my career, that changed my professional life. John gave me *Ice Pirates* to help me grow and *Prizzi's Honor* to help me shine. He restored my confidence when I, more than anyone, did not believe in myself.

John prolonged Dad's life. When others were wary of hiring him, or deemed him too old or unfit to direct a film, John stepped up with a quality project. John cared more than anyone and made it look like water off a duck's back.

John's funeral service was held at Westwood Memorial. Michael Caine told funny stories about being on set with Foreman and Huston, and Polly Bergen sang "I'll Be Seeing You," which, in the words of John's daughter Julie, "brought us to our knees."

CHAPTER 25

In the summer of '93, I was shooting a miniseries in Toronto, a quite beautifully written piece called *Family Pictures*, about an autistic boy, Randall Eberlin, whose disorder severely disrupts the people around him. I played his mother, Lainey, a woman increasingly dependent on alcohol as she struggles with the impossibility of helping her son. It was a good part, with a demanding range of emotion. Dermot Mulroney and Kyra Sedgwick were my children, and a fine young actor, Jamie Harrold, played Randall. Sam Neill was the conflicted father, faced with the choice between putting his son in an institution or allowing the family to painfully self-destruct.

Sam and I hit it off in the first few days. He was empathetic and lovely to work with. We compounded our friendship by going to see k.d. lang in concert. Although the workload was intense and I was tired, Sam's theory that listening to great live music was better than a full night's sleep held out. Our director, Phillip Saville, was British, and, although very nice, he shot the movie slowly and conventionally, always starting with a master, inevitably followed by medium and close-up shots to cover each detail of a scene. It was a little frustrating to shoot by the numbers after the experience and freedom of working with Woody Allen, who was more prone to cut in the camera, economically and efficiently, like Dad.

We were staying at the Sutton Place Hotel, a limbo away from home for many actors working in the city. Bob came to stay with me a few weeks into production and took up all the room in my suite by building a full schematic maquette of our future home in Venice. But it was exciting to be planning a domestic space together.

Mittoine had come with me to work on *Family Pictures*, and I was increasingly worried about him. He had become terribly thin. Although he would order a lot to eat if we went out to dinner, he was never able to finish what was on his plate. I pretended not to notice that his hands were shaking when he did my hair. After we wrapped, before we left Toronto, Mittoine went to the most expensive department store in the city and maxed out his credit cards on lavish end-of-movie gifts— cut-glass perfume bottles and cashmere blankets.

Woody Allen wrote to me around this time, asking if perhaps I would like to work on his new movie, *Manhattan Murder Mystery*, because I would both solve a murder and get to kiss him. It was a very pleasant if short assignment. Alan Alda, Joy Behar, Ron Rifkin, and Diane Keaton were all in the film, and although Woody was still in child-custody litigation with Mia Farrow, he seemed in a good mood. He obviously enjoyed Keaton's company. Every morning she arrived on set looking like she had walked out of the pages of *Vogue*, and that was before she even got into wardrobe.

As was Woody's habit in the nineties, we shot all over New York. The dialogue was especially difficult when we were all in a scene, as I had most of it and it was scripted that my character should be smart and come up with the solution to the crime. The part required some fast talking. Some of the actors were prone to taking long pauses before or during the take, and I was panicked that I might miss my cues, but somehow I got through.

And the Band Played On, directed by Roger Spottiswoode from a book by Randy Shilts, was an HBO film about AIDS, from the first signs of its inception through the early days of the mysterious disease that was decimating the gay population. A number of actors had agreed to participate in the film for no fee, feeling that whatever they could do to defray the cost of making it would be worthwhile. I joined a cast that included Alan Alda, Matthew Modine, Bud Cort, Richard Gere, Glenne Headly, and Ian McKellen. I was playing the part of Dr. Betsy Reisz, an AIDS researcher, for just one day.

They sent a limousine to take me out to Long Beach for the shoot, and Mittoine was coming with me to do my hair. He had been staying in a friend's apartment in Los Angeles since *Family Pictures*, but I hadn't seen him in the hiatus.

When he got into the car, I could see that things had become much worse. His complexion was the same unnatural orange that I had seen before with others who had been diagnosed with AIDS. He was even thinner than the last time we'd been together. We rode along in a silence so thick I thought I might scream. Mittoine's eyes were hollow as he stared out the window.

"How are you feeling, Mitti?" I asked him.

"Fine," he said unsurely, with a little grin.

When we got to my camper, I entered first. Then, hearing Mittoine's bag crash to the floor, I turned around to see every imaginable pill roll out in full view on the chocolate-brown carpet. There were hundreds—blue and red and yellow and green—all combinations of containers, sizes, and colors, like a pharmacy. Mittoine and I just burst into tears.

"I couldn't tell you," he said. "I wasn't brave enough."

When Vice President Dan Quayle made a speech in 1992, following the L.A. riots and the aftermath of the beating of Rodney King, he attributed the discord in the city to a breakdown of "family values." He also criticized the character Murphy Brown, a role played by Candice Bergen on television, for bearing a child out of wedlock with the intention of raising it on her own. There had been a considerable outcry in reaction to his statements, and he was the subject of much derision by the Left. Paul Rudnick wrote a sequel to *The Addams Family,* cleverly entitled *Addams Family Values.*

Two years had passed since the first movie, and there were some changes in cast and crew, but overall, Scott Rudin and Barry Sonnenfeld held to the high standards that they had previously established. Every frame was composed and considered, and our lighting cameraman, Donald Peterman, painstakingly lit Morticia hotter than anyone else on-screen, so that her luminous pallor would seem otherworldly—all this before the age of color correction. Fern Buchner was doing my makeup again, and Toni-Ann Walker, with whom I had not worked since *The Postman Always Rings Twice* and *Frances*, was doing my hair. She was unchanged after all these years, soft-spoken and intelligent, with an upturned nose in a doll's face.

Theoni Aldredge did the costumes for *Family Values*; her approach to costuming was more forgiving than Ruth Myers's, and the dresses themselves were more lavish, with different textures and shades of black, embellished with jeweled insects, bats, and arachnids. One piece, a silvery cloak, transparent as a black widow's web, was particularly spectacular.

When I entered a rehearsal room at Paramount with most of the former cast members from *The Addams Family*, I noticed a few changes. My friend Carol Kane had taken over the part of Granny, and Joan Cusack had come aboard as Uncle Fester's maniacal love interest. Shockingly, the children were now adolescent; Jimmy Workman was grazing at the craft service table under the approving eye of his mother, and Christina Ricci had somehow matured without having visibly grown. Raúl was back as Gomez, enthusiastic and good-natured as ever. He had lost a little weight because of an appendectomy. But it was exciting for us to be working together again.

Soon after we started, Raúl and I went into dance rehearsals for "The Mamushka," a hot tango composed by Marc Shaiman, in which Gomez spins Morticia like a dervish and she throws a kitchen knife that he catches in his teeth. In a particularly funny gesture, Fester tries to woo his girlfriend by shoving breadsticks up his nose. There were fresh oysters for the scene being shucked offstage, and Raúl tried a few for lunch; soon after, he was violently sick. It began to be apparent that Raúl was having trouble eating, and he was becoming increasingly thin. At no point did he ever complain. Raúl's wife, Merel, and their handsome sons visited the set on several occasions. Raúl was very proud of them.

For a week we were on location up at the Sequoia National Forest, about twenty miles from my farm. I invited my hair-and-makeup team to stay at the farm, along with Raúl. For a few nights, Yolanda cooked Mexican food, and Raúl seemed to enjoy it. In the evenings he would sit outside on the porch, smoking a good cigar and singing along with the bullfrogs.

That is how I love to remember him. Raúl made more than thirty movies, including the amazing *Kiss of the Spider Woman*, before he died after complications from a stroke.

Mittoine had been in and out of the hospital while I was working on *Addams Family Values.* Soon after I finished, he went into a hospice in the Valley and died just a few months later, on March 17, 1993, at the age of forty-four. He was one of the sweetest men ever born, and I miss him every time I go to work on a movie.

I sold my home to a young couple from a hit television show, and as the Venice house was not quite ready after escrow closed, Bob and I went to the Miramar Hotel in Santa Monica for a brief stay. Bob had been asking all along what I wanted for the plan of the house, and designing it just so. The building wrapped around a central courtyard. It had high domed ceilings, outdoor walkways, recycled pine floors, and French doors that opened to the ocean breeze. Oxygen flowed through the house, and even on the hottest days, there was no need for air-conditioning. Bob had managed to include a lap pool and a Jacuzzi in the courtyard, and frescoes by his friend the painter David Novros lit the outdoor walls. The house was a perfect backdrop for my possessions—everything I had held on to throughout the years, from my collections that began in Ireland and London.

While the house was still under construction, Bob and I had gone to an arboretum in Gardena and chosen a coral tree with a sculptural trunk to fill the central space. It was lowered into the courtyard by crane, its roots sunk deep inside a metal container to stop the concrete patio from cracking around it. Bob laughed and said that after we died, the roots would break loose from their confines and the house would crumble, something from a story from Gabriel García Márquez.

Every spring the tree grew a full two feet. In summer it blossomed with fire-red flowers, and in winter it dropped black pods with red beans that the birds devoured, in spite of the constant threat of being pounced on by one or more of the eight local stray cats I had adopted.

My understanding with the cats was that if they chose to stay, I would have them neutered. Often kittens would show up hungry or abandoned. I always took them in out of pity, but because of malnutrition and their feral pasts, they generally cost a fortune in veterinary bills. They also proved difficult to train to kitty litter and ruined many of my best rugs and plants. At night they slept in the garage, and in the daytime they loved to hang out with Dora in the kitchen, especially when she was making chicken enchiladas.

Across the outdoor walkway from our bedroom was my office, and above it, a guest room. On the top story was a little parapet from which one could see the whole of Venice Beach—from the flags of the many nations on the roof of the youth hostel next door, above a faded sepia mural, to the Townhouse bar across the street, the tattoo parlor, Animal House, the hippies and the homeless, the vendors, the performance artists, the swami with his turban and electric guitar on Rollerblades, the runaways, the snake-charmer, the rappers, the chalk and sand artists, the weight lifters, the addicts, the Jehovah's Witnesses, the tourists and the surfers, the skateboard kids, the guy who played "Eye of the Tiger" relentlessly and did crazy stuff with a chain saw for eight years.

Bob had designed our bedroom with a balcony overlooking the courtyard. It met the coral tree about twenty-five feet up, and when we were moving in, a family of doves nested in the tree's branches, until the starlings came en masse, trilling and squeaking for cat kibble. Then came two stern ravens who produced an angry chick each May, which the cats would circle and consider for a while before eventually abandoning the exercise, leaving the nestling to flop around in the empty lot by the side of the house as its parents screeched in distress. If it was evident that the deck was stacked against the fledglings, I'd put on gloves and make a rescue. I would put them in a big cage I'd bought for the first casualty and raise them on cat food and fruit and boiled eggs. If they were incapacitated, I would take them up the coast to a wildlife sanctuary, where they were placed with others of their kind in a huge aviary called "Crowatia."

Birds, for some reason, seem quite attracted to me. Every spring up at my farm, babies fall from their nests and need saving or rehab. Occasionally, a morning finds me chopping up a frozen mouse at breakfast for a baby screech owl. It's not a pretty sight.

The house on Windward became the embodiment of Bob's and my mutual aesthetic, as well as a home and sanctuary for our menagerie. On weekends in the summer, we gave parties in the courtyard and played instruments. Bob and Steven were great on congas. The house was always filled with music.

CHAPTER 26

In answer to Dad's question: Yes, Irving Lazar would be missed and his generation, too, ardently so. Swifty died at the age of eighty-six in December 1993 of complications from diabetes, and was laid to rest in Westwood beside his wife, Mary, who had died in January of that year from liver cancer.

When Irving Lazar and Ray Stark and John Foreman died, a large part of the order of how things worked on the social scene in Los Angeles was gone forever with them. The graceful evenings at Chasen's restaurant, once the background to almost any good Hollywood story of the fifties. Parties with the Wilders, the Walds, the DeCordovas. The senior affluent, with their spotless white carpets and silver-framed photographs of famous friends, their porte cocheres, their sweeping staircases, their gilded mirrors reflecting the confirmation of early hopes and opulent dreams, where summer trumped all the seasons with purple jacaranda lining the streets of Beverly Hills and coral trees that grew like weeds outside the mansions on San Vicente Boulevard, the old-growth bougainvillea wrapping the Spanish walls in shocking pink. A way of life beginning to fade—like nocturnal dreams—in the harsh light of a new day.

*   *   *

Sean Penn sent over a script that he'd written called *The Crossing Guard*. Jack was starring. I think Sean asked me to play the part of Jack's ex-wife because of our history. In the film, I was to be married to a new husband, played by Robbie Robertson, but still suffering the loss of my and Jack's daughter to a traffic accident. Sean's kids were young at the time; emotionally, he always seemed concerned with the subject of the death of a child.

I hadn't seen Jack in some years; there was a formality to the reunion, and I felt shy. We worked together for only a few days, and he was brilliant as ever. It always broke my heart when Jack played damaged men. On our last day, Jack asked if I'd like to have lunch, and over a very delicious pasta in his camper cooked by our old friend from *Prizzi's*, Tommy Baratta, Jack said, "You and me, Toots—we're like *Love in the Time of Cholera*." Which for some reason pleased me, probably because that is one of my favorite books, by one of my favorite authors, about one of my favorite subjects—hopeless, enduring love.

It was a hot June in Coral Gables, Florida. I was there to work with Marisa Tomei and Alfred Molina on Mira Nair's *The Perez Family*, the story of a Cuban exile whose wife disappeared in the Mariel boatlift and who arrives in Miami having fallen in love with a young whore on the passage over, only to discover that his wife is still alive. The situation is not so unlike *Enemies, A Love Story* in that over the course of the film the wife becomes a mother figure to her husband as he draws closer to regression. In both cases, the woman makes the choice for him, then releases him with love. In *Perez Family*, my character, Carmela, the exile's wife, goes on to a new relationship with Lieutenant John Pirelli, played by Chazz Palminteri.

I had looked forward to working with Mira ever since we had talked about it years before on Bernardo Bertolucci's jury at Cannes. In the interim, she had married Dr. Mahmood Mamdani, a professor and author, and was living in Uganda near the mouth of the Nile River. The war in Rwanda had left many victims floating downstream near where they were living. She was now the mother of a beautiful little boy, Zohran. I have always been drawn to Mira and to the way Indian women carry themselves—their perfume, their jewelry, their saris and shawls, the nuance of their movement, their attitude.

No woman I have ever met had the talent of Mira's mother for being perfectly attired for all occasions in traditional sari, with the almost spooky talent of a chameleon. If we were under banyan trees, she would visit set wearing the colors of the bark and leaves. If we were at the beach, she would appear in layers of blue or turquoise. Mira always promised that she would show me India. We agreed that maybe we would work together there one day.

But when it came to the scenes on *Perez Family*, I felt that our styles were a little at odds, in that I was not achieving what she wanted from me. I was sensing her impatience and feeling a certain discomfort in performing actions without having found my own original impulse.

Bob and I took the train from downtown Los Angeles to Santa Fe, where I would be shooting *Buffalo Girls*, a Western miniseries for CBS. We'd packed a lovely dinner and some wine and had a fine picnic before we bedded down. In the morning we passed the red rocks of Gallup, Arizona, glowing in the sun. I'd taken a beautiful traditional house belonging to a friend, up a long, icy, winding road in the hills above Santa Fe. The next day I woke up sick with the flu. The costume designer Van Ramsey came over with my dresser, Nava Sadan, and Tzetzi Ganev, who'd made my Oscar dress and now was throwing me into buckskins, long johns, and overcoats until I thought I'd pass out. After this I had to meet with the director, Rod Hardy, at a wild and distant location in the mountains outside Galisteo, where I was to read through some love scenes with Sam Elliott, who was playing Wild Bill Hickok. The set was frigid and I had a big crush on Sam and all I could do was cough and blow my nose.

In the days that followed, there was a party for the cast. I met Gabriel Byrne, a handsome, brooding Irishman who was to play Melanie Griffith's lover, Teddy Blue. Melanie shared the title with me. I was playing the part of Calamity Jane, and Melanie was playing the part of her best friend, Dora DuFran. We were always sympathetic friends, and we were happy working together. It was never hard to love Melanie.

I was wearing many layers of clothing with cross-belts so packed with ammunition that it was hard to even get up on a horse. Bob had always had a pet peeve about the inappropriate guns featured in movies and had taken it upon himself to arm me to the teeth personally: I had double-barreled Remingtons, buck knives, pearl-handled, silver-dipped revolvers, and a bullwhip. Boots and spurs and hats and gloves and buckskin jackets with a lot of fringe completed Calamity's look.

I was introduced to my mount, a big black stallion named Satan. We were shooting the first scene in the movie, a crane shot where Calamity appears below camera and jumps a small stream as she gallops across the landscape. The wranglers had offered to let my stunt double do the ride, but I had volunteered. Rod Hardy called, "Action," and Satan and I took off at a good pace. Unfortunately, the pommel of the Western saddle became lodged under my gun belt and got stuck there, pounding into my stomach below my rib cage. I was worried for a few minutes but managed to strip it off at full gallop and save myself. After that, I was much more careful about riding with all that steel hanging off me.

Jack Palance and Tracey Walter were playing a couple of mountain men. Jack was tall, with a strong body. He looked imperious and tough and scary; he was very proud and might bark once in a while, but he was extremely game. No one really appreciated what the guys were going through. Apart from no longer being young men, both Jack and Floyd Westerman—who was playing Calamity's friend, the Native American scout No Ears—had emphysema and were having a lot of trouble breathing in the high altitude. One day when Jack was running in a scene with Tracey up in the high desert with a wad of tobacco in his cheek, he hit the ground hard and didn't get up. It took longer than it should have for anyone to approach him—they all seemed to think he'd bite. Jack and I got along very well, however, because when we were out in the middle of the icy landscape, side by side on his mule and cart, I'd slip him a shot of whiskey in Dad's silver flask, the one from *Moby Dick* engraved with the words PULL, BOY, PULL. And he'd tell me stories.

The first day we worked was in a full-on blizzard at a three-thousand-acre elk farm above Los Alamos. Bob and I stayed up in the mountains in a log cabin on the property the night before. We had awakened at daybreak to see hundreds of bison in an open snow-covered landscape outside our door, like a Charles Russell painting. A few days before, Bob had left for San Jose, where he celebrated the dedication of the winged serpent Quetzalcóatl, which he had been commissioned to make for the city. He had decided that he would return in his gray limousine all the way back to Santa Fe, with Nick at the wheel. This turned out to be a terrible decision. The roads had been ghastly, with icy winter conditions and trucks overturned on the highway. When I came home from a particularly ardent love scene with Wild Bill Hickok, Bob had just arrived at the house in Tesuque from his horror trip and was still shaking with fear. Sometimes I wished that Bob were more physically intrepid, but he was not a country boy.

I was taking bullwhipping lessons from an expert called Anthony De Longis, who had also taught Michelle Pfeiffer to wield the lash as Catwoman. I got really good at snapping a cigarette out of someone's mouth or double-cracking the whip above my head, although in the beginning, when I was in L.A., I hit myself so hard on the temple that I fell into a swimming pool. Frustration with my costume and the laws of nature finally got to me. It was freezing in Santa Fe, and the toilet in my camper had gone unfixed for three days and I was irritated by having to ask Melanie if I could use hers. I decided to brave the outdoor Porta-Potty, which required that I disentangle myself from my firearms along with several outer layers of chamois leather and Pendleton wool. But I hadn't reckoned on having to strip off the top half of my long johns, which unfortunately came to dangle in the blue toilet water. I finally bailed out of the latrine in utter fury, dragging the sodden long johns after me like a horrible soiled tail, and proceeded to attack the Porta-Potty physically, kicking at it brutally with my spurs in front of a bunch of slack-jawed teamsters. But despite the occasional physical discomfort, I loved making *Buffalo Girls*. It was a gift to work in Santa Fe. As Jack Nicholson always said, one should do a Western every summer.

I had heard from Jeremy that our friend Tim was very weak and might have only a few days left. He did not want to go to the hospital; he was up at the farm, surrounded by our animals and friends. A few days later, I was in the kitchen in Tesuque when I received a call from Jeremy. He said, "Tim wants to speak to you."

There was a rustle, a pause, and an intake of breath. Then a faint voice whispered, "Well, Anjel, I guess this is it."

I told him I would never forget him. I told him I would love him to the end of the universe and back, forever and ever. The next day, December 14, 1994, Tim passed on from this life.

On a frozen morning a day later, on the way to the location at dawn, my driver, Harry, stopped by some railway tracks at the foot of a mountain in Las Vegas. Not to be confused with Las Vegas, Nevada, this was a small redbrick Victorian town with a main square and little else, in a corner of New Mexico still wild enough to tolerate the occasional exchange of gunfire at midnight. We were waiting for a train to go by when I saw a movement and a brown-spotted face that looked like a bear cub with two-toned eyes. After the train passed, I got out of the car and discovered two puppies in the grass. They were tiny, whimpering, and cold, but with big thick coats like mountain lions. Farther up the tracks, we found their mother;

she was stiff from rigor mortis. It only occurred to me half-way up to the location on the mountaintop that there might be more I'd left behind. All day I worried, and on the way down from set that night, Harry and I found two more puppies. One, a little female, was dead; the other, a male, was very weak but alive. I took the three survivors back to my hotel room on the square, fed them some steak I'd obtained from catering, and as the others dozed, I watched the little male strut up and down on the counterpane, full of himself, as proud as he could be. He knew that he had survived. I called him Billy, after Wild Bill Hickok, and his sister Crazy-eyed Jane, after my character, Calamity. The other pup went to live with a member of our crew.

After we got back from Santa Fe, Jane developed some issues and went to live at my farm and eventually ran away, but Billy was a great and noble companion to the end. He disliked walking on a leash, which he found humiliating. He always walked two steps directly in front of me, like a body-guard, glancing at me over his shoulder from time to time to see if I was all right. The dogcatchers would recognize him and sometimes give me a break when they caught him off-leash. On the Venice Beach boardwalk, Billy was christened the Chairman of the Board.

After working on *Buffalo Girls*, I was diagnosed with a basal cell carcinoma on my nose. Following several months of radiation, the doctors discovered that the treatment hadn't worked, and I was forced to have the carcinoma removed surgically on May 24, 1995. This scared me and proved to be something of an ordeal, because when the swelling went down, I had a visible hole in my nose. It was necessary to fill the scar with wax before going on camera. I shed some tears of self-pity over my misfortune. It wasn't easy to deal with, and it made me very self-conscious, especially under scrutiny for work, when I had kissing scenes, or when the lights were hot.

Two years later, I had my nose reconstructed with cartilage from my ear, but it remained a problem to photograph and looked bumpy until Dr. Arnie Klein administered Restylane to smooth it out, for which I am forever grateful. It's still not perfect, but it could have been much worse. I don't know why, but my nose always takes the hit first. Maybe it's from having a boxer for a father.

CHAPTER 27

During the course of making any film, with directors both great and indifferent, I have found myself wondering how I would have cast this or that part, or how I might have imagined the look and feel of the film. What would it be like to stand outside the action as an observer and not always be in the thick of the plot and subjectively involved as an actor?

Knowing the difficulties and drawbacks—apart from the obvious one of being a woman—such as finding and seeking out the financing for a project, I had not put much effort into the idea other than to tell Toni Howard that I wanted to direct one day. Nothing ever came of it until one weekend in the fall of 1995, when Toni told me that she had an interesting prospect for me, a movie for Turner Network Television based on an autobiographical novel by Dorothy Allison called *Bastard Out of Carolina*. The director had dropped out, and they needed an immediate replacement. Was I interested in directing the film? They would need an answer by Monday.

That night I read the script with mounting excitement, and the next day I pored over the book in its entirety. It was undoubtedly one of the most moving and profoundly upsetting stories I had ever read—about a young girl called Bone, growing up in South Carolina, who is raped by her stepfather with her mother's consent. The problem, I thought, would be finding a girl of the right age who could convey the anguishing fear and the dilemma of a ten-year-old child trapped in a vicious cycle of abuse. What child, I wondered, could possibly take on this role? And how would one explain it to her?

The personal thrill of being selected for this assignment obliterated any fear I might have entertained as a neophyte. Because the material was so good, with a solid beginning, middle, and end, I had confidence and did not contemplate what the response might be to my decision to direct, or any unfortunate comparisons with my father.

The film's producer, Gary Hoffman, and I set about making some changes with the scriptwriter, Anne Meredith. Jennifer Jason Leigh, one of my favorite actresses, was already attached to play the part of Bone's mother, and we were to have a week's casting session before leaving for Wilmington, North Carolina, to do a location scout.

On the first day of auditions, a small, slender, pale girl with straight brown hair came into the office. She was wearing a blue flower-printed thin summer dress with puff sleeves that was a size too small; her legs were bare, and she had knowing green eyes and a beautiful, sad, lopsided smile. Her audition was amazing. I couldn't believe that finding Bone could be this easy. Just to be sure, I went on looking at other girls, but no one fit the part like Jena Malone. At the time I met her, she had been living in Lake Tahoe with her mother, who was working in regional theater. Jena told me that she had gotten used to being onstage as a toddler and singing show tunes with her mother.

Soon Gary and I were scouting locations with the cinematographer. I had called Nic Roeg and asked whom he might recommend. "Tony Richmond will take care of you,"

he said. Gary hired Tony's wife, Amanda DiGiulio, as our
production manager.

When we began to scout for the movie in rural North
Carolina, I was appalled by the poverty, the derelict conditions, and the evidence of meth and alcohol abuse in the area.
When we pulled over to the side of the road to inspect a house
as a possible location, small children would appear with hands
outstretched, begging for soda and cookies. In one woman's
home, the tangle of discarded clothes, newspapers, and garbage belied the message of the poster above the bed, depicting
an egg frying in a pan with the slogan THIS IS YOUR BRAIN ON
DRUGS, written in bold type above the image.

This was a country of endless fields and wet timberland,
with great distances between dwellings. Broken-down cars
and bits of discarded machinery stood on cinder blocks or just
rusted out by the side of the road. In the kitchen of a house we
eventually used in the film, a whole side of beef was marked
"not for sale" on the fat in blue ink. It was covered in flies. In
the hall, panty hose hung from a light fixture. A suture held
the red living room curtains closed against the light of day as
FOX News droned in a continuous loop on a battered TV.
Cockroaches climbed the walls, and out back the owner had
created a pyramid twelve feet high of Pabst Blue Ribbon beer
cans. The general lack of pride or initiative was astonishing,
but I understood for the first time how a life can amount to a
hill of beans, without a faint glimmer of hope or investment
in the future. Just isolation and moonshine and the shadow
of abuse.

Soon the cast was assembled. Finding the actor to play
the part of Bone's stepfather, Daddy Glen, proved more of a
challenge for me than casting the women. I wanted his sick-

ness to come from a real place that the audience could identify with. I didn't want to cast him as an evil man, more like
an out-of-control baby. And Ron Eldard, a fine actor, understood this perfectly. Pat Hingle was set to play Ron's father.
Diana Scarwid, whom I had loved ever since *Mommy Dearest*,
Glenne Headly, and Susan Traylor—the daughter of my acting teacher Peggy Feury—were cast as Bone's aunts. I found
a lovely four-year-old local, Lindley Mayer, to play Reece,
Bone's little sister. It was an outstanding group that also
included Michael Rooker and Lyle Lovett as Bone's uncles,
Grace Zabriskie as the grandmother, Dermot Mulroney as
Bone's beloved first stepfather, who dies in a car crash, and
Christina Ricci as a visiting cousin who gives Bone a taste of
freedom. Laura Dern would later narrate the film.

Many of the crew had worked with me before, such as Van
Ramsey and Julie Hewett, who did key makeup. Tony Richmond was everything Nic had promised and looked after me
beautifully. The optimistic and resourceful Nelson Coates
was our production designer, and Van Dyke Parks came on
to do the music. Éva Gárdos wrote me an irresistible letter
and became my editor.

On the first day of filming, in Wilmington, I arrived early
on set and ordered bacon and eggs in my trailer. Then I sat
and waited for my call. No one came. Eventually, I thought
maybe I should just go to set and see what was going on.
When I made my way down there, the first assistant director,
Mary Ellen Woods, looked at her watch and then at me with
raised eyebrows.

"I'm late?" I gasped. "No one told me."

She took me to one side and explained that only actors
get summoned to set; the director should be among the first

to show up. I was terribly embarrassed, but it broke the ice. Now everyone knew what a novice I was, and it would never happen again. Every day I learned more. Given that my father was a prolific film director and I had worked for more than twenty years as an actress in movies, it was shaming that I didn't know more about the technicalities of making a film. So I survived on instinct and by surrounding myself with great people from whom I could learn.

Mary Ellen Woods was very protective and helped me save face a few times. When it came time to film the rape scenes, Ron Eldard, Jena, Tony Richmond, and I were prepared. I had put Jena and Ron together with a stuntman weeks earlier, so all the action was carefully choreographed. I didn't want Jena to have a moment's uncertainty about her safety, and I needed her and Ron to become accustomed to physical behavior. By taking this approach, the action became as syncopated as a dance. The image of Jena as she went about her task was amazing to all of us. She was extraordinarily gifted and a dream to work with. I can't recall ever having to tell her what to do. She was a natural, with an innate understanding of what was required.

The filming played out over twenty-eight days. Each evening the dailies would go to the network, and although Gary was playing it close to the vest with me, from what I understood, everyone at Turner Network Television was delighted with the footage.

When I came back to Los Angeles from Wilmington in January 1996, Éva Gárdos and I worked on the cut for about a month. We were shaping it to come in at exactly the time allotted, to the minute. I had found some original Baptist music that I liked, by Ronnie Dodd and Ruby Vass, along with tunes from Lefty Frizzell, Johnny Cash, Merle Haggard, Kitty Wells, and Blind Willie Johnson. When we gave our final cut to TNT, we felt proud of our accomplishment.

A few days later, I was asked to come to the Turner offices for a meeting with Scott Sassa, Ted Turner's top executive. "It's a wonderful film," he said shortly after our introduction. "But there are two problems—the masturbation and rape scenes."

I looked at him in shock. "But that's what the film is about," I said.

"Nevertheless, the scenes have to go," he said. "We can't put that on the air."

"Has Mr. Turner seen the film?" I asked.

"He doesn't generally do that, but if that is what you would like, I guess I can ask him to look at it."

"I'd appreciate that," I answered, nose in the air.

Later that week, I got a call from Scott Sassa. "Well," he said, "they actually watched it, Mr. Turner and Miss Fonda, they watched it together."

Ted Turner was dating Jane Fonda. I felt sure she would weigh in on my side. "And?" I said proudly, knowing that I had won the round. "What did they say?"

"They didn't say anything. They screamed."

"What do you mean?" I gasped. "They didn't like it?"

"Mr. Turner said it will never show on his network."

I went directly to bed, which, as I said earlier, is generally my way of dealing with things when the world gets too complicated. That night Bob and I were hosting a party for an art event at the Museum of Contemporary Art, and he offered to call our friend Wendy Stark to fill in for me, which she kindly agreed to do. I stayed upstairs that evening, listening to the chatter rise from below. At one point, I peered over the balcony; the courtyard was a sea of people. It actually felt kind of great, hiding at one's own party. Bob came up to check on me a few times and brought me some of Dora's *pupusas*.

One of the great things about Bob was that he understood the nature of artistic crisis. He never bullied me when I was in a fix but always allowed me to work out my problems in my own way, even if it was not to his advantage, such as my not behaving like a perfect wife and hostess.

The following morning as we were sitting at the breakfast table, the phone rang. A voice with a French accent came on. "Monsieur Gilles Jacob, the president of the Cannes festival, would like to speak to Miss Huston."

There was a pause as Mr. Jacob came on the line. "I would like to show your film at Cannes," he said. From zero to one hundred miles per hour in just a moment—my luck had changed.

In May, I presented the movie in the Un Certain Regard selection at the Debussy Theater in Cannes. The enthusiastic response to the film was a moment of triumph for me personally. Subsequently, Jerry Offsay, the president of the cable company Showtime, bought the film and aired my cut without asking for any changes. There were some offers to buy the film for foreign distribution, but Turner refused them all. I guess he closed the movie down after he'd gotten the return on his investment.

In December 1996, it was my honor to be nominated by the Directors Guild for Outstanding Directorial Achievement in Dramatic Specials, and also nominated for an Emmy Award for Outstanding Directing for a Miniseries, Movie, or

Dramatic Special for *Bastard Out of Carolina*. Making movies is a bittersweet business.

Joan Buck had been working since 1994 in Paris as the editor of French *Vogue*. I had seen her parents, Jules and Joyce, whenever Joan had come to Los Angeles to visit them and to stay with me. They were living in reduced circumstances in an apartment overlooking some big dark pines on the edge of a golf course in Santa Monica. It was as though all the stuffing had gone out of their lives, and suddenly here they were in post shock, with the memories of their former existence still embodied in a few good pieces of salvaged furniture and fine china from their heyday in London, where they had lived the high life in the sixties. They gave me a mahogany makeup box that had belonged to the actor Edmund Kean. I treasure it to this day. Joyce was working at Pratesi in Beverly Hills, selling linens. Jules was speaking of old times like a reel-to-reel tape that you couldn't turn off. He had been the cameraman on several of Dad's documentaries about the war, and all of his stories centered on that subject.

One day I got a call from Joan. "I'm coming to L.A.," she said. "Mom's sick."

Joyce had lung and liver cancer, and it had spread to the brain. Things went very fast from there. When we went to visit Joyce at St. John's hospital on my birthday, she was sitting up in bed. A nurse came in to offer her lunch. "I think you should have caviar," I said.

I ran to the car and drove to Santa Monica Seafood, where I picked up a tin of beluga, a little mother-of-pearl spoon, and a split of Dom Pérignon. When I got back to the hospital, Joyce ate the caviar and sipped her champagne. We had no idea this would be Joyce's last meal, but a couple of days later she slipped into a coma and never reawakened. Joyce passed away on July 13, 1996. Joan spoke wrenchingly of her love for Joyce at the Little Chapel of the Dawn in Santa Monica. When Joan returned to Paris, she took Jules with her.

I was now in my mid-forties, and this was my last chance to consider motherhood. Bob and I talked often about having a baby—whether we should try implanting and what, if any, our chances might be. Maybe a child could be part of our new adventure together. The doctors recommended surgery to remove scar tissue, and I had a second laparoscopy, followed by a hysteroscopy a year later, followed by in vitro fertilization some months after that. It was something of an ordeal. I felt like a human pincushion, giving myself shots of progesterone and Premarin several times a day, as well as going to Alhambra for fertility acupuncture with a Dr. Peng. I remember praying that the outcome would be positive. Bob and I made the attempt to implant several times, but it had not worked. I felt like an animal experiment; the whole process was a trial and felt unnatural.

The last time I underwent in vitro, at St. John's Health Center in Santa Monica, it was with several of my own fertilized eggs. The doctors recommended that I lie on my back for a week following the procedure. Everything felt good until day five, when I felt a change and knew instinctively that the effort had failed. I believed that it was not meant to be, and decided that I was not going to try again.

I had been speaking to Gordon Davidson, the director of the Center Theatre Group, for some time about doing a play at the Mark Taper Forum, but between the time commitment and my stage fright, movies generally took precedence.

However, following the positive reception for my reading of Yeats's poetry at UCLA, I proposed to Gregory Peck that we do an Irish poetry reading and ask Gabriel Byrne, Fionnula Flanagan, and Nóirín Ní Riain, an extraordinary singer and musician who sang with the monks of Glenstal Abbey in County Limerick, to perform excerpts from Seamus Heaney, Flann O'Brien, and Thomas Kinsella at the Taper. I had recently become aware of Nóirín's work through Michael Fitzgerald, who produced *Wise Blood* and *Under the Volcano* for Dad, and it seemed right to ask Michael to come aboard to organize the evening. December 16 turned out to be a perfectly wonderful night; "And Wisdom Is a Butterfly—A Celebration of Irish Poetry, Prose and Song" supported Amnesty International and Project Children, an organization that provided summer holidays in the U.S. for both Protestant and Catholic kids from Northern Ireland. It should not have surprised me that I was vilified by some members of the British press who suggested that I was supporting the IRA, which could not have been further from the truth.

On May 2, 1997, Bob and I drove from New York to Washington, D.C., with Bob's favorite New York driver, Paul Cuomo, who always kept us laughing and entertained on the road. We were on our way to celebrate President Bill Clinton's dedication of the Franklin Delano Roosevelt Memorial. Bob's contribution was a large bronze bas-relief of Roosevelt riding in a motorcade at his first inauguration. In a series of outdoor "rooms" designed by the landscape architect Larry Halprin, several monolithic standing cylinders and a bronze wall described the fifty-four social programs instated by FDR's government following the Great Depression.

A month later, I accompanied Bob to New York for the dedication ceremony for his memorial to Duke Ellington at 110th Street and Fifth Avenue. The celebrated cabaret singer and pianist Bobby Short had worked long and hard to get the project going, and it had involved many meetings and a lot of persuasion to get the Harlem community to approve the installation.

One such meeting took place at an uptown museum in a room filled to capacity with mostly outraged church ladies, upset that the maquette that had been presented to them by Bob depicted a number of nudes on a plinth, supporting the Duke's piano. As the voices grew shriller and the conversation more heated, we began to worry for the future of the monument. Suddenly, an older gentleman stood up and began to speak. "I knew the Duke," he said, "and I am sure he would want an end to this controversy. I was with him when he played on Vine Street in Kansas City, I was with him when he traveled to St. Louis, and here in New York. Duke Ellington loved it when, after he played a set, the ladies of the night would come out to see him and wave to him from their balconies. It is my conviction that no one would be more pleased than he to be supported by these beautiful nudes."

The room was silent for a moment, then it erupted in cheers. The monument had gained approval and passed the board. Bob and I rushed down with Bobby Short to his haven, Bemelmans Bar at the Carlyle Hotel, and ordered a succession of martinis to commemorate the triumph.

In the spring of '98, Bob was commissioned to create another piece for the FDR Memorial, a life-sized bronze portrait of Roosevelt in his wheelchair. Because Roosevelt always refused to be portrayed as handicapped in photographs or illustrations, there was a good deal of controversy leading up to the final decision. Following a particularly heated discussion between the lobbyists, pro and con, the outcome proved positive for the statue, which was dedicated on January 10, 2001, in West Potomac Park. Today the FDR Memorial is one of the most popular in Washington and has close to three million visitors each year.

On our last trip to Mexico City, when Bob was working on his show at the Museo del Palacio de Bellas Artes, a small busload from his studio went to the private museum and residence of Señora Dolores Olmedo. She was an art collector, an artists' model and businesswoman, known for her friendship with and patronage of Diego Rivera, having sat for some twenty-seven of Rivera's drawings and paintings. She was also a collector of Frida Kahlo. When interviewed by *The New York Times*, she said she was never a friend of Frida's. "Frida Kahlo liked women. I liked men." Rumor was that Dolores Olmedo was also a mistress of Rivera's. Before he died in 1957, he named Señora Olmedo as administrator of his and Kahlo's estate. The Olmedo collection now includes some of the most highly regarded Riveras and Kahlos—137 works of his, 25 of hers.

Her estate at La Noria spread out over several acres. The museum was, in effect, a shrine to Dolores herself, with fabulous jewelry and pre-Columbian art in glass vitrines and several commissioned Rivera portraits in oil of both her and her daughter.

A building next door was being prepared for dedication as

a library, and a third edifice, a fortress built of lava stone, was her residence. The interior was on a monumental scale; the rooms, though few, were vast, with white polished-marble floors and high ceilings. Light flooded through tall glass doors out to a tropical garden, where peacocks preened and a pack of hairless dogs in a variety of sizes prowled the grounds. It was explained to us that Señora Olmedo was more often than not confined to her bed these days but that she would be pleased to receive us in her private suite.

We were shown by the valet through several rooms of impressively carved chinoiserie—huge sculptures of jade horses and ivory goddesses, giant vases enameled and inlaid with mother-of-pearl. Throughout the house were extravagant flower arrangements of banana leaves, tuberose, and shocking-pink ginger. When finally we entered the señora's sanctuary, I was startled to see a raven-haired woman in her late eighties, fully recumbent on a chaise longue, her small puffy hands, with long scarlet nails adorned by three of the largest, whitest diamonds I'd ever seen, tugging at the hem of an Hermès blanket. Her makeup was spectacular—hair scraped back from brightly rouged cheeks, with finely arched, penciled eyebrows and a curtain of false lashes from under whose veil she contemplated Bob. "I like him," she said. "He's handsome."

Señora Olmedo was fiercely independent. When asked once how she would like to be remembered, she said, "Just as I am, a woman who did whatever she felt like doing and, luckily, succeeded at it."

Following this trip, Bob decided that we should acquire a Xoloitzcuintli, a hairless dog from Mexico. It also happened to be the favorite breed of the painter Toledo, who lived in

Oaxaca, and whose dogs, I believe, are descended from the Diego Rivera–Frida Kahlo strain. They are said to weep real tears when sad, and have an appetite for chocolate, which makes most dogs very sick. They are also prone to smile.

Guillermo Olguín was enlisted to help satisfy Bob's desire, and a puppy was duly air-freighted on Aeroméxico to Los Angeles on April 16, 1998. It was a very busy time for us, and taking on a puppy seemed overly ambitious. We decided to offer the dog to Steven, who met her at the airport. She cried big tears when he took her out of her cage on the median by the parking lot, gave her chocolate, and christened her Lola.

Steven and Lola were a great match. Later, when he mated her, it was with another hairless Xoloitzcuintli that he had located in Palm Springs. Lola had five puppies, all different. Steven kept a little male with a shock of white hair atop his head, and Bob chose a female with a fine silvery coat. He named her Mecha, short for Mercedes, his aunt's name; it also means "cowlick" in Spanish.

CHAPTER 28

The valley of the Dordogne is one of the most beautiful places I have ever been. My assistant, Cristen Kauffman, and I arrived there in the summer to start shooting *Ever After*, with Drew Barrymore attached to play the role of a feisty Cinderella. I was to play her stepmother, Rodmilla. Initially, I wasn't sure of the tone of the piece; it was the familiar fairy tale reimagined with modern dialogue and an updated storyline with creative touches, such as an appearance in the script by none other than Leonardo da Vinci, who attempts to walk on water and conceives of Cinderella as the Mona Lisa.

However, I enjoyed the chance to play Rodmilla not just as the usual wicked stepmother to Drew's Danielle but as a thwarted and disappointed woman whose reaction to pain and fear is to lash out. Finally, there was a chance to make a case for her. It was great fun to explore her backstory— her reaction to her husband's death and, consequently, the extreme necessity of seeing her daughters married. This hitherto one-dimensional character had become human on the page, like a bad-tempered Mrs. Bennet from *Pride and Prejudice*.

The Dordogne is ravishing. Castles abound in its valley, home not only to the Lascaux Caves, which contain the earliest petroglyphs known to man, but to the strongholds that defended France from England for more than three hundred years, until the end of the Hundred Years' War in 1453.

The landscape is epic and open, with soft rolling hills, lush and green, and the local stone used in all the masonry glows apricot in the pink sunlight. Along the wide river, there are ancient caves carved into the canyon, and the valley is so fruitful it is not hard to imagine primitive man roaming there with ease, feeding on bison and berries and running from the occasional saber-toothed tiger.

Sarlat, the little town where we were based, is also the home of foie gras. In the shops, almost everything pertained to goose—cans of confit, goose fat, Mason jars of pâté, drawings of geese, ceramics. There was a cobblestone square where the locals met for coffee and a little dog circus performed throughout the afternoon; these dogs seemed to enjoy a very social life all their own in the village. One of our locations was a castle and farmyard some ten miles from town. I had met the owner's dog, a massive deerhound, so I was surprised when I saw him coming alone out of the local art shop and walking up the street. It turned out that the sister of the people who owned the castle ran the store, and every day at noon the dog would make his own way into town to visit her. Few of the dogs in Sarlat were leashed and all seemed independent and smart. Often I would see a number of them congregate in the square to watch the circus dogs, like an audience at the theater.

It was a lovely bucolic summer. Working with Drew was a pleasure; she was extremely intuitive and sensitive. One day, however, I felt she was not taking me seriously. We were working on a scene that I felt required a strong reaction on her part—the first time Danielle rebels against her stepmother. Drew seemed uncomfortable and giggled.

"All right, missy," I snapped. "I've had it!"

This made her laugh even harder. "Missy?" she said. "I can't believe you're even calling me that!"

We finished the scene and I stalked off. The next day, a huge bouquet of daisies arrived. The card read, "Thank you for making me a better actress. Love, Drew."

Cristen was ensconced upstairs in the old farmhouse I was renting, and I was occupying a large bedroom downstairs with an enormous fireplace that backed up at night, causing me to cough violently—in retrospect, I think it probably was carbon monoxide poisoning—and French doors that opened onto a wide walled garden. We had a surly chef called Mr. Poisson who cooked delicious meals for us straight from the local farmer's market.

On Saturday nights the cast and crew would all go to the local nightclub outside Sarlat and dance to bad French disco music. Dougray Scott, who was playing Prince Henry, had some fun parties at his house as well. At the house Drew shared with her makeup and hair artists and her assistant, Gwenn, she decided to decorate the beams on the bedroom ceiling with swaths of leaves and flower stems. All the Americans on the crew were missing Mexican food, so the producer threw a Day of the Dead party with candy skulls and candles and lots of tequila. Gwenn liked to go antique shopping, and Cristen and I would get up early on Saturday mornings to go with her to the local Marché aux Puces.

One of the joys of *Ever After* for me was being around horses. I have loved them all my life, and riding was a big part of my growing up. We had two sets of horse wranglers—a handful of Irishmen who had come over with a stable of hunter-thoroughbreds, and a bunch of Spaniards who trained the Andalusians, big high-stepping creatures with flowing manes and tails. Being up on those horses was like riding a floating dinner table. I soon made friends with this group, and on days when we were not working I'd drive up to their horse barn and the arena they used as a base and help put the horses through their paces. It was particularly fun to ride dressage on the big Carthusian warmbloods with flamenco playing over the loudspeakers in the arena, and to take the Irish horses cross-country out into the hills and forests. Sometimes the Spaniards' wives would cook paella for us afterward, or strips of pork dipped in honey and peppers roasted on the grill. On my days off from the movie, I would drive over to the stables and go riding with the Irish boys. I developed a crush on one of them, Dolyn, and in spite of knowing better, I succumbed to the temptation of location romance.

One Sunday some of us decided to go on a long ride to a deserted castle we had spotted on a map. It rose above a forest some four or five miles west of Sarlat. At the last minute, two of the Irishmen canceled, but Dolyn and two French riders who were working at the stables decided to come along. The day was perfect. We took off in the morning and cantered gently over the lush green fields. One of the French riders, Annick, was familiar with the countryside and eventually guided us to a path leading into a wooded area where, above us on a hill, a castle became apparent, glowing in the midday sun. We had been out on the trail for several hours.

As we left the bridle path and entered the shaded forest, I noticed that the ground was very loose and wet, and before I knew it, the lovely chestnut mare I was riding was sinking fast—the mud was up to her knees. We had inadvertently entered a swamp, and it was taking us down like a suction cup. By now the mud was over my boots. I looked up and saw a tree limb, thick as an elephant's leg, above the mare's head. When I jumped down from the saddle, I sank instantly up to my waist in muck. All around, the same thing was happening to the others. I heard Annick cry out and saw her mount submerged up to its neck. I was holding on to my mare's reins, pulling them over her bridle to the front. Even if I were physically capable of pulling her out, the branch above her head would make it impossible. We were trapped; the situation looked utterly hopeless.

I called out to Dolyn and saw that he was preoccupied with his own horse, which also appeared to be sinking rapidly. "Hold on," he called to me, "I'm coming."

Annick was panicking now. It seemed we didn't have a chance. Suddenly, Dolyn, in a flash of brilliance, managed to pull his horse onto a bank of brackish earth; the animal was covered in gray silt and shaking from exertion. My mare was sinking, almost up to her shoulders now and groaning; the effort she was making to free herself had left her exhausted. Dolyn sprang up the tree and started kicking violently at the overhanging branch. Unbelievably, it broke loose, so that it was now possible to make a concerted effort to get the mare out, although the possibility of extracting her still seemed very remote. I was convinced that she would break her back. Every attempt she made was met with failure; she was tiring, her breathing deep and hollow.

Dolyn was behind her, trying desperately to lift her buttocks out of the mud with his own brute strength, and I was at her head, pulling her bridle for all I was worth. In desperation, I said a prayer: "Please, God, get us out of this." Prayer is an extraordinarily powerful thing. I am not Catholic, and I do not pray as a rule, but these words escaped my lips uncensored by thought. And as sure as a miracle, the horse reared out of the bog water as if she had wings. I don't know how she circumvented me, either, as I was directly in her path. She had leaped sideways across me to stand shivering on the edge of the swamp, her knees half buckled from the effort, but she was alive and mercifully unscathed.

Dolyn moved on to rescuing the remaining two animals, laying a platform of twigs and branches, attempting to give them a foothold. Together we motivated the horses to make the effort to save themselves. It seemed like hours, but it could have happened in a matter of minutes. Eventually, all the horses were safe on dry land. There is no question in my mind that God was looking down on us that day.

We limped back to the stables on foot, leading the exhausted horses behind us. We had washed them down in the river on the way home, but their tack was full of mud, and we were a mess. What might have happened was so dire that we could barely speak of it afterward.

Bob had made arrangements to fly in from Los Angeles. It was essentially two days of travel, and I would be working on the afternoon of his arrival. I sent Cristen to the train station, but when Bob arrived in Périgueux, there was no one there to collect him. Cristen told me that she had ducked into a café for a croissant and missed meeting him. Two hours later, he arrived at the farmhouse, having come all the way in the back of a taxi in a dreadful mood. He broke a pane of glass in the front door to get into the house. He always resented Cristen after that.

The truth was that Bob had the instinct of a greyhound

when it came to lies or duplicity. He was no doubt aware that I had developed a set crush, but he didn't mention it. I was not in a confessional state of mind, and the romance wasn't going anywhere. Dolyn and I were married to other people, and he was the father of a little girl.

After several days Bob relaxed and fell under the spell of Sarlat, and we made some wonderful outings to castles and churches and to see the guarded treasures of the caves— paintings on the walls in vegetable dyes of ocher and black, of bison, antelope, and oryx, and the earliest depictions of man ever drawn, so fresh they had a childlike quality, yet you could tell they came from the hand of a master.

As the shooting drew to a close, Bob preceded me to Paris. I was sad that the idyll in the Dordogne had ended, and I shed tears on the needlepoint tapestry I had begun in the early days of shooting. When I said goodbye to Dolyn, he reminded me of a conversation we had shared about Ireland. "Maybe your work there is not finished," he said.

I took the train to Paris to join Bob. We were staying in the Meurice Hotel in a room with dark red wallpaper, over-looking the rue de Rivoli. I remember taking a long bath and falling into a deep sleep. It was difficult to resume my real life after working on *Ever After*. I felt like a racehorse after a liberating run, returning with silent resignation to her stable. I was aware I had brought this upon myself.

CHAPTER 29

I was on Long Island at the Hamptons Film Festival when I ran into Jim Sheridan, the brilliant director of *My Left Foot*. "What are you doing here?" he asked. I invited him to see a special screening of *Bastard Out of Carolina* that evening. Afterward, over a Guinness, he said in his Dublin accent, "I think we should find something to do together. I could produce, you could direct."

This sounded like a great plan. Jim had an idea for a film based on a novel called *The Mammy*, written by another Irishman, the comic Brendan O'Carroll, about a widowed mother of seven children. A few weeks later, Brendan was in my office in Venice, dressed like Jimmy Cagney in a straw boater, with a tiny black mustache.

After much deliberation, I had decided to offer the lead role of Agnes Browne to Rosie O'Donnell. I wanted the quality that Lynn Redgrave had brought years before to her part in *Georgy Girl*, and I had no doubt that Rosie would provide it.

Three weeks before going into production, I got a call from Jim. "It looks like Rosie's dropping out," he said. "We'd better go see her."

Soon after, Jim and his co-producer, Arthur Lappin, and I were driving from the airport to Snedens Landing, Rosie's enclave across the Hudson from New York. A pretty girl called Kelli answered the door; Rosie was playing with two small children in the kitchen. She greeted us affably but seemed at a remove. My instinct told me that it would be a fatal mistake to embark on this endeavor with a reluctant actress. Jim attempted to capture her attention, and I rather lamely tried to persuade her that she was making the wrong decision.

On the way back into New York, we agreed that I'd blown it. "I think if you went after her again, we might get her," said Jim, who has a reputation for being a pit bull when it comes to getting what he needs for a film.

I was obviously a disappointment in this regard. "I think we should look elsewhere," I said.

It was evident that we had no time. It came down to a question of postponing or calling off the production entirely. Later that week, Jim called from Dublin. "What will we do?" he asked. "We only have a few days left to cast the part."

"*I'll* do it," I said.

I knew that this idea had the potential to backfire, in that I had directed only once before, and the character of Agnes Browne would be on-screen throughout the movie. I was excited but also apprehensive as Cristen and I packed for Ireland.

My first days in Dublin were spent in production meetings with Arthur Lappin, moving into our offices near the Quays, finding a place to live, and assembling a cast and crew. On the first read-through, I was struck by two actors in particular: Marion O'Dwyer, from the Abbey Theatre; and Roxanna Williams, the little girl reading the part of Cathy Browne. There were two sets of twins in the script and seven children total, of various ages. I was cross-eyed when I came out of casting sessions. Arthur Lappin finally had to sacrifice his delightful, ruddy two-year-old, James, for the part of Trevor Browne, simply because he was the most delicious baby in Ireland—and that's saying something.

We had sent the script out with an offer to Gérard Depardieu, who had subsequently fallen off his motorbike and broken a leg. He did not feel he could do the film.

Ultimately, our casting director found a lovely actor, Arno Chevrier, also a Frenchman, to play the part of Agnes's love interest, Pierre, the baker on Moore Street, where she has an outdoor stall. Agnes's other passion in the film is for the singer Tom Jones. This posed something of a dilemma. Since the story takes place in the sixties, the question came up as to whether we were going to attempt to find a younger version of Tom Jones. My belief was that Tom Jones was iconic and impossible to replicate, and that soul and authenticity were more important than small details like the age of a character—my rationale being that, in any case, it was a fairy story. So I cast him.

Once again, I chose Tony Richmond as my director of photography. I had learned a lot from Tony on *Bastard Out of Carolina*, and I knew how important it would be to have his support and input on *The Mammy*. I trusted Tony's instinct and admired his professionalism and expertise. On occasion, I would be in the makeup chair and unable to divide my time to line up the shots, so although it was not optimum, in several instances Tony would have to make directorial decisions for me.

Éva Gárdos, who had worked with me on *Bastard*, came from Los Angeles to set up our editing rooms in Dublin. The action in the movie centers on Agnes's workplace, and we had taken over a street in Ringsend on the south side of town to double for the famous vegetable market on Moore Street. It was quite a rough neighborhood, with betting offices and smoky bars. From the first day on set, it was evident that my work was cut out for me. It is understood when you shoot in Ireland that it is bound to rain at some time of the day, so every morning in anticipation we had to wet down the streets for the camera.

Jim Sheridan had handed most of the day-to-day production decisions to Arthur Lappin and visited the set only sporadically. I think that this decision was a gesture of respect, in that he did not want to tread on my feet.

I asked Paddy Moloney of the Chieftans to score the film. The last time I had seen Paddy was during our visit to Dad's set on *Sinful Davey* in 1968, when, at age sixteen, I had danced a jig in a riding habit for a busload of visiting Russians.

While we were working in Dublin, some friends and I went up to Belfast one weekend to see Van Morrison play on a double bill with Bob Dylan. Van, in all his brilliance, wailed on saxophone. It was my first time in the North since the seventies. We stayed at the Europa Hotel, in the center of town, opposite bombed vacant lots and burned-out buildings. A very different story from the West, or the Wicklow Mountains, where sometimes we would meet up for Sunday lunch to hang out with Paddy and the Chieftains, or with Garech Browne and John Hurt and Marianne Faithfull at the Roundwood Inn, singing from lunch until nightfall.

It felt great to be back in Ireland, although this was a different place in many ways from the one where I grew up. Apart from that one short visit to Belfast, which was like visiting another country, I was unable to take the time to relax or drive through the landscape, or to visit my old home, St. Clerans, in County Galway. Everywhere there was evidence of construction, and gated communities had sprung up aggressively on the outskirts of Dublin. Already there were signs that the economic gains trumpeted by the Celtic Tiger might collapse.

It was definitely a challenge to both star in and direct the film. I felt hampered at both tasks, and sitting in hair-and-makeup was irritating when I wanted to be on set, answering questions and setting up shots. The best times I had on set were with the children. Occasionally, I felt thwarted by a lack of enthusiasm from some of the technicians in the crew. I don't think they liked being told what to do by a female director. Once, after spending hours on the simplest of special effects for a scene, I almost cried in frustration. The days were long and chilly, and I often had to change clothes on the street in a pup tent that housed the monitors.

Bob was in California and had just been commissioned to create the Great Bronze Doors for the Cathedral of Our Lady of the Angels on Temple Street in downtown Los Angeles. It was to become the new home of the archdiocese and the seat of its archbishop, replacing the Cathedral of Saint Vibiana, which was damaged in the Northridge earthquake. Bob and I were speaking on the phone daily. He told me that he was coming to see me while I shot the last couple of weeks of the film. I asked him not to. I was in my own world and wanted to savor my independence and not have to consider his needs. I had seen Dolyn again and was relieved not to be tempted to revive our romantic moment in the Dordogne. But Bob insisted on coming; he was suspicious. I felt that he was invading my space. This led to Bob's deciding that he would move to the Shelbourne Hotel for a week, until after the wrap party, and then, if I was game, we'd fly to Italy to stay at Marlia, Earl and Camilla McGrath's fifteenth-century villa in Tuscany, and decide what, if anything, we needed to do about the state of our relationship.

When we arrived at Marlia, Bob and I spent a good deal of time walking in the gardens and talking about what had occurred between us. I decided from that moment that whatever might happen, thick or thin, I would be honest with him and do my best to be more considerate of his feelings.

When we returned to L.A., Éva Gárdos and I went into our former suite at Soundbox to begin the final cut. I had to brace myself every day before I went into the editing room to watch the film. I have always had trouble looking at photographs of myself, and even though Tony Richmond had photographed me in gentle light, it was hard to confront my own image in practically every scene.

Shortly after we handed in the film, word came that Jim Sheridan and October Films, having made a cut of their own, had decided that some reshoots and additional scenes could improve the film. Although it is not usual for a producer to commandeer a cut without the permission of the director, I agreed that we needed a scene to deepen the impact of Agnes's losing her best friend, Marion. However, if we were to accomplish the work in such a short time, I would need Jim's help as a director.

Jim hired a local cinematographer whom I was assured was top-notch. Jim helped me get through the work, and in just a few days we shot half a dozen additional scenes. But when I got back to L.A. and viewed the footage, it looked like a different movie. Tony Richmond's careful lighting looked luscious and golden compared with the new scenes, which looked crude, with a documentary pallor. It was evident that Jim and I did not share the same vision for *The Mammy*. Although I admired his films enormously, Jim was making tough movies about socioeconomic problems and the political atmosphere in Ireland, and I was making a fairy tale, an ode to the country I grew up in at a more innocent time.

When the film was sold from October Films to USA Films, I did not understand that we would be left at the curb. First the company announced that it would be changing the title to *Agnes Browne*, because of the negative connotations *The Mammy* might provoke, and then they opened *Agnes Browne* a week before the Academy Awards in a letterbox theater with no title above the door. It was a major disappointment, and I felt deflated by the experience. On a more pleasant note, *Agnes Browne* was chosen as part of the Directors' Fortnight at the 1999 Cannes Film Festival, but I no longer had an opinion about the film, as I was incapable of being objective.

After Cannes, Bob and I stopped in Paris on our way to San Sebastián. Joan was still the editor of French *Vogue* and was now living in a grandly proportioned apartment in the 8ème arrondissement, and had employed a full-time nurse to look after her father, Jules, in a flat nearby. She gave us a dinner party one evening. Jules spoke exclusively about Dad and their experiences during the war; he seemed terribly diminished and lonely without Joyce, like a turtle dove that has lost its mate.

On our first morning in San Sebastián, Bob and I awakened and ate breakfast in our lovely turn-of-the-century room at the Hotel Maria Cristina, with windows overlooking a canal that ran under delicate white wrought-iron bridges, out to the wide gray Atlantic. I had a series of interviews scheduled all over town, and I was meeting the PR person downstairs. As I came down the staircase, I became aware of a large group of children in the lobby, mostly dark-eyed little girls, many of them dressed in black. Some were inside a roped-off area, while others formed a crowd in the plaza outside.

A whisper came up like wind through trees: *"La bruja! La bruja!"* I looked around, but no one else was there, and suddenly I realized they had come to see me. They were the children of the Camí del Mig school, with their teacher, Lola Casas. I had enjoyed a wonderful correspondence for many years with Lola's students; these children were all fans of *The Witches* and had traveled from Barcelona to see the *"bruja"* in person.

That year, at the 1999 San Sebastián Festival, I received the Youth Jury Award for *Agnes Browne* and the Donostia Award for lifetime achievement, presented to me by the Spanish star Marisa Paredes. Jeremy Thomas and Hercules attended, and Herky gave lunches at the yacht club, his favorite spot. We had fine times with Chema Prado, the artistic director of the festival, going to tapas bars and spectacular four-star restaurants between the film presentations.

In December *Agnes Browne* had a screening in Rome. I remember little about the trip, only that Michelangelo Antonioni came to the premiere and the acute embarrassment I felt. My confidence was very low; I was so sure he would hate it that I left before I could see his face when the lights went up.

* * *

Early in 2000, I returned to England to work on *The Golden Bowl* for James Ivory and his producer, Ismail Merchant. Nick Nolte, Uma Thurman, Kate Beckinsale, and Jeremy Northam were starring in the movie, based on the classic Henry James novel about marriage and adultery. I was playing the part of Fanny Assingham, the meddlesome friend of the four main characters. We were on location in some of the great houses of Britain, including a castle near Richmond.

At one point we stayed in a hotel in the countryside, a stuffy institution that didn't encourage actors in the dining room. It was vexing to be told at the end of a long day's work that there was no food left in the kitchen or tables available in the restaurant. I guess they hadn't heard that we'd been emancipated.

Jim Ivory was a calm, understated American in his early seventies. After the first day's read-through in London, he had announced that he was not a demonstrative director, and please not to expect that from him. At the time, I had thought that this would be fine, but I always felt insecure when he called "cut" at the end of a scene and had nothing to say. He rarely commented on performances.

Ismail Merchant was just the opposite. A loquacious and outgoing man, he was a most enthusiastic host on set, often cooking up curries for the crew and giving cameo roles to visiting society ladies. I had met with the cameraman, Tony Pierce-Roberts, to discuss their vision for the film. I was still self-conscious about the scar on my nose and was hoping he could bleach it out somehow.

Uma and Kate looked spectacular in their costumes, designed and cut with astonishing detail by John Bright at Cosprop. For sheer beauty and authenticity, I think they were the most exquisite I've ever seen. And yet when I saw the makeup tests, I looked plain and frumpy as Fanny Assingham, and I felt the absence of light had much to do with it. Both Bob Richardson and Bob Graham used to say, "Light is almost everything." And I think that is true for the visual arts. Light is capable of making you look good or bad. I have an angular face, and when lit from the side, my bones cast shadows that I don't like, unless I also have a key light. I've had some differences of opinion over the years with cameramen who don't like to light an actress from the front, preferring a more "realistic" approach, but I am never fully happy without my key.

The first man ever to steal my heart, James Fox, had been cast as my husband. When I was a schoolgirl in London, he used to pick me up in his purple Lotus Elan at the gates of Holland Park comprehensive. I had seen him briefly one evening in Los Angeles at a tribute to David Lean, but until this moment I hadn't met his wife of nearly twenty years, the mother of their teenaged children. And yet here we were in the movie, playing a happily married middle-aged couple. It was odd and not just a little ironic.

CHAPTER 30

I was going to be in New York and had heard through Toni Howard that the director Wes Anderson wanted to meet me. I was excited about this, as I had very much liked his most recent films, *Bottle Rocket* and *Rushmore.*

We met in the opulent restaurant of the Carlyle Hotel for breakfast. Bespectacled, with pale brown hair brushing his shoulders, Anderson was rail-thin, in a tan corduroy suit cut high on the forearms to expose a full shirt cuff with a few inches of sleeve above it, a knotted silk tie, and brown suede lace-ups. He seemed both serious and droll at the same time. I guessed he was still in his twenties.

I ordered eggs Benedict. "What is that?" he asked. I had figured him to be a bit more worldly; perhaps he was just not interested in food. He said he was from Texas, which, given that he had no accent and didn't dress in any way like a cowboy or an oil man, seemed a bit of an anomaly. He spoke enthusiastically about his project. Within minutes, I was charmed and agreed to do his new movie, *The Royal Tenenbaums.* It was the story of a fictional New York family of misfits with a dangerous rogue at its helm.

It was obvious from the beginning that Wes was the sole author of his film. At the Tenenbaum set, a gracious, albeit narrow, house in upper Harlem, everything was chosen carefully and generated by him; his eye was on every frame. Wes wore his heart calmly on his sleeve. At once I felt the desire to both please and protect him.

Wes sent me some drawings he had sketched of my character, Etheline. The matriarch of the family, she had a distracted air, a wispy bun on top of her head with a pencil stuck through it, the sleeves of her jacket too short, and a locket around her neck. My wardrobe was to consist of six identical cashmere suits in pastel colors, all with skirts too long and jackets too small. The locket I used was my grandmother's.

Wes is extremely responsive to actors and ready to do anything he feels will improve his script. To that end, at my request, he wrote a beautiful scene for the end of the movie, in which Etheline forgives Royal all of his transgressions.

The cast was impressive—Ben Stiller, Bill Murray, Owen Wilson, Luke Wilson, Gwyneth Paltrow, Danny Glover, and Gene Hackman, who played the head of the family, Royal Tenenbaum. I was nervous about Gene, because I'd heard he had a temper, and I knew that in our first scene together, I would be required to slap him in the face. It was a sharp, brisk morning in deep winter, and we were out on the street. In rehearsal I had faked it, and in the camera lineup, I had simply batted Gene on the lapel. But when the cameras rolled and Wes called, "Action," I realized I had no choice but to go for it and strike Gene on the cheek as indicated. The slap landed hard. I was actually wearing kid gloves in the scene, but I think they only made it sting worse. My hand came down on his cheek like the crack of a whip. Gene's eyes teared up, and a livid red welt rose on his face in the shape of my hand. "Goddamn," he muttered.

I prayed that Wes wouldn't ask for us to go again, and mercifully he didn't.

It became apparent through the days that followed that Gene was generally much more tolerant of the fairer sex. Sometimes he got really tough, once telling Wes to "pull up your pants and act like a man." I think he was just furious at having this youth telling him what to do.

I liked Billy Murray a lot. One night we went out to the Brooklyn Academy of Music to see *Hamlet*; it was a flimsy performance, but we had a lot of laughs. Occasionally, he would come by my trailer and put my coffee on to brew in the mornings. We did a scene outside Gwyneth's bathroom in the movie, where we stooped down to pick up a key she shoves under the door. And when we came up with our heads together, Wes said, "I've just had an idea. You two would be good in a movie I'm planning." That movie turned out to be *The Life Aquatic with Steve Zissou*, three years later.

Bob came and we stayed at his favorite hotel, the Stanhope, from whose windows he could gaze at the Metropolitan Museum, which he so loved, and plan his next tour of her galleries. He decided during his visit to do a group of drawings entitled "The Stanhope Series." For an exhibition at Earl McGrath's New York gallery, he drew portraits of friends and faces who came through our rooms upstairs, everyone from Gwyneth to Lauren Bacall. My niece Laura and my nephew Jack welcomed the subjects and helped make them comfortable.

I posed, too, after Bob asked me somewhat formally if we might do a portrait. I was shy when I asked him what he wanted me to wear, and he chose a black crepe evening dress with a halter neck and a slit up the side. When I sat down in the armchair he indicated, my breath was short and I was very nervous. I saw that his hand was shaking; it was an intimate moment. I think we were both very excited. After the portrait was finished, we were both gasping for air. Bob had to open the window. But the ice was broken.

Going to the Met with Bob was always a learning experience. He loved to pop in just to look at a couple of things each day. It was the Pompeiian marble busts that had given him the idea for the Stanhope drawings. He used to say, "Only look at what you need."

Allegra was renting a house in Taos. She had first gone there to visit Tony in 1995. She had been living in London in a pretty little mews house in Notting Hill Gate and hadn't reckoned on moving to the wilds of New Mexico permanently when, on a subsequent trip to visit Tony in 1999, she met Cisco Guevara, a renaissance man and owner of a river rafting company on the Rio Grande. He was from a long line of Spanish and Zapotec ancestry, and one of his great-aunts purportedly was married to Pancho Villa. This seemed like an interesting match for Allegra, who has the same attraction to travel and exoticism as our mother.

In February 2002 she called to tell me they were expecting a baby. I was thrilled for her. Finally, Allegra would have a family of her own. I knew that having a child would transform her life and allow her to feel again the deepest connection that exists, between mother and child, having endured the loss of our mother at such an early age.

Working with Clint Eastwood was a breeze, because that was the way he liked it. Surrounded by his loyal team at Malpaso

Productions, Clint's set was all about good food and no fuss. He had invited me to participate in *Blood Work*, a film on which he was doing double duty as actor and director. In Clint's case, it just seemed to afford him more ease. His approach was cool and relaxed; if he went off-script, he would merely ask for the line and continue the dialogue without pausing. I was to play Dr. Bonnie Fox, a stern cardiologist who gets on his case about maintaining a healthy lifestyle after his heart transplant. Throughout our scenes, Clint would whisper, "Beat me up! Give me what for!" I guess I was a little intimidated.

We had some lines by his hospital bed, where I took his pulse and inserted a stent. Sometimes I would look at him and choke, because he reminded me so much of my father when he was sick, especially if I was standing behind the hospital bed on set, watching Clint work, with his long arms with their bony elbows stretched behind his head. Also, he called me "daughter," just like Dad, which I adored. Clint would often shoot rehearsals when the actors did not know the camera was rolling.

One day when we were in a tough scene, he leaned forward—I thought he was going to give me direction—and whispered, "There's steak and lobster for lunch today." There is much to love Clint for, not least of which is the swimming pool I built up at my farm with the earnings from my short time on his film.

Having directed several movies, my brother Danny was now acting as well, working repeatedly with his friend and collaborator Bernard Rose. They had just completed *Ivans Xtc*, one of the first digital movies ever made, in which Danny was starring to much acclaim. He was living across the street in an apartment that had functioned as a design studio while Bob and I were in the process of building our house. We had not met her yet, but there had been sightings of a beautiful girl in the parking lot. Helena, having moved from Mulholland Drive, was now living next door to Bob's studio in Venice and had taken to breakfasting with them both. The girl's name was Katie Evans. One evening Danny brought her over to meet Bob and me. She was slender, with aquamarine eyes, pale ash-blond hair, and high cheekbones. She was English and spoke like a debutante, shy and sweet and self-deprecating, and came across as quite serious.

Not long afterward, Katie left for London. I was in the back of a production car on the Long Beach Freeway, driving home from location on *Blood Work*, when I got a call from Bob. "Are you on your way?" he said. "Danny is coming over to the house in an hour. There's something he wants to tell us." I asked what he thought Danny might want to discuss. "I'm not sure," Bob said, "but I have a feeling Katie might be pregnant."

When I heard the news from Danny, I cried. It was like saying goodbye to him as a little boy. "I could never imagine this before," he said. "It feels right. This baby will belong to all of us."

That night, in separate countries, Danny and Katie both looked into the starry night sky and individually decided to christen their unborn daughter Stella.

They went to Puerto Vallarta to get married. Bob was having trouble with headaches on airplanes, so we didn't go down for the wedding, which took place in the center of town in front of a statue of Dad on Isla Rio Cuale, with the mayor and several of Dad's old poker cronies in attendance.

* * *

I began work in August 2002 on *Daddy Day Care* at a very beautiful old Spanish house on the edge of West Adams in Los Angeles. Eddie Murphy was the star of the show, and in the parking lot where our campers were based, his four trailers were at the center of a cluster of motor homes surrounded by a twelve-foot plywood wall with video cameras. I guessed that if we came under attack, his place could double as a stronghold.

Eddie was sleek and burnished when he came to work, and expected everyone to be there before him. It was hot waiting on set, so I preferred to stay in my air-conditioned trailer until the last minute. But when I asked if we might get our call at the same time, the answer came back, "Ladies first."

It had taken Bob more than four years to create and render the iconology of the Great Bronze Doors, and many more months to address and commit to bronze the attributes of the Virgin Mary that would adorn the entrance. Each day Rafi drove Bob on the freeway to an engineering company in San Dimas that made hydraulic parts for amusement-park rides and was contracted to take on the function of the doors. Rafi had been with Bob since 1989. He was our houseman, bodyguard, gardener, floor finisher, driver, and general all-around go-to guy.

Making the trips back and forth to San Dimas, Bob spent almost half his waking time on the road. He confided that his joints were aching and his feet were getting numb from the physical inactivity. He bought a van with ergonomic seats and decorated it with a Persian prayer rug, two Indian leather ottomans, and a large ceramic ashtray.

ANJELICA HUSTON

After the doors were finished and ready to travel and Bob had completed the Madonna, he gave a big celebration at San Dimas for the many workers and technicians who had helped bring the project to fruition. Ten beautiful female mariachis in white played Mexican songs, and many of our friends and his fellow artists came to salute Bob's accomplishment before the doors made their final journey to downtown Los Angeles.

Joan Buck was staying with us at the time, and we rode together in the van with a police escort, beside the huge flatbed truck that carried the Virgin through the night, bound to the trailer with ropes and chains, to be released and raised high on a crane to take her place above the cathedral doors at dawn.

On September 2, 2002, the cathedral had its dedication mass in a powerful and moving ceremony. Cardinal Roger Mahony poured holy oil on the altar as fifteen bishops helped him consecrate the space in the presence of a pipe organ, a large vocal choir, and a troupe of dancing Vietnamese nuns. So began Bob's work with the Catholic Church. He had found a way to circumvent the traditional choice of working with galleries, or so he hoped.

Later that month, on Monday, September 30, 2002, Allegra and Cisco welcomed their son, Rafael, into the world. And two months later, on November 4, after a difficult labor for Katie, my niece Stella was born. Because I had contracted the flu, I met Stella a week later at Danny and Katie's house. When I first held her, her little head was tiny, cupped in the palm of my hand.

Allegra and I were on the phone, discussing her baby boy's christening. "He's Rafael. Rafa for short," she said.

"What else?" I asked. Never having been equipped with a middle name, I was anxious that he not come up short.

"Well, I was thinking Patrick for Ireland," she said. I agreed. Patrick was a lovely name. Then she added, "He was born on the feast day of San Geronimo."

"Now that you mention it, there's no question in my mind but that you have to name him Geronimo as well," I replied.

And so, on June 8, 2003, I gathered together all of my character's flowing silk dresses that I had kept from my wardrobe on *The Mists of Avalon* and, per Allegra's request, traveled to Taos, New Mexico, with Danny to preside over the christening of my new nephew, Rafa, on the banks of the Rio Grande.

The christening was to be a nondenominational event, which meant in this case that there would be a group of guardians to welcome Rafa—Cisco's best friend, Louie Hena, war chief of the Tesuque Pueblo; Steve Harris, a colleague of Cisco's; and me.

Danny and I had flown in from L.A., landed in Albuquerque, and rented an SUV to drive up to Taos. We were meeting Joan Buck and her new boyfriend, Kim, who had driven up from Santa Fe the day before, and Jeremy and Yolanda, who had flown in from Los Angeles with boxes of long-stemmed sunflowers that I had ordered. Danny and I had rented a casita on the north side of town.

The next morning we arrived at the appointed bend in the river where the christening was to take place and were surprised to see my brother Tony dismounting from his vehicle, carrying a giant staff and wearing little other than a shoulder-length curly brown wig and a deerskin. He explained that he had come as John the Baptist. As the crowd assembled on the shore, I recognized faces that I had not seen in the longest time: Allegra's father, John Julius Norwich, with two of his adult children, Allegra's half siblings Artemis and Jason, and my mother's best friend, Gina Medcalf. Another dear friend from London days, the American artist Jay Hutchinson, was there, along with Lillian Ross and her son, Erik, and the producer Michael Fitzgerald and his wife, Kathy.

A cluster of us were standing under a processional banner that spelled out Rafa's many names in gold on blue when a barge bedecked with garlands appeared, floating toward us. Everyone on the bank applauded, including an inebriated stranger who had just appeared on the scene. As the dinghy drew closer, we saw Rafa in Allegra's arms, a Hawaiian lei hanging around his little neck and shoulders, with an expression of wide-eyed wonderment. We guardians made our speeches and welcomed him into the world as his full name was pronounced: Rafael Patrick Geronimo Niño de Ortiz Ladrón de Guevara. The stranger with the tequila bottle lurched to his feet and declared, "Don Rafael!" to the crowd. According to Cisco, if one is proclaimed a don at christening, the name will stick.

Early the following day, Danny and I traveled to Albuquerque through the Sangre de Cristo Mountains with Joan and Kim. As we drove up to the high green fields, we breathed the fresh air and agreed that all beautiful places looked to us like Ireland. We stopped at the sanctuary in Chimayo, where the earth is curative and the sick and weak come from all over to drink the waters, and ate in a little restaurant close to the chapel. The air was sweet with a perfume I did not recognize; the chain-link fences surrounding the grounds were laced with flowers and crosses made of twigs and reeds, with prayers and letters to the saints.

* * *

A few days later, on June 11, 2003, the silver *Torso* that Bob created for Rodeo Drive was unveiled. The mayor of Beverly Hills declared that date Robert Graham Day. And on Monday, June 23, I watched as Bob was inducted into the Knights of Malta by our friend and his patron Prince Rupert Loewenstein at the Brompton Oratory, in South Kensington, London, during a solemn ceremony. Sabrina threw us a party at her flat and we had dinner one night in Mayfair with Hercules, Jeremy Thomas, and Michael White. Hercules was oddly fretful; Bob and I wondered if he was unwell.

CHAPTER 31

In September, I arrived to stay at a boutique hotel in Rome. I wasn't partial to my room, which overlooked an outdoor restaurant. The scent of food and the clattering of dishes below reminded me I was hungry. Jaclyn Bashoff, who had been my assistant for three years, and I had just arrived to work on *The Life Aquatic* with Wes Anderson. We had been picked up by a unit car, but otherwise there was no welcoming note from production in my room, no flowers, no phone message, no customary box of inviting chocolates. I asked Jaclyn to get hold of someone on the crew. "They're all out at sea," she said, hanging up the telephone. Apparently, Wes and his crew were filming on an island off the coast and had no cell-phone reception.

The next morning the hotel management announced that the building was having serious plumbing problems and offered to relocate us. There were scores of unhappy, unwashed tourists in the lobby when we came downstairs. The management offered to send us to the Hotel Hassler, atop the Spanish Steps, the best and most luxurious hotel in Rome, free of charge for the week, which softened the blow enormously.

At liberty for several days, Jaclyn and I retraced the old steps I remembered from my time with Dad on *The Bible*.

Visiting museums and churches and Caravaggios, having lunches at fine trattorias, and shopping at Missoni, Prada, and Fendi along Via Condotti, we had almost forgotten why we were there in the first place when Wes and the boys finally got off the boat. They had been out on the charming but funky fishing vessel, *The Belafonte*, that was serving as Bill Murray's craft in the movie.

Milena Canonero was designing my look as something of a sea creature. I was thrilled to finally collaborate with Milena after so many years of following her work, from *Barry Lyndon* to *Chariots of Fire*, and my years of friendship with her and her husband, the actor Marshall Bell.

Wes invited me to come to dinner with the cast the following evening. That day I met my hairdresser, Maria Teresa Corridoni, who, from reputation, had worked on the great heads of Magnani and Callas. It was decided by Maria Teresa that the work should begin then and there. Another woman and an assistant attacked my scalp with breathtaking zeal, attaching long swatches of black and blue waist-length extensions, and sealing them to the roots with boiling-hot resin. It was a prolonged and painful process.

When I arrived for Wes's dinner, I was still somewhat in agony but sporting a thick waist-length blue mane. I was very happy to see Wes and Bill Murray and Bob Yeoman, Wes's director of photography. A beautiful man in a turban introduced himself as Waris Ahluwalia, and Owen Wilson stopped by with his charming steel-colored hound, Garcia, who was enjoying a fine adventure off-leash in the piazzas. I couldn't sleep a wink that night, which is often the case before a first day's shooting, and the shards of resin pierced my scalp like teeth. But I was excited to be working once again with Wes.

The Life Aquatic centered on the character of Steve Zissou, a disaffected documentary filmmaker and oceanic researcher based loosely on and in the spirit of Jacques Cousteau, played by Bill Murray. I was his estranged wife, Eleanor; Owen Wilson was Ned Plimpton, his possible son; and Jeff Goldblum was Alistair Hennessey, Eleanor's first husband and Zissou's archenemy. Willem Dafoe was Klaus Daimler, a German boatman, and Cate Blanchett was set to play Jane Winslett-Richardson, a British reporter and the boys' love interest. The Brazilian singer Seu Jorge was in the movie and contributed to the sound track.

Our location was an hour or so from Rome in Torre Astura, a peninsula in Nettuno that housed a medieval tower and the remains of a villa. This set was the Zissou compound. The cast and crew were put up in a small beach town down the coast called Sabaudia, which had at its center a postwar square with fascist architecture and a concrete cathedral. Our hotel was on the sand, and had two levels of open stairwells with turquoise tile and a delicious little restaurant downstairs where everything on the menu was traditional and fresh, right out of the sea. I was in the habit of eating mozzarella and seafood every night after work and going to sleep lulled by Seu Jorge's guitar and the Brazilian songs floating up from his room downstairs. I made good friends with him and his wife, Mariana, and I went bicycling with Waris Ahluwalia; he, too, was playing a member of Team Zissou.

Overall, everyone was very pleasant, but I couldn't always tell where I stood with Bill. On one of our first days in Sabaudia, he asked everyone but me out to dinner at a restaurant nearby, and it hurt my feelings. Maybe it was because he is a Method actor and our characters were divorcing in the movie. I never knew why, since he had been considerate of me when we worked on *The Royal Tenenbaums*. But one of my dear friends from London, Melissa North, was staying at Bernardo Bertolucci's summer house up the beach, and we had a lovely reunion.

It may be overly sensitive of me to say this, but that job in Italy was partly overshadowed by feeling strangely like an outsider. The previous outing with Wes, on *The Royal Tenenbaums*, had felt more family-oriented and inclusive, but this was a much bigger, more complicated canvas. We were also on the move for much of the time, from the Amalfi Coast to Naples, then back to Rome. After a few days filming out at sea, my blue hair was bleached ash-white by the sun. It had to be replaced, which took another seven hours of hot tongs and boiling resin. And the "eye specialist" who was to put in and remove my aqua-green contact lenses somehow managed to scratch my cornea, which required that I wear blackout shades in some night scenes. The work on the film was deceptive in that it looked simple, but a great deal of effort went into the sets, the costumes, the locations. Ideally, they should have started shooting in the late spring, because we were now entering September, the sea air was getting very chilly, and much of the action was out at sea.

There was a dog wrangler on set whom I could not tolerate. I was to have a clutch of Irish wolfhounds in my scenes in Torre Astura, and I sometimes witnessed this man abusing the dogs, kicking and shouting at them. The abuse of animals is criminal, and to see this guy profiting from it made me furious. I got into squabbles with him a few times. One scene required that my bedroom be filled with hundreds of finches and budgerigars. As scripted, the wolfhounds were to be seated in a corner. On "action," the birds were released, and one inadvertently flew right into the open jaws of one of the wolfhounds. I would have felt worse, but it seemed like such a good moment in that dog's unhappy life I couldn't help but rejoice, even at the expense of the unfortunate bird.

Bob came to visit, and we traveled up to Ravello to film some scenes at Gore Vidal's villa, La Rondinaia—the Swallow's Nest—high above the Gulf of Salerno. Bill and I did a scene on a balcony overlooking the precipitous drop. I thought I'd pass out from vertigo. It was where Gore entertained throughout the sixties and seventies; there were faded photographs of Princess Grace and Noël Coward and Rudolf Nureyev on his walls looking like they were having the time of their lives. In our hotel room, Bob would answer the phone "Beyond the clouds," and everywhere in the little hilltop town there were references to Dad's film *Beat the Devil*, which he had made in Ravello in the early fifties with Humphrey Bogart, Jennifer Jones, Gina Lollobrigida, Robert Morley, and Peter Lorre. Off the square was Dad's old production office, commemorated with a plaque.

For me, traveling in Italy is always like going home. We visited the little village of San Pietro, where Dad made a documentary film about its liberation by the Americans in World War II. My mother's parents, Grandpa Tony and Mama Angelica Soma, were from the north, near Lago Maggiore, but we didn't get to go there on this trip.

Sofia Coppola was in Rome presenting her film *Lost in Translation*, with Bill Murray starring—a brilliant, deeply felt, extremely funny love story. I was very proud of her. Sofia had been unfairly criticized by the press when she had agreed to act in her father's last film in the *Godfather* trilogy in 1990.

I felt sympathetic, because I had endured the same negative reception after *A Walk with Love and Death*, but I wonder if she would agree that in some way that experience had formed us.

In the last few weeks of the film, we shot in Naples, where there was a garbage strike and the best pizza I've ever eaten. The town was beautiful but rough, full of gypsies and sailors. Bob and I went to see the ruins at Pompeii and some marvelous Etruscan carvings at the Museo Archeologico Nazionale, which gave Bob the idea to do a series of bronze portraits of artists and actors and other people he was interested in. When we had last seen Wes in California, Bob had playfully asked him for a cameo in *The Life Aquatic*. Milena had gone to great lengths to outfit Bob beautifully as a mysterious South American dictator; he looked fabulous but unfortunately got only a few seconds of camera time, in a party scene at the harbor on *The Belafonte*.

Bud Cort, who was playing an accountant taken hostage by pirates, went to the beatification of Mother Teresa at the Vatican and brought me back a rosary. On the Day of the Immaculate Conception, Jaclyn and I happened to be standing atop the Spanish Steps watching as, way below, purring up Via Condotti, came the little Popemobile, with Pope John Paul II inside, giving a benediction under a warm yellow light. He was dressed all in white with a red sash, and people were packed on the sidewalks and reaching out to him from behind the barricades. I became very emotional watching him; he had a radiance, something vulnerable, that moved me to tears. I wished I believed in God enough to be Catholic.

CHAPTER 32

Hercules came to L.A. for his annual cocktail party at the Bel Age in January 2004. One of Herky's great talents was keeping track of all his friends, discovering and sharing what was best in other people's cultures. Everyone showed up for Herky's evening, people I hadn't seen in a long time. It was always great to catch up. Bob and I didn't stay long, because the rooms were crowded and we were going on to dinner. As I was getting into our car, a voice rang out. I recognized the owner and hardly dared to turn around. When I did, I was dismayed by Bert Schneider's appearance. Where once he had been the handsomest of men—tall, slender, and elegant—now he was bent over, twisted, and misshapen. His face was gray and his eyes were bloodshot; he looked like a cadaver. I'd heard that he'd blown his mind on drugs. I did not know what to say to him.

Later that week, Bob and I had lunch at Orso with Hercules and Helmut and June Newton, on their annual visit to town. Bob and Helmut liked each other and were admirers of each other's work. Bob had been a photographic subject of Helmut's, as indeed had I, long before Bob and I had ever met. Bob and Helmut shared a passion for the female form and a dry sense of humor.

We talked about how June and Helmut had photographed

each other all their lives; they had even published a book called *Us and Them.* Helmut had been working with movie stars that morning at the Chateau Marmont, where he and June always stayed.

A few days later, there was a fashion show in the front lobby of the hotel. I was seated beside Helmut. One sad, slight model after the next weaved down the runway. Helmut turned to me. "The models are so ugly, you have to look at the dresses," he said. Helmut always had a healthy disdain for fashion.

Two days later, I was driving on Robertson Boulevard when I got a call from Joan Buck. She had been staying at the Chateau on assignment for *Vogue.* "Have you got Mrs. Davis's number?" she asked, referring to Barbara, Marvin Davis's wife. "She's on the board at Cedars. Helmut has had an accident." She went on to say that his car had slammed into a wall opposite the garage at the Chateau Marmont. I made the call and drove over to the hospital.

The owner of the Chateau, André Balazs, was there, sitting with Joan and June in a children's waiting room, which was decorated with decals of caterpillars, toadstools, and Alice down the rabbit hole.

"Helmut is gone," said June stoically. "Go and see him."

Helmut was on a gurney in a darkened room. He looked peaceful and unscathed. When I came out, June had gone back to the Chateau for her camera to take his final photograph.

On October 19, 2004, Laila asked if I'd read something of Hunter Thompson's at the Taschen bookshop in Beverly Hills. She said that Benicio del Toro and Harry Dean Stanton would also be reading and that Hunter would really appreciate it. I decided to bring my nephew Jack, who was always fascinated by Hunter lore. When we got to the bookstore, I could tell that the night had in place all the ingredients and promise of a rich gumbo; Hugh Hefner and three blondes were seated on a banquette on the second level, drinking pink champagne in a fog of paparazzi; the crowd was thickening; and Hunter, in spite of a very swollen leg from having undergone surgery a few weeks before, was self-anesthetizing with bourbon, modestly but cheerfully, with a caution unusual to him. It was strange for me to see him outside the confines of the Rockies.

Predictably, this mood was not to last for long. During the reading of his book, when someone suggested audibly that perhaps he should go outdoors to smoke, Hunter launched a lead-glass ashtray that hit the little makeshift stage where Harry Dean was standing and glanced off the edge, skimming across the floor toward one of Kelly Lynch's open-toed sandals. It was merciful that it didn't break, and the room heaved a collective sigh of relief.

The after-party was at the Chateau Marmont. Hunter ordered me a sugary drink and told me to sit on his lap. He took off his silver totem, the one he always wore, with the squash blossom and the peyote button, and placed it around my neck. I was feeling dizzy from the margarita and the champagne and asked Jack if he would take me home. Laila told me that later that night up in Hunter's suite, he had rushed toward the balcony as if he might jump and turned back at the last minute. I woke up the next morning with Hunter's medallion still around my neck. It seemed terribly wrong for him to be without it, so I sent Rafi to take it to him at the Chateau. I would never again see or be frightened by Hunter. He shot himself in the head on February 20, 2005.

* * *

Robert Roussel, an American author and filmmaker living in Mexico, suggested to Danny that the Huston family participate in a film festival to take place in Puerto Vallarta in our father's name the following year. Danny and I flew out to Mexico and met with a group of business owners and local denizens who would be active in the creation of the program. The festival sounded like an interesting idea and one that, at the very least, would allow the extended family to spend some time together. We all cheerfully shook hands and agreed to make a go of it.

Danny and I went on vacation for a week in the Costalegre region, visiting Alix Goldsmith and Goffredo Marcaccini at their resort, Cuixmala, an extraordinarily beautiful and biodiverse estate full of exotic animals imported from Africa years before by Alix's father, James Goldsmith. This proved to be a wonderful holiday, riding their horses through the wilderness alongside herds of zebra and impala and oryx, seeing crocodiles slide into the water from the riverbanks.

There was a hatchery on the beach where they incubated baby turtles and one day we sent several out to sea, their tiny bodies so soft and vulnerable one could only pray for their survival. Every night Goffredo would cook delicious pasta, and we went to sleep in cabanas under the stars to the songs of night frogs and cicadas.

In November 2004, according to plan, the Hustons descended in force on Puerto Vallarta. There were about fifteen of us, friends and family, including Danny, Katie, Allegra, Tony, Cisco, baby Rafa, my nephews Jack and Matt, Laila, and Kate O'Toole. But soon it became evident that the festival might not survive to enjoy a future as an annual event in Dad's name. With all good intentions, the screenings were mysteriously canceled or moved to different venues without notification.

Notwithstanding, it was lovely to be in Puerto Vallarta, just a stone's throw from where Dad had spent his final years. Jack and Matt had never seen his place, and Allegra and Danny and I had such great memories of Dad in the midst of the jungle, with no walls between him and nature. I suggested that we hire a panga and a boatman and make a little pilgrimage to Las Caletas.

We sailed out from an unfamiliar mooring at Boca de Tomatlán. When I'd gone to visit Dad in the old days, the harbor was just a bay with a grass shack and a few rowboats tied up. We motored out to a channel between two rocky cliffs that rose from the ocean floor, and dove in to circle the rocks in masks and snorkels and watch schools of exotic fish and a white octopus dancing underwater.

Soon after we reboarded the boat and sailed on beside the coast, Las Caletas appeared in front of us all at once like a mirage. Dad had said he hoped that after his death, it might return to the jungle. Evidently, just the opposite had happened. From a distance, it looked like a termite hill or like cupcakes left on a windowsill covered in ants. Las Caletas was swarming with tourists; sailboats and Jet Skis lined the beach, and a sign for a gift shop and café bar halfway up the cliff read JOHN HUSTON MARISCOS. Scuba tours were being advertised, and Thai massage. Allegra's eyes met mine. "Let's not stop," she said.

I said, "Let's go to the Von Rohrs'. It's just around the bend. Things will be better there." Von Rohr had been Dad's closest neighbor on the coast, the owner of a pristine stretch of white sand beach halfway to Xalapa.

As our panga turned a bend past an outcropping of black rocks, we saw a couple of people in the water, and on the beach a man in shorts and a straw hat was nailing something to a fence. Allegra and I climbed from the boat onto shore, wanting to introduce ourselves to whoever was in residence. As we walked toward the house, in a grove of palm trees, a voice called out to us. By now we had crossed the strand and reached the terrace, where a man in a Hawaiian shirt stood in the shadows. "Get out of here," he said.

I was so shocked that somehow it didn't register. "I don't think you understand," I said amiably. "My father was John Huston; he used to live next door."

The man walked toward us menacingly. "I don't give a damn who you are," he said. "Get out of here. Now!"

As fast as we could make it, Allegra and I ran back to the boat, and as we pushed back out to sea, we related our story to the others. Allegra and I were both sobbing. Jack and Danny and Cisco wanted to go back to talk to the guy. We begged them not to. The whole experience felt too dangerous.

On April 2, 2006, I had my last cigarette. I had smoked since I was fifteen. In so many of my early photographs, I have a cigarette as my constant prop; I don't think I ever did a photograph for Bob Richardson without one in my hand or clouds of smoke billowing around my face. Just recently, I checked to see if the old carton of American Spirits is still in the drawer in my office. For some reason, I like to keep it there, like a road sign I passed eight years ago.

Katie had told me that she and Danny were going to a seminar to quit. It was called "The Easy Way to Stop Smoking," and I announced that I wanted to go, too. I was smoking two packs a day and was sick and tired of my old habit. The cost of the session was six hundred dollars—enough money to make you pay attention. When I sat down in a hotel conference room with the ten other people, my expectations were quite low, particularly since our counselor encouraged us to leave the room every fifteen minutes or so for a smoke break.

We'd troop outside and light up, sucking on our cigarettes ever more urgently, as six hours dwindled down to one. Eventually, the counselor brought us all back together, and we joined in a prayer and dumped our cigarettes in a wastepaper basket. Having said goodbye to everyone, I went to the parking lot and opened my car door. This would have been the moment to settle behind the wheel and light up. Extraordinarily, that wasn't my impulse. I drove home and repeated the same thought process in the kitchen. Whereas yesterday I would have walked into my house and paused for a smoke before going upstairs, now it was suddenly no longer part of my repertoire.

I haven't had a cigarette since, and I have had no desire to smoke. Possibly I was hypnotized, and evidently the prayer worked.

Danny left for New Zealand in August to act in *30 Days of Night*. Although Katie didn't confide to me in detail, she and Danny were not getting along; she seemed off-balance and was very thin. We met in the valley on Ventura Boulevard one morning in September to look at a potential school for Stella, who would be starting kindergarten. Katie was downcast but defiant and had bought a diamond ring to cheer herself up. She had just come into a family inheritance and was in the process of buying a new house in the Valley, to be close to the school we had chosen for Stella. When Danny returned for a brief hiatus in filming in November, they began divorce proceedings.

I was invited to go to Norway in December as a cohost with Sharon Stone for the Nobel Peace Prize Concert, a televised event that celebrates the recipients of the medal. That year, the winner was Muhammad Yunus of the Grameen Bank in Bangladesh, the leader of the organization Raúl Juliá so passionately supported.

Jaclyn and I stopped first in London, where I attended a special evening at the British Film Institute to screen *The Dead* and participate in a Q&A. I also reconnected with David Bailey and sat for him in his studio in Brownlow Mews. The studio was bustling as usual, with several squealing stylists who had just had their picture taken for *GQ*, hairdressers, art directors, and two small, plump dogs lying on a daybed amid piles of couture—a beautiful contained chaos specific to Bailey. Portraits of Mick Jagger, Damien Hirst, and Jean Shrimpton gazed down on the influx of models, actors, and personal assistants. Sir Ian McKellen, Sir Peter Blake, and Trevor Nunn were being photographed. Bailey was working with rhythm and energy.

Norway, from above, looked like the opposite of California—long fingers of land reaching into an inky black sea. The plane rose and dipped like a boat in the turbulent sky.

Oslo was a clean, refined city. On our first day, Jaclyn and I ventured out to a park that had been the life's work of a sculptor named Gustave Vigeland, whose pieces included legions of round people in shiny bronze, erotic configurations at various stages of their lives; his bronze baby, *The Angry Boy*, a whinging, whiny child, is the most famous of his sculptures.

We visited the Norsk Folkemuseum, with its farmhouses and an ancient wooden church with a straw roof, and the Viking Ship Museum, which had the most beautiful longboats, wood-slatted and sleek as sea serpents.

But there was no daylight in Norway; it was dark when you woke up. At midday the sun made an appearance for a couple of hours, then retreated into night. We ate copious amounts of salted and pickled fish, and reindeer was on the menu in every restaurant, which made me sad. Before going home, I bought troll dolls for everyone at the farm for Christmas, and a sailor suit for Stella.

The peace concert, attended by the king and queen of Norway, offered an amalgam of talent from Rihanna, John Legend, Lionel Richie, and the former Cat Stevens (now known as Yusuf Islam) to Wynonna Judd, Simply Red, and Renée Fleming.

But the best time of all was on our final night in Oslo, when the artistic director of the concert, Petter Skavlan, gave me a small, intimate dinner at his house and invited the great actress Liv Ullmann. We stayed up laughing and drinking red wine until after 3 A.M. I'd always wanted to meet her, having admired her collaboration with Ingmar Bergman for years. And she was everything I'd hoped for and more.

CHAPTER 33

My first vision of India was when I was landing on a British Airways jet in January 2007, through a murky stretch of morning smog above a patchwork of gray and rusted tin shanty roofs, spread out between foothills and coast like a filthy blanket. These were the slums, a network of paper-thin huts, a warren of noise and activity and squalor. Jaclyn and I had flown through the night from London, and the airport in Mumbai was modest by contrast to Heathrow. There were no concession stands and no shops, and the floors and walls were the color of sour milk and made of solid concrete. I was excited to be on my way to Rajasthan to work again with Wes Anderson, this time on *The Darjeeling Limited*. My part would be that of Sister Patricia, a nun. Wes had been sending me small metal replicas of Mother Teresa for some time to get me in the mood. The backstory was that I had deserted my three sons after my divorce from their father and run away to India. My sons were now on a quest, traveling through that country, to attain spiritual understanding and to reunite with their mother.

The boys were being played by Owen Wilson, Adrien Brody, and Jason Schwartzman, with appearances from others in Wes's fold, such as Waris Ahluwalia and Kumar Pallana. The opening scene would involve a race through city streets with Bill Murray in the back of a taxi, rushing to make his train.

Jaclyn and I passed through customs, and an envoy from the film met us and helped us with our bags to a parking lot. It was still early, but the sun was starting to come on strong over the sea of tin by the side of the runway. Children darted around us, pulling on our sleeves, begging. One small boy tried to insert a dog-eared copy of something by Somerset Maugham through the open car window; another sang "Jingle Bells," even though it was late January.

I was staying at the Taj Mahal hotel for two days before flying north to meet up with Wes Anderson and the cast and crew of *The Darjeeling Limited*; they had already been filming in Jaipur, and I had come to finish up the final weeks with them. The Taj, which was beside the Gateway to India monument, was on a grand scale, with a distinctly Victorian air—an imposing building with arches and domes, gray stone streaked with soot on the exterior, the downstairs a series of expensive galleries, jewelry and fabric shops, and restaurants. There was a large open-air central patio, decorated in tile with palm fronds beside an outsized pale turquoise swimming pool. I noticed several ravens flying randomly above our heads and found their presence a little menacing.

That afternoon we attempted to shop a little, but we were jet-lagged, and the city was so active and crowded that it seemed almost impenetrable. We had heard of a particular gallery close by that had wonderful antiques, but we almost got killed crossing the road. The population drove at top speed to a cacophony of horns and car engines; the tuk-tuk trucks raced forward, accelerating for pedestrians and red lights. The "antiques" were indeed lovely, but when I asked if I might use the bathroom, the shop owner guided me to a second-floor toilet in the next-door building, which had multiple reproductions of everything we had seen downstairs. "Some antiques are older than others," he explained.

We went down some crowded streets to an outdoor market under a bridge—stalls selling pith helmets from forgotten wars next to skinned sheep heads. Around us were women in shawls, burkas, and veils, young men sleeping on bales of hay in the back of trucks, animals being led to slaughter. A skinny old man in the gutter, naked to the waist, dropped his arm down an open drain up to the shoulder and came up with a handful of black silt, which he poked through with his fingers.

That night we ate at a trendy rooftop restaurant not too far from the hotel. Later, as I tried to sleep, the ravens outside my window croaked and cawed, and when I got up and looked outside at 3 A.M., I saw their shadows batting above my window in the amber streetlight; two stray dogs were asleep in a gutter. I looked forward to getting out of the city.

We left for Rajasthan at 4:30 A.M. and flew north over open expanses of dry, hilly land dotted here and there with bushy trees. No water to speak of. When we arrived at the small airport in Udaipur, we were told the film unit had been shooting there and most of them had moved on to another location. However, it was nice to see a few familiar faces from *The Royal Tenenbaums* and *The Life Aquatic*. Our driver welcomed us to the town of Udaipur. "It's clean here," he said. "Not like Mumbai." But as we drove through the outskirts of the city, we remarked on the number of cows chewing on plastic bags and the men in their jewel-colored turbans and heavy blankets warming themselves at small bonfires of acrid black smoke by the side of the road.

The car climbed a hill on the outskirts of town, and a lake like a black mirror spread out before us; there were several small, canopy-topped barges anchored in the early-morning haze. A beautiful girl in a beige silk cheongsam sat silently with us in the back of the motorboat as we skimmed across the misted expanse of water toward the hotel. Wes had chosen a spectacular location. It felt like *One Thousand and One Nights*.

Udaipur, known as the City of Lakes, was created in 1559 by Maharana Udai Singh II as the final capital of the former Mewar kingdom, and many of its Rajput-era palaces now serve as luxury hotels. The Lake Palace Hotel, constructed of white marble, is situated on an island in the Pichola Lake; another palace has furniture made entirely of lead crystal. The City Palace, which remains the residence of the present maharana, is a gray stone fortress accessible by land and water, with an immense fortified gateway on which, one was informed, an opposition army's elephants might have impaled themselves if the castle was under attack.

Now the gates were opened to a citadel behind the palace. Monkeys dangled from the trees, women strung marigolds on the pavements. Shops, temples, barbershops, souvenir shacks, and shrines lined the narrow winding streets.

Our cast was staying at the newest edifice on the lake. The hotel was very beautiful but somehow not site-specific—a fusion of Oriental influences, like a free-floating Shangri-la. My room was at the end of a long outdoor cloister; ribboning around the exterior of the building was an ocean-blue swimming pool where Owen Wilson swam his laps each morning. Beyond my room, at the end of the corridor, was a chain-link fence that protected a wildlife reserve. On my first morning, I saw vultures picking at a carcass on the other side. Often I saw deer, monkeys, wild gazelles, and peacocks. Another morning as I was having breakfast at the restaurant, a pack of some twelve to fifteen jackals tore across the nearby golf course, barking and chattering at high pitch.

Upon arrival in Rajasthan, I had received a formal invitation from the maharana of Udaipur to dine at the City Palace. The maharana lived in an apartment where time stopped at the Raj. A photograph of Her Majesty Queen Elizabeth II sat in a silver frame on the mantelpiece, and beside it one of Lord Mountbatten. The private rooms curved around a cylindrical center wall, and on the outer perimeter, a streak of taxidermied tigers—most shot down in previous centuries and pale with age—were cut in half and appeared to be emerging from the wall as if by magic. In his garden, some two hundred feet above the lake, a cluster of ancient exotic trees stood close to fountains and an ornamental rose garden. Farther out in the lake, the marble palace, white as a pearl, floated like a dream on the still water.

Under Wes's new policy, we were not to have wardrobe or hair and makeup artists on set during the shooting of this film. Essentially, we were to costume ourselves each morning at the hotel, go through the works, and travel to set by minivan, dressed, coiffed, and ready to work. The situation on set was a little difficult in that my wig kept trying to pop off, and there was no one to help me with it; no one even seemed to have a mirror. To compound the problem, there was a scene of intense weeping with no one there to mop up my tears. I looked like a drowned raccoon.

Owen's and Adrien's real mothers, both photographers, were with their sons on location, their necks draped in long-lens cameras. They were always taking pictures of their boys amid the temples and the ruins. The movie was shooting high in the hills, almost two hours from town, at an ancient monastery. The catering consisted of curry and rice served on the floor in bubbling vats next to the Porta-Potties. Soon Owen's assistant, Steve, was doing back-and-forth duty to the hotel to get boxed lunches for the cast. I didn't see Wes eat the whole time I was in India.

For research, I had gone to a Catholic mission in Udaipur that had been very inspiring. Part asylum, part old people's home, part orphanage, it was a quiet, peaceful place. Everyone there, young and old, seemed supportive and caring for one another. There was a manger in the compound with a healthy milk cow whose sweet face was rubbed affectionately by the nun who was showing me around. I gave the mission most of my per diem. It felt nice to give it to the nuns, who had asked for nothing.

My days on the movie were not many, and I had some time to visit Ranakpur, a few hours' drive from the hotel. When Jaclyn and I set out with our driver, he suggested we buy pencils and paper as gifts for the women and children in the villages along the way. We passed a town where there was a festival, and all the women were wearing dresses with tiny mirrors sewn into the material, so that the main street danced with their reflections. We passed jackals gnawing inside the rib cage of a long-horned cow, and a parade of girls in orange saris near a poppy field with brass urns on their heads and flashing smiles that lit up their faces. Everywhere in India were contradictions of savagery and beauty, fullness and deprivation, life and death. I never knew what to expect next.

Ranakpur's Jain temple is constructed of more than fourteen hundred marble pillars, all carved differently. The high priest took Jaclyn and me to visit the small Kama Sutra temple on the grounds; he said a special prayer for us, Wes, and *The Darjeeling Limited*. After the prayer, he told us he was cast in a scene in the film. On the way back to Udaipur, we turned a corner in a forest and saw about two hundred monkeys hanging out by the side of the road; they were being fed by a forest ranger, and each had his own individual carrot in hand.

One morning I went out riding with our producer, Alice Bamford, and Owen's mother, Laura. We rode the local breed of horse, the Marwari, interesting because the breed moves at a fast shuffle on long legs and has ears that curve like an ornament. My best buy in India was a large silver replica of a Marwari horse that happened to decorate my hotel room.

January is peak wedding season in Rajasthan. At night, the streets of Udaipur almost levitated with music and dancers, the grooms being led out on white horses or some astride painted elephants. Festooned with marigolds and roses, the brides wore jewels on their foreheads, noses, and ears, anklets with tiny tinkling bells, and armloads of colored bangles. One afternoon out shopping with Jason Schwartzman, we went to an obscure fabric store that he claimed had outfitted Gandhi and then into a small glass-bangle shop where a score of young women sat on a dirt floor in front of the proprietor. From a floor-to-ceiling stack of cardboard boxes, to which her two minions flew back and forth like an organ grinder's canaries, the proprietor amassed different combinations of bracelets in specific choices of size, design, and color for each girl to match her wedding sari. Jason sat on the floor among them. They giggled but paid him little attention. The bangle seller's focus never wavered; her eyes barely acknowledged his presence.

At one point, Mick Jagger arrived in Udaipur with his

daughter Jade. I had some days off and went shopping with them, and was surprised how good at haggling they were. He was buying fabric to decorate his summer house in Mustique. Later that night we went to a most beautiful Jain wedding. As we were sitting waiting for the maharana to appear, his floating motorcade drew up to the plaintive strains of "Loch Lomond," as rendered on a pair of bagpipes. The ceremony, which went on for hours, was gorgeous. The bride wore a red sari, and her feet were washed in rose water. The priest poured honey onto the palms of her hands and bound them to the hands of the groom with silk and banana leaves.

After I returned from India, I was pleased to learn that the Library of Congress deemed Dad's *The Asphalt Jungle* "culturally, historically, or aesthetically significant" and selected it for preservation in the U.S. National Film Registry.

I remember speculating at the time as to whether the ruling in 1991 by the French courts preventing Ted Turner from colorizing *The Asphalt Jungle* had possibly "colored" Turner's view of my film *Bastard Out of Carolina*.

I visited Katie and Stella at their house for lunch. Danny had left for London. When I walked in, both of them were dressed in white. The windows were open to the canyon breeze, and, disconcertingly, a dozen candles were burning on the living room table. I told Katie that if ever she should need peace and quiet, she had an open invitation to visit the farm at all times, but to watch out for fire. A few weeks later, following a visit she made there, her friends became alarmed about what she was confiding to them on the phone. Soon after, they persuaded Katie to enter rehab.

For the couple of weeks that Katie was in rehab, Danny was still away working. Stella's nanny, Christine, received a call from Katie, asking if she would bring Stella to visit. Christine said that she would feel more comfortable if I came along.

It was a facility in Pasadena, an old Spanish estate, and groups of hard-eyed people were sitting outdoors drinking coffee and smoking cigarettes. Stella was only four and held on to Katie in a long embrace. Katie told her to stay with Christine while she and I went for a walk on the grounds of the clinic. When we were out of earshot, she paused under some tall pines and said, "Watch after Stella for me." She was frail but resolute that she would get well.

When Danny returned from filming, Katie had left rehab, sold her new house, and moved to a condominium in Manhattan Beach. I wanted to stay in contact with her. I feared that because she and Danny were having problems, she might decide against my seeing Stella. I wrote her a letter on December 15 saying that I hoped we could continue to reach out to one another in friendship, saying how saddened I had been by the spiral of recent events regarding her relationship with Danny, and telling her how much I cared for her and Stella.

CHAPTER 34

Whenever I listen to the voice of Maria Callas, I think of Bob. That explosive sound, soaring to the vaulted ceiling of our living room. On either side of the high window above the fireplace, where the Mexican Madonna that Dad had given me after *Prizzi's Honor* bestowed her benediction, the arches that Bob had designed curved overhead in the shape of angel wings.

Bob awakened punctually at seven o'clock each morning, showered, put on a starched white cotton shirt and cargo pants, and walked downstairs for breakfast. He would read the newspapers, drink coffee, eat an egg tortilla with hot sauce that he called *lo mismo*, light a cigar, rant for a short while on the politics of George W. Bush, and by 8 A.M. be in his studio, ready to work.

There were exceptions to this routine, as when he was commuting to San Dimas to oversee the fabrication and the engineering of the Great Bronze Doors, or if he was warming up to tai chi with his Chinese master.

Bob would have done well during the Renaissance, when an artist might have worked for a patron or the church. He felt that art belonged to everyone and that artists should be supported by the state. He did not believe in ownership, in art as an asset, yet he worked with galleries all his life, using whatever monies he made to partially underwrite his public art projects, for which the cost often exceeded the budget. He had it both ways.

Although he rarely invited me to do so, watching Bob work was fascinating. I see Bob, in the act of observation, dipping his head, peering over the rim of his glasses. This look was acute, searching, porous. He was relentless in his quest for the true essence and shape of things in an ever-changing light. Sometimes he would labor with the clay, fight it, complaining about its consistency and weight. He would take a mallet to break down a compromise he'd made, and start again.

Soon after I met Bob, he was commissioned to sculpt *Source Figure*, a monument for downtown Los Angeles, fourteen feet tall and cast bronze; the expression on the woman's face is rapturous, with an inward contemplation. It was, I felt, a departure for Bob, who some years later again explored spirituality, in the transcendent expression of the Madonna of the Angels. With these two pieces, Bob had become increasingly involved with evidence, character, and what was taking place emotionally. I think this outlook was behind his empathy with my work as an actress. His later pieces became all about the spontaneity of the moment; the figures dance, leap, jump, spin cartwheels. They are exuberant, physically animated, and involved with their surroundings.

Bob lived modestly and elegantly. His only indulgences were Cuban cigars and, for a few whimsical months when he tried to give up smoking, a brand-new pair of white socks every day. He liked to experiment with modern technology and materials and was using computers to measure, cut, and build with resins and polymers. He talked about making new inventions. He loved women; he sculpted naked girls at the zenith of their beauty and physical allure. He was a consummate artist. I posed for him only a few times; the prospect was unnerving to us both.

Bob usually returned from his studio at seven in the evening. I would sit opposite him on a white sofa in the living room of the house he had designed for our life together, and he would light another in the series of cigars that he smoked throughout the day. He'd pour himself a large tequila and play a tape of Callas very loud, leaning back on the couch and allowing his gaze to travel skyward with her voice.

The song was "Vissi d'arte," from the opera *Tosca* by Puccini:

> *I lived for art, I lived for love,*
> *I never did harm to a living soul!*
> *With a secret hand*
> *I relieved as many misfortunes as I knew of. . . .*
> *In the hour of grief,*
> *Why, why, Lord,*
> *Ah, why do you reward me thus?*

The smoke billowed about him. He could remain silent like that for hours. "Thinking," he would say. So many elements can fill a silence. Sometimes I felt a rising frustration, a wave of panic. What was unspoken between us had begun to disturb me. Something immense and frightening was present in the ether. Though often I thought it would drive me mad, I said nothing. I did not know why, but I was terribly afraid of the answer to my unspoken question: What is happening here? What is wrong? More and more we seemed to be drifting into a consensual forbearance to communicate;

we had developed a strange tolerance for the elephant in the room.

Bob was mysterious, but it had become increasingly evident that he was not well. A few years before, he had begun to complain of neuropathy and had been going to a doctor in Beverly Hills who was giving him something he described as akin to shock therapy for his feet. Bob's general physician had died, and Arnie Klein had been recommending doctors, but they were specialists, and no one seemed to have formed a diagnosis for what was ailing him. I offered to take him to my doctor, but he refused to go.

Across the street from our house on Windward Avenue, the Townhouse bar disgorged its customers at 2:30 A.M. to yell and sing and fight or throw firecrackers for a full hour and a half until their cars were located, or even on occasion to shoot at each other. I had read that the sound of car alarms at night could induce a heart attack.

Often I would peer out from a tiny glass bedroom window like a keyhole in the fortress into the interrupted night, full of flashing neon and raised voices. My having chosen to live in Venice seemed like a faraway flight of fancy, and now we were stuck in the middle of it. Anger and distress generally made it impossible to return to sleep, so more often than not, Bob would turn on the television and say, "Let's have a mini-day." Oddly, these were some of the best times in memory, striding the hours of 3 to 5 A.M., watching classics on TNT or reruns of *Ab Fab* or Sacha Baron Cohen. Finally, we would lie back down, Bob would turn his back to me, and I would take his shape, cupping his body with my own, my hand over his heart to feel it beating into sleep.

I was asked to serve as president of the jury at the San

Sebastián Film Festival in 2005, and when we arrived Bob had accidentally walked into a pillar at the Bilbao airport. He was mad at me for rushing ahead when I was actually walking slowly ahead of him to the customs hall. Where just a few years before we were going out to dinner and salsa dancing, now Bob was complaining of numbness in his extremities. Apart from that journey to Spain, Bob was refusing to go out anymore, and socializing was generally confined to home, other than a few dinners we were invited to at other people's houses.

At night I would awaken to find Bob sitting bolt upright in bed, his head bent forward on his chest. If I spoke his name or touched him, he would flinch or jump as if awakened from a nightmare, and his eyes looked panicked. I wondered if he was being overly dramatic, but something was mysteriously affecting him.

Steven and Bob decided together that Bob should see a doctor for a full physical. By now he was complaining of back pain as well; we had already endured several MRIs and X-ray imaging. I don't know how aware Bob was of the seriousness of his condition. I have heard since that medical records from previous years had warned him of a weak heart, and that he had been advised to quit tobacco and alcohol, but this information was never imparted to me. Many of the people who loved Bob, including me, suspected that he was something of a hypochondriac, always worrying about this symptom or that, but as his friend David Novros later commented, Bob was in fact a stoic.

It was late in the afternoon on August 7, 2008. Bob and Steven returned to the house after their visit to the doctor; Bob was diagnosed with rheumatoid arthritis and had been given a large dose of steroids. His hands and feet were massively swollen. When I touched the skin on his ankle, it bounced back like a marshmallow. We were in the living room; Bob was sitting on an armchair between Steven and me. At one point, he looked around dazedly. "I think I'm really sick," he said. There was wonder in his voice.

I was very worried, but he had just been prescribed medication, and I was confident it would work.

The following evening was the opening-night ceremony of the Summer Olympics on television. Bob and I watched on the flat-screen above our bed. The Chinese drummers were extraordinary; their syncopated sound was like thunder, and they beat out the changing rhythms as one. Such precision in such a vast number of musicians was daunting, almost mechanical. I drifted off to sleep.

I was aware of something terrible in the split second before I actually awakened. When I reached consciousness, Bob had already exploded from the bed and was standing at the foot, gasping in panic. "I can't breathe, I can't breathe." I thought maybe he was having a nightmare. I emptied the brown paper bag of Chinese medicine from the bedside table and told him to blow into it. "I'm calling the paramedics," I said.

"No," he said, "don't." He stumbled into the bathroom. I was calling his doctor. The answering service said he was unreachable in Canada, but if I would care to hold on, I could speak to his substitute in an emergency. A male voice came on.

"Doctor," I said, "Robert Graham is in crisis. He says he can't breathe."

"Do you have diazepam in the house?" he asked.

"Valium?"

"Yes," he said. "Give him one of those. He sounds like a nervous patient."

Bob was doubled up. I called Steven, then I called 911.

It seemed that the paramedics came in seconds. Like ministering angels, they laid Bob on the bed, gave him oxygen, and took his vitals. He was in full heart attack. Steven arrived and left with Bob in the ambulance. I locked up the house and the dogs and followed them to UCLA Medical Center in Santa Monica. Bob's heart stopped twice in the ambulance and they had to administer cardiopulmonary resuscitation using a defibrillator.

When I got to the hospital, Bob was in intensive care. The doctors had given him a blood thinner, and where the IVs penetrated the skin, watery blood was seeping through bandages and towels. I stayed with him, talking to him, telling him I was there and that everything would be all right, but it wasn't. Bob was now having a stroke. He had already undergone kidney failure.

At three o'clock in the morning, I traveled with him to the Ronald Reagan UCLA Medical Center in Westwood. It was dangerous but crucial to move him, because they had a better capability to treat him there. They would not allow me to be with him for several hours, as they were doing tests and biopsies. Jaclyn came and we tried to sleep in the waiting room. How awful those rooms are! Windowless, dark spaces with bad lighting and two small couches, like an afterthought. Following those first hours, the nurses were kind and allowed me to stay with Bob unless a procedure was taking place for which they might prefer I not be present. I felt that the care at the hospital was excellent.

I called David Geffen, whose name decorates the UCLA School of Medicine, and the kind and concerned head of the hospital, Dr. Gerald Levey. I called the mayor, Antonio Villaraigosa, a friend of Bob's, and I called Cardinal Mahony, for whom Bob had made the cathedral doors at Our Lady of the Angels. I wanted all thoughts and prayers to be with Bob. Both the mayor and the cardinal were kind enough to come see him.

The elevator doors opened one day and I beheld dozens of Tibetan monks in saffron robes outside intensive care. I learned that their spiritual master had suffered a heart attack. In the days following, whenever I walked down the glass corridor to see Bob, I would pass the priest's room, where two acolytes were stationed, one with prayer beads and the other spinning a prayer wheel. It made me feel that Bob was a little bit more protected.

At the end of the ICU corridor on the fifth day of his crisis, I saw a doctor sitting in a glass booth, studying a computer screen. He had a bemused look on his face. He introduced himself as Dr. Saleh, a kidney specialist.

"I think," he said, "that we have an overall diagnosis for your husband."

"What do you mean?" I asked, confused.

"Your husband has a disease. It's called Wegener's granulomatosis."

"Is there a cure?" I asked.

"We have a treatment we generally reserve for cancer patients, but in this case, we bomb his kidneys with Cytoxan and hope that they start to function again. Until then, he will have to do dialysis—first every day and then every other day until we get results."

Bob was in intensive care for a month before they moved him across the street to the acute physical rehab unit. I was with him every day. As a result of the stroke, he had to learn to use his left side again to walk and to read. They were teaching him to climb stairs, and he was making valiant efforts.

On Bob's birthday, August 19, the doctors allowed him to go outside in a wheelchair to visit with Mecha and my little dog, Pootie. After that I would bring the dogs to the hospital grounds regularly to have picnics on the lawn outside the Jules Stein Eye Institute next door, which reminded me of Dad, because it was where I first read him the screenplay of *The Dead*.

Bob was very weak, but they still had him on masses of steroids, so, deceptively, his appetite was enormous. I had always associated having an appetite with health, but in Bob's case, his sudden immense urges for lamb gyros or doughnut creams were the result of his illness. One was under the illusion that he was getting well, but it was an insane appetite—hunger fueled by the drugs. At least it took his mind off things. I would sit with him and we would choose three-course dinners from take-away menus and an array of ice creams from the best gelaterias in Westwood. Bob was having fantasies about Mediterranean food, something remembered and treasured from his time in London, living as a young artist in Notting Hill, and a dish his mother used to make for him, a Mexican stew called *mancha mantales*—literally, "tablecloth stainer."

On Saturday afternoons at the hospital, when the patients were being evaluated and the staff turned over for a few hours, Danny would drive me to Manhattan Beach to pick up Stella from her mother's rented condominium and take her down to the seashore. Sometimes Katie would be there, and a couple of times she came with us to an ice cream parlor and we all ordered big cones. She seemed sleepy or distracted, drinking a lot of coffee and smoking a chain of cigarettes. She was sharing the house with a girlfriend from London and an assortment of dogs adopted from the pound. She said she loved life at the beach, that she had been to visit a burlesque nightclub, and that she was doing a lot of dancing. There were several pale young women in her employ, both tattooed and pierced. Katie introduced one of them as Stella's babysitter. Danny and I would take Stella down to the beach and watch her beautiful lithe body splashing in the waves. For those few hours, it was possible to breathe again.

At last, after seven weeks in the hospital, Bob was allowed to come home. The Cytoxan had not worked, but we were still hoping that his kidneys might return to functioning. He was spending every other day in dialysis, seven hours a day. I had redone the ground floor for him so he would not have trouble with the stairs, and installed a big flat-screen television and ordered a king-sized bed.

After daybreak, before having breakfast, I'd leave Bob with his private nurse and walk with Pootie and Mecha one block down to the beach, past the bars and hostels on the boardwalk, then south toward Washington Boulevard, over the lumpy hillocks of grass and sand under the palm trees, their trunks the color and texture of an elephant's legs, stopping to look out to sea at the surfers dotted on the waves. Each day I said hello to the neighborhood's homeless and displaced: the Joker, Eugene, Frederick, Old Papa John, who read paperback crime stories and Westerns sitting in his wheelchair under a tarp in the pouring rain, his back to the seawall, where his epitaph now reads FLOW ON HOME in half-concealed graffiti. And Wino Bobby, who wore a yellow top hat and had his "wine goggles" on; for a few dollars, he'd recite a poem for you. Bob used to give him a few hundred dollars once in a while so he could go to his favorite place in Manila in the Philippines. Bobby was black, but he had a girlfriend there who had persuaded him that he'd fathered her white son. Now Bobby, too, has passed on.

Most of these men were veterans of wars in Korea, Vietnam, Iraq—victims of post-traumatic stress, living out the years. Although they never asked for money, I slipped them a few dollars once in a while. I was reminded that Bob Richardson, the man I'd left at the baggage carousel and from whom I had learned so much about life, had until recently been living among them out there on the sand.

For the first time in two months, on October 16, I left Bob at home and went out to a friend's birthday party in Hollywood, an all-girl outing to a lingerie shop called Kiki de Montparnasse; they were serving caviar and champagne. No sooner did I arrive and sit down at dinner when I felt my phone vibrate in my pocket. I answered; it was Jaclyn. "It's Katie," she said. "She committed suicide."

I left the party and rushed to Danny's house in the hills, only a few minutes away. Some friends of Danny's had already arrived. Stella was asleep, oblivious that her mother had jumped to her death off the roof of their Manhattan Beach summer rental earlier that day.

I got home late. Bob was asleep. I lay awake for the rest of the night, staring into the dark in disbelief. In the morning, when I told him what had happened, Bob just covered his eyes with his sleeve. Danny and Stella came to stay with me through the weekend.

Katie's funeral was at Hollywood Forever Cemetery. It

was one of those pale days that turn into brilliant sunshine. Zoë and Katie's family had flown in from England. We were all in shock. The ceremony was at the chapel on the grounds, the same chapel where we had congregated for Dad's funeral. After Katie's coffin was lowered, Stella dropped into the grave some pink roses she had picked in the garden of her house.

CHAPTER 35

When Bob got sick, the world turned mean in ways that were totally unexpected. His sweet private nurse Mary was not on duty one night, and although her substitute said she was watching him, Bob fell to the floor at six in the morning so hard that it shook the whole house. It woke me up and I ran downstairs. He had gone down on his face; his eye was swollen shut, and a black bruise was already traveling to the other eye.

"I don't want to go to the emergency room," he said.

I called his doctor. He was at home; it was Sunday. "How bad is it?" the doctor asked.

"Why don't you ask him yourself," I answered, and handed the phone to Bob, who by now was looking at himself in a hand mirror.

"I've got a bruise the size of a tennis ball," Bob said ruefully, then paused. "Well, okay, like a golf ball."

When I got back on the phone, I asked the doctor what I should do. The response was typically unhelpful. "Keep him propped up," he said. "If he passes out, call an ambulance."

I went upstairs and stepped into the shower. My heart was beating very fast. I was unspeakably angry and upset. As I dressed, I decided to take Bob to the hospital. I was not going to wait and see if he fell unconscious. When we passed the kitchen on the way out of the house, I heard Stella screaming. I looked through the porthole window in the kitchen door to see her on the floor, her hands between her legs, rocking back and forth. When I opened the sliding door and asked her what was the matter, she held up her little hand to show it was bleeding; she'd shut it in the doorjamb. Danny's face appeared. He had come running down from the guest room when he heard her cries.

"Stella's okay," I said. "I'm taking Bob to the emergency room." Bob, meanwhile, had leaned down to the sobbing child and, putting his bruised and blackened face close to hers, made a mocking sound, as if to say, "You think you've got it bad, little girl." Danny and I exchanged a look of disbelief, and then Bob, his nurse, and I drove to UCLA Santa Monica. Eight hours later, they told him he had a fractured eye socket. They didn't tell him he had cracked three ribs and had several compressed discs in his back—that information came later. Or maybe that injury had happened previously. I never knew fully what to believe.

Bob refused to stay in the hospital that night or any other. He resumed his rehabilitation and formulated a plan to deal with his dialysis: He estimated that by getting up at 3 A.M. and going to Santa Monica for treatment in the middle of the night, he could actually survive two days in a row without it. He claimed that this would keep him sane, and that he would be home in time for breakfast, and for me to read the morning newspapers to him. He told me he would lose his mind if he had to spend seven hours on the machine every other day. So this became our routine for a couple of months. Dialysis, speech therapy, physical therapy, occupational therapy, occasional visits in the courtyard with friends and family over tea and biscuits.

Hercules was in from London. I had heard that he was ill as well, that he was in all probability having a relapse of the lung cancer that had challenged him years before. We had lunch at the Lobster in Santa Monica and sat at his customary table overlooking the Pacific Ocean. He kept the conversation light and agile, as always. We talked about our mutual friends, from Bernardo and Claire Bertolucci—he was having a back operation, she was buying them a new flat in London—to our dear friend and his partner in film, Jeremy Thomas. And we talked about Bob. That afternoon Herky came over to see him. They conversed quietly for a considerable length of time; soon after, Herky left for London.

Bob had great elegance—he wore the white Sulka pajamas I had given him as a ritual every birthday and at Christmas, with his initials on the pocket, RPG, Robert Pena Graham— and such extraordinary dignity under pressure. The doctors told us that his disease was rare, basically unheard of in black- or brown-skinned people, and that it was a vascular disease. This explained why for years Bob had pain and numbness in his feet and headaches whenever he rode in airplanes. He had gone to many specialists for these problems. Even though his hair was now falling out from the treatments, he had so much that one could not see it was thinning. Bob was a beautiful man at all times.

There was a day when his doctors wanted to perform a kidney biopsy, and Steven called to say he didn't like the sound of that. The gurney was already in Bob's room, about to take him to surgery. There is such anguish in having to make these decisions. Ultimately, I felt that Steven should have power of consent, and I gave it to him out of respect for the father-son bond. But throughout Bob's mystifying illness, it became apparent that none of the doctors had an answer for the unified diagnosis of Wegener's granulomatosis. It was as if we had entered a medical dead zone. Nothing seemed to work.

One night when Bob was downstairs in the living room and I was upstairs, awake at four in the morning in the bed we used to share, Mecha came upstairs for the first time since Bob became ill to lie beside me. It was then I realized that she was transferring her allegiance to me. Mecha had always been obsessed with Bob—she had always stayed by him and had never chosen to leave his side until that moment.

Late at night on December 12, the television was on downstairs, as it usually was, and we had just finished watching a movie. Bob's back hurt so bad that he couldn't lie down, so I was lying on the rented hospital bed and he was at the foot of it in a big white armchair. "I think it's time we went to sleep," I said.

"I don't feel so good," said Bob. He was dizzy and disoriented; his forehead was hot and damp. He said he couldn't focus or stand up. I called the paramedics immediately. They arrived in minutes. Bob began to cry out that his back was killing him. They transported him by ambulance back to UCLA Santa Monica. Two days went by. Bob was fighting for breath. His doctors were confounded; it had become startlingly evident how little they knew about his condition.

Steven was with him one morning when the dialysis machines broke down; his blood was thickening and his body was rejecting the treatment. The ports in his arms by which they could administer intravenous drugs had blown.

*   *   *

On December 15, Bob was inducted into the California Hall of Fame. Noriko Fujinami and Steven accepted the honor on his behalf in Sacramento. Bob always described Noriko as the most intelligent and most informed studio director he had worked with; they reflected each other's aesthetic. Her calm presence was always comforting.

On December 16, Steven stayed with Bob at the hospital, and I spent much of the day working with the photographer Terry Richardson. I hadn't seen Terry in many years, although he had published a book on the work of his father, Bob Richardson, to which I had contributed some early pictures—mostly Polaroids that I had saved, of Terry as a child. Bob had, for the most part, lost or destroyed the original prints of many of the fashion photographs we had made together in the seventies.

I met Terry at the Chateau Marmont. It was a very emotional reunion for me. Terry was tall and thin and looked very much like his father did when we first met. The pictures we worked on that day, for the British fashion magazine *Love*, were an homage to both Bob Richardson and Bob Graham— two huge influences in my life. I'd always imagined that Bob Richardson might do something flamboyant in the end. I thought of him and our crazy, volatile relationship and, later, his sad finale in 2005, when he sat down in front of Terry's television one evening in New York after a long drive back east from California and died quietly of a heart attack. His final pictures, from that last cross-country drive, are among the saddest images I have ever seen.

A few days later, I was scheduled to do a print ad for Badgley Mischka with Annie Leibovitz. It would keep me from being at the hospital for a whole morning, which I regretted, but I hadn't worked in the four months since Bob first got so sick. When I went to see Bob that morning at UCLA Santa Monica, he said, "Don't go." I told him that I would be gone for only a couple of hours and would come straight back to the hospital when I was finished.

I left his room in tears. When I got to the studio in Hollywood, I ran up to Annie. There were a group of women in the photograph. I asked Annie if there was any way she could shoot me out first so that I could rejoin Bob. "Absolutely," she said. "I'll have you out of here as soon as your makeup is ready."

When I got back to the hospital, I asked Bob's primary doctor if they were going to give him more Heparin to thin his blood.

"We were thinking of administering something like that, possibly," said the doctor. He looked baffled.

"He's dying, isn't he?" I asked him.

"It seems we've done all we can for him."

When I entered his room in the ICU, Bob's eyes were closed, but he was thrashing in his bed. "I'm here," I said. "Do you know who this is?"

"My Honita, as beautiful as ever," he said.

I held his hand. "Shall I sing you a song?" I asked.

"Yes."

I sang Gladys's song to him, about the three little fishies that go over the dam, one of my favorites growing up in Ireland. He seemed to listen closely. "Shall I sing you another song?" I asked.

"Yes."

I started to sing "Sweet Baby James."

"No, not that," he said. Then he asked, "Am I dying?" He asked the question like a child. There was mystification in his voice.

"No, of course not," I replied.

He turned his cheek on the pillow and seemed to relax a little. Then he left his body. I watched his spirit go. I marveled at how beautiful he looked in his white pajamas—his artist's hands, his caramel skin, his silver hair thrown back upon the pillow. The doctors told us that they wanted to put him on a respirator, to give him a chance to regain his strength, but it was clear to me that this was just life support.

Joan Buck flew in from New York to hold my hand. Danny and Stella came to stay over the holidays, and Yolanda brought a Christmas tree from the farm. Mitch and Kelly came, too, and I remember almost nothing else, just that gaudy little pine in the studio, all lit up and full of ornaments from the past—golden angels and dancing skeletons, a cigar made of glass. I opened a bottle of wine, Château Mouton 1982, with the label Dad had painted of a dancing goat, and we drank to Bob.

When I went to the hospital the next morning, Bob was still unconscious. He remained hooked up to the ventilator for another day. Then, with the doctor's counsel, Steven and I made the decision to turn off the machines. We called Bob's best friends—the artists, his ex-wives, and his staff. They all came to the hospital to say their goodbyes. On December 27, 2008, he left his life gracefully and peacefully. A pretty red-headed nurse came into his room in the hospital to detach him from the respirator that was pumping oxygen into his lungs. The room was filled with the people he loved. In its way, it was as ceremonial as a wedding—Bob's head resting on a white cotton pillow, his hair like mother-of-pearl, his eyebrows arched above closed eyelids, his eyelashes long and dark. When the nurse removed the oxygen mask, he wore no expression at all.

As she detached him from the machines, a last exhale blew softly through his lips, the clouds outside the window parted, and the sun glanced off the sea beyond Santa Monica, bathing him in a golden light. It was such a beautiful scene that we actually started clapping. Bob had passed.

Rafi drove me home from the hospital. He had held my hand and comforted me and prayed for Bob throughout his illness, always raising my spirits and always keeping the faith whenever I was confused or despondent. When I walked into the house, the dogs ran to greet me. I sat down on the ground in the courtyard and let them sniff me all over. Mecha was thorough and put her nose up to mine. Pootie licked the salt tears from my face. I looked up under the canopy of the coral tree. The sun was filtering through the leaves. Joan was in the kitchen. Kelly Lynch was answering the phone. Susan Forristal was coming with Susanna Moore. Allegra was flying in. The world as I knew it had ended, but I was surrounded by loving friends.

The morning after Bob died, I woke up as if some sort of decision had been reached for me in the night. I decided that, to commemorate his passage, I should take all the flowers Bob's friends had sent to the house and place them at his public monuments, starting downtown at the Coliseum. It was there that I had first become aware of his work, when I saw the two headless bronze athletes towering above the gateway to the Olympic Games in 1984, never dreaming that we were destined to live together for the last eighteen years of his life.

Susan Forristal came with me, and with Rafi at the wheel, we drove from one end of the city to the other, laying roses at the bases of Bob's statues and floating gardenias in the fountain at the feet of his *Source Figure*, on Bunker Hill. We went to the UCLA sculpture garden, to the cathedral and the Music Center, and to visit his silver *Torso* on Rodeo Drive, where someone had already laid flowers. In New York and Washington friends and admirers were doing the same for Bob—Boaty Boatwright, Laila's mother Martha, and our New York driver, Paul Cuomo, all sent pictures of the statue of Duke Ellington, the base covered in lilies at 110th Street and Fifth Avenue, on the northeast corner of Central Park. In Washington, D.C., Franklin Delano Roosevelt's lap was strewn with roses. Allegra had called Miguel Norwood, one of our old friends from Skataway, who was calling a cousin of his in Detroit to place a bouquet of blue flowers by the fist of Joe Louis.

On the first Sunday after Bob died, I found myself alone in the house. I walked out to the half-lot beside the kitchen where the studio used to store scrap metal, grabbed a spade, and began to dig. Three hours later, I had made a four-foot hole in the hard dirt. There I placed an avocado tree, three feet high, that Rafi had grown from seed.

When the staff arrived for work on Monday, Rafi and I went to a local nursery for mulch and grass seed and flowers. I bought two wide concrete bowls and filled them with water hyacinths and goldfish. For days afterward, Dora, Rafi, and my housekeeper, Rebeca, helped me to plant shrubs and sow grass. That was the beginning of our garden for Bob.

It was a comfort for me to dig holes in the earth, to bury

plants and watch them grow. One morning as dawn was breaking, I awakened to an unusual sound and walked downstairs. Two large ungainly seabirds were balancing on the ficus trees above the garden. They were white, the size of swans, with yellow bills and pink feet. The branches buckled under their weight. When I looked in the Audubon guide later, I was unable to identify them; it is possible that they were snowy or cattle egrets. This was their only appearance in the garden, and it felt like magic.

Hercules had returned from London and was staying at the Bel Age Hotel with Jeremy Thomas. He called asking if I would meet him for lunch. He needed the name of a good chiropractor. His back was killing him, he said. We met at the Lobster in Santa Monica. He tried to rise as I approached the table; he was terribly thin. He ordered a glass of water, no longer his customary beer.

"Jack's coming to Bob's funeral," he announced.

"Really," I said.

"Of course," replied Herky. "He wouldn't miss it for the world."

I knew that Herky had most likely persuaded Jack to come. I was very touched. He followed me in his car back to my house. The chiropractor, Dr. Schwartz, was waiting for us. Herky went upstairs for about an hour, came downstairs, gave me a kiss, and left.

I went up to see the doctor, who said, "You know your friend only has a short time left, don't you, Anjelica?"

"Yes," I said. "I know."

* * *

Cardinal Mahony offered to hold Bob's funeral mass at the Cathedral of Our Lady of the Angels. On January 7, 2009, a large congregation gathered outside Bob's Great Bronze Doors.

Allegra had come down from Taos with Cisco and Rafa; Danny brought Zoë and Stella. The children were so young, it was hard to see them attempt to grasp the enormity of the situation. It was hot on the plaza, and Stella's little face was pinched. Rafa knelt on the steps outside the cathedral, pitching some pennies with Miguel Norwood.

Bob's pallbearers were his patrons, his fellow artists, and his closest friends, Jack Quinn, Doug Wheeler, Roy Doumani, Earl McGrath, Tony Berlant, Tom Holland, and Ed Moses; his assistants and co-workers, Rafi, Juan Carlos, Noriko's son James, and Raul; and his family, my nephew Jack, my brother Danny, and Bob's beloved son, Steven. Joey, Steven's mother, placed Bob's Knight of Malta medal on the coffin; Dora, Noriko, Rebeca, and Yolanda placed roses picked from the garden I planted at Windward.

Mayor Villaraigosa, Governor Arnold Schwarzenegger, and Maria Shriver were all in attendance. Steven, Danny, and Jack Quinn read. Roy Doumani spoke; Earl McGrath talked of having introduced me to Bob; Maria described how she had brought her very Catholic mother, Eunice, to Bob's studio when they were planning the Governor's Medal for the Arts in California. Eunice had taken a long, doubtful look at all the beautiful bronze nudes and proclaimed, "That poor wife!" Hercules brought Jack, who was a prince and stayed by my side throughout.

People had come from all over the country—Steven's

mother's family, Bob's cousins, and many friends near and far; even Bill Murray showed up. It seemed that everyone was there but Bob. I read a poem from Yeats, "He Bids His Beloved Be at Peace."

> *O vanity of Sleep, Hope, Dream, endless Desire,*
> *The Horses of Disaster plunge in the heavy clay:*
> *Beloved, let your eyes half close, and your heart beat*
> *Over my heart, and your hair fall over my breast,*
> *Drowning love's lonely hour in deep twilight of rest,*
> *And hiding their tossing manes and their tumultuous feet.*

CHAPTER 36

Before Hercules left L.A. for the last time, Jeremy Thomas threw a dinner for him at the Chateau Marmont. I was sitting in a booth at the restaurant watching June Newton, herself a widow, reflected in a candlelit mirror. I was thinking about what was real and what was not, and how ephemeral were our quicksilver lives. Although the party was beautiful, it was melancholic, for some of us knew we would not see Herky again. He left the gathering early, passing along the aisle between June's table and mine, and blew me a farewell kiss before he went upstairs.

Herky died February 21, 2009, in London, mourned by the many people who adored him, not least by almost every blonde in Britain. His passing was an inconsolable loss to his friends.

If death weren't what it is, it would be magic, and there might be an explanation for why my mother disappeared one day in 1969 in a car wreck and why my father left his body in 1987 in that rented house in Rhode Island. Why the sun came out from behind the clouds to kiss Bob goodbye as his body lay under white sheets at UCLA hospital in Santa Monica. These ties, these blind attachments! These love affairs! Why, we ask, why must they leave us? When will we join their ranks? Is life truly meaningless? I guess not as long as we remember the influence of the people we love: that manna that flows from the stars!

In the five months from October 2008 to February 2009, four people to whom I was deeply connected died—Bob, Katie, Sam Bottoms, and Hercules Bellville. I did not hear from my brother Tony. Our shared experiences were what Tony and I had in common, but we related to them quite differently. Whereas I was more of a people pleaser, he was perhaps more inclined to please himself, which on occasion can look selfish but in many ways is a more honest approach to life.

I didn't hear from Jeremy Railton, either. I do not want to speculate as to how it happened that Jeremy decided not to be my friend—the loss of his companionship and the deterioration of our relationship still bewilders me. Life takes strange turns into backwaters, and we learn to let go.

I first really came to know my brother Danny when Dad was sick and we would rally around him at the hospital—the frightening episodes when he was diagnosed with a heart aneurysm, when the doctors worried he might not survive an operation with only one functioning lung, when his oxygen was so low that falling asleep was life-threatening: the hellish and continuous narrative of his ill health and failing body. Danny's inherent sweetness and courage were my comfort.

Allegra wrote a book, published in 2009, about her upbringing and titled it *Love Child*. In it, she describes the mysterious conundrum of her earliest years, following the death of our mother, being raised by Dad, and meeting her natural father, John Julius Norwich, when she was twelve.

It was always my wish to protect her, even though I was ill prepared to take on the full responsibility of a child in my early twenties. I did as much as my own singular agenda allowed. There were times I know I disappointed her.

These days Allegra lives and writes in Taos. Rafa skis the black-diamond runs and is an avid soccer player. He makes beautiful jewelry and wants to be an astrophysicist.

Tony's son Jasper lives in New York City. He is almost thirteen years old and loves to draw and paint. His mother is the actress Jodie Markell. Matthew, Laura, and Jack are grown with children of their own—respectively, Noah, Mathilda, and Sage.

Stella sent me a drawing she had made of a girl with butterflies for eyes that she titled "See-through Nature." On one occasion, a conversation was going on and someone said, "You can't buy love." And Stella said, "No, but you can buy a puppy!"

At twelve years old, she excels as a runner; has long, lean limbs, wide shoulders, honey-brown skin, gold hair, and pale aquamarine eyes that draw a lot of attention. People often remark on her beauty or ask where she got those eyes. She tells them she got them from her mother, Katie.

Stella and I spent a lot of time together after Katie and Bob died. I took her to the theater and to the ballet. We saw *The Nutcracker* and *Cinderella*, *Wicked*, and *Mary Poppins*. When I took her backstage to meet the corps de ballet of the Hispanico dance troupe, the dancers asked what she wanted to do when she grew up.

"I want to be a waitress," she replied.

Most artists are involved in overcoming some form of childhood heartbreak. I don't know if Stella will be an artist, but she is already a rider. For the past two years, she has been going to school in the English countryside and living with

Danny's mother, Zoë. She wrote me a letter saying, "Today I galloped by myself, it was a wonderful feeling." Her grandfather John would be proud.

I was at Dr. Klein's office in Beverly Hills. Arnie had been in the news because it was no secret that he was one of Michael Jackson's doctors, as well as his friend and confidant.

Arnie said, "Michael's here. He wants to see you. Shall I order you lunch?" He ushered me down the corridor into an adjacent room. A large Baldessari print of a man with a yellow nose hung on the wall. A few moments passed, there was a gentle knock on the door, and Michael walked in.

On the rare occasions I'd run into him of late, it had been shocking to see how thin he was, how white his skin had become. The tiny nose, the tattooed mouth, the high-slanting cheekbones, the sadness in his dark eyes.

"I'm so sorry about Bob, I know how much you loved him," he said.

I thanked him. "It's a cruel world," I said.

"I want you to know that none of what they claimed about me is true," he said. "I love children, I always have, I would never in my life hurt a child."

I know that many people thought otherwise, but I believed him. Michael died just a few weeks later, on June 25, 2009, the victim of a broken heart.

Whenever I fly to London, I try to stop at Sabrina Guinness's cottage in Hampshire on the way into town. In spring, the woods are resplendent with bluebells, and I love to work in her garden, dig in the wet earth, and let the sun hit the back of my knees. They say it helps you to get over jet lag. In the year that followed Bob's death, I had struggled with anxiety and moments of panic and had not a few dark nights of the soul.

In July 2009 I was in London on my way to Ireland to receive a "Hooker" award at the annual Galway Film Fleadh. This award is not, as one might imagine, for excellence in streetwalking but, rather, is named for a fishing vessel native to this part of the West of Ireland, along with the curragh. Going back to Ireland was to remember a time when we were sailing on Galway Bay, before loss became part of my landscape.

Leaving Heathrow, Sabrina, Jaclyn, and I walked the endless distance to the Aer Lingus gate at the end of the terminal. Dad always said that his vision of purgatory was to be in transit on one of those long corridors. The last time Sabrina and I had come to Ireland was for Jasmine Guinness's wedding at Leixlip Castle outside Dublin, when I had been challenged by Paddy Moloney of the Chieftains to dance a reel in front of a marquee full of assorted guests—my only excuse for accepting the challenge being that the Guinness made me do it!

This time I was going back to the west to be among the places and people I had grown up with. We landed at Shannon. The road to Galway had become a sleek highway; the signposts were painted green and had the Irish translation written beneath the names of towns—Ardrahan, Ballinasloe, Gort, Tuam, the sounds of my childhood.

I was staying in Galway as a guest of the festival for a week, which gave me just enough time to touch base with many friends from the past. Even Michael Burke was there, whom I hadn't seen since I was nine, when he and Tony were playing hurley in the back field behind the primary school in Carabane.

We traveled up to Huston Beach in Connemara, named

for my father, where Dad once owned a cottage by the sea. Leonie King asked us over to Oranmore Castle for champagne. As we arrived, her father, Bill, wandered into the kitchen. He was, at ninety-nine years old, small and resilient, like a seabird. There was a lot of loose poetry in his head, of the water and of the wars; though he could recite long stanzas of *The Iliad* and *The Odyssey* by heart, he could not remember who my father was. He knew his daughter, Leonie, but recognized few others. He was living in a bathrobe in the cellar of Oranmore Castle, drinking coffee and eating chocolate ice cream. As he walked from his monastic little bed into the kitchen with the aid of ski poles, he said sweetly, "You may be an aunt, a sister, or I may not know you at all! Please forgive me if I don't remember, for I believe that I am quite old."

I spent a lovely afternoon touring the Galway campus of the National University of Ireland and visiting the Huston School of Film and Digital Media. Although Dad never received formal training, the Huston School is something he would have liked very much. Established in 2003 as part of NUI Galway, it occupies a building on the north side of town. I had received an honorary degree from the school in May 2005.

Jaclyn had made an appointment for us to visit St. Clerans, my beloved childhood home. This time we were invited only to the Big House, as the land had been subdivided. Where once the estate was of a piece, now there were walls, and gates, and boundaries. The stone lions outside were long gone, the fountain was still.

We walked into the main hall of the Big House; its beautiful fossiled black marble floor was carpeted wall to wall in red. We were met by Anne, a warm woman who, along with her husband, was in the process of packing up to leave St. Clerans, which they had been running as a boutique hotel for its late owner, the TV host Merv Griffin. After Griffin's recent death, the family had decided to move on. Anne offered us tea, and we entered the drawing room. No more pale gold, although the sunburst Dad had brought from Mexico still adorned the ceiling. Anne returned with small cakes she had baked specially, and offered me a little book about St. Clerans called *Portrait of a Manor House.* Inside there were prints and pictures of the house dating from the eighteenth century and on through Dad's tenure. There were some quotes from Leonie King and my old playmate Mary Lynch about the grand old days. It was almost uncanny, like coming back as a ghost.

I was offered a tour of the house, and although the prospect frightened me, I agreed. Most of the furniture had been packed up except for the beds, and there were a lot of those. Every door upstairs and down led to a bedroom or a bath. The color scheme in Dad's suite was yellow and lime green, colors that might have been good in Barbados but were somehow unthinkable without the benefit of sun. And yet the beautiful bones of the room were still in evidence. It reminded me of Greta Garbo in a bad dress.

In the St. Clerans of my youth, no other domicile was visible from any window. Now, with the subdivisions and the excesses of the eighties, the forests had been chopped down and cheap housing had sprung up all around, occupying the view from most of the windows. The Japanese bath no longer existed; nor the Grey Room; the Napoleon Room, with its splendid mahogany emperor's bed; the Bhutan Room, with its violet walls and embroidered curtains; the Red Sitting Room; nor the pre-Columbian art gallery. Only in the Mexican tiles in the kitchen and the abandoned Waterford chandelier suspended over the staircase were there small indelible traces of the past.

In the spring of 2010—in London and ensconced at Claridge's, Dad's favorite hotel—I introduced a beautifully restored print of *The African Queen* to members of the British Film Institute. Many friends came, including Nic Roeg and Stephen Frears. There was a Q&A after the show, with the amazing, ageless Angela Allen, who had been Dad's script supervisor on the film. I waffled on for a bit in answer to the question "What makes this film unique?"

Stephen Frears was adamant afterward. "It's the most conventional movie ever made," he said. "But it took John Huston to put it in the jungle."

CHAPTER 37

In New York, making *When in Rome* in March 2008, I was introduced to Michael Mayer, who had directed *Spring Awakening* on Broadway. We agreed that we would like to work together one day, but nevertheless it came as a surprise several years later when he and NBC asked me to act in a pilot for a new television series called *Smash*. It was a bright and unconventional idea for a network show—the back-story of how a musical based on Marilyn Monroe makes it to Broadway. My part would be that of the show's producer, Eileen Rand. The contract demanded that should the show be ordered to series, I would have to commit for up to six years. I had never before played a character for that long a time.

In early March 2011, I signed on for the role of Eileen Rand and within twenty-four hours was on a plane to New York to shoot the pilot over three weeks. When I got the news a month later that the show was picked up, I returned to New York for a publicity ritual called the "upfronts," which involved many interviews and endorsements for television affiliates. After a whirlwind forty-eight hours, I flew home to L.A. The reality of the situation sank in. I would have to leave the house in Venice that I'd built and shared with Bob and relocate to New York. What would I do about the dogs?

Seized with trepidation, I called Sue Mengers and asked if I could come over for some advice.

Sue was sitting in her usual yellow silk chair, wearing her usual kaftan and wreathed in marijuana smoke. "Tell me about it," she ordered in a measured voice, tossing back her ash-blond mane.

"Well, Sue, I'm nervous. You see, it would be a total change of lifestyle. A series. New York. I'm just really worried." I was pretty worked up.

Sue eyed me for a moment and, without missing a beat, growled, "Are you kidding? It's a fucking miracle."

I stayed for lunch. It was just the two of us in the living room. Susan Forristal always talked about re-creating Sue's living room as a public space and calling it "Sue's Salon." I took measure of the color of the walls, salmon pink, and the ceiling, stormy gray like the sky in a Fragonard. I knew it would be one of the last times I would see this room, with Sue at the center of it, her little white hands with their manicured nails fumbling to light a joint with a Georgian silver table lighter.

I got up to leave and moved to kiss her goodbye. She smiled wryly and turned her cheek. "I love you," she said. "Now beat it!"

On July 8, 2011, I celebrated my sixtieth birthday. Many beloved friends were there. Mary Lynch came from Galway and Joan Buck from New York; even Jack came. It was a fine evening at the house on Windward. The only element missing was Bob, which, in a way, was everything. It had never occurred to me that we would not share a future.

* * *

I put the house and studio up for sale and moved to New York for *Smash*.

Sue was right—doing the pilot was exciting. My character Eileen Rand's office was filmed in the glamorous Brill Building, a longtime home to some of the most powerful and prolific producers on Broadway, its windows framing the heroic tableau of the Great White Way.

When the show went to series, a perfect replica was built at our Long Island City location, and even though its windows there looked out to green screen, I always felt like a female Harold Prince, sitting in my power chair. Working in the streets of New York, in cafés, bars, restaurants, and theaters, dealing with the vagaries of bad traffic and worse weather, walking in sleet and snow with crowds milling around was a challenge, daunting but often rewarding just to get through the scenes.

One challenge of a different nature was singing a version of "September Song," from my grandfather's famous role in 1938's *Knickerbocker Holiday*, for composers Scott Wittman and Marc Shaiman, whom I first met on *The Addams Family* when I danced "The Mamushka."

The crew was located in sound stages in the remodeled interior of a redbrick warehouse in Long Island City, and in a studio in Greenpoint, Brooklyn, above a plastics factory with a chicken farm on the roof. The top floor was being reconfigured as writers' rooms, conference rooms, and production offices, which often doubled as locations for the show; sometimes it was hard to tell what was real and what was *Smash*.

Initially, there was a great energy to the series, and it was always a pleasure to be among the performers—the actors, dancers, and singers who threw themselves into the work with total commitment. The show ultimately lasted only two years, during which time my dogs and I endured two hurricanes, Irene and the daunting Sandy, and enjoyed the vast resources of the city, including sun-filled days aboard a beautiful pleasure boat in Sag Harbor in the summertime with my friends the Buffetts. But as much as I love the East Coast and seeing my friends in New York, I always look forward to coming home to the open skies of Southern California.

I have worked on more than seventy movies and television shows, but I always feel that going back to work is like the first time. It's new and scary, and I wonder if I can do it. I find that the older I get, often the last thing I'm in the mood for is learning lines, but that's really what acting is all about—knowing my lines so I don't have to think about them. This is sometimes harder than it looks, and it's almost impossible for me to memorize under stress. I occasionally wonder what I was thinking when I decided I wanted to be an actress.

I have never felt that the camera automatically loved me, but in a way this forced me to develop my career as a character actress, which has enabled me to do the work that gives me the most pleasure. Sometimes it feels almost like alchemy—calling out and channeling spirits; you can inhabit many lives and never get bored. Movie sets are safe but temporary worlds. Dad always used to say, "It never happens in quite the same way twice."

Television has been very good to me, from my first outings on *Laverne & Shirley* through *Lonesome Dove* and *Buffalo Girls* and *Iron Jawed Angels* to my guest appearances on *Huff* and *Medium* and my regular role on *Smash*. Television has less patience than film; the work moves fast. Sometimes I have the sensation that I'm running from a big man-eating machine and feel overwhelmed, but I have learned to persevere.

I've had some great tributes, among them my selection as the 2000 ShoWest Female Star of the Year; the 2003 Harvard Hasty Pudding award, which involves being paraded down the streets of Boston by a raucous army of cross-dressing students and graduates and subjected to intense ridicule; the Women in Film Crystal Award; and the awarding of a star on the Hollywood Walk of Fame, presented to me by Wes Anderson, Danny, and Stella in torrential rain, surrounded by my friends, as well as Allegra, Cisco, and Rafa, who flew in from Taos.

When I began working on *Smash*, a lot of people asked how it felt to "be back." Of course, when you are in your own company, you never go away—it's just a matter of to what extent the public is aware of your existence. Although I guess that visibility for an actor is devoutly to be wished for, I have always treasured the idea that I could, if I wanted, take a break, disappear from view, and go walkabout from time to time.

I can't say that I have ever been deeply hurt by inaccurate reportage, but many of the stories conjured by the tabloids were invasive and untrue, and the tactics employed by the British press were particularly relentless. I've had photographers jump out at me from behind bushes and follow me home in their cars. I've heard people say that celebrities deserve it; they get paid too much and make their living in the public eye. But there is hardly anything more barbaric than being hounded by other human beings. Tony Blair called a halt to fox hunting in England in the eighties, but it's still open season on famous people.

Some moments when I've wanted to move under the radar, I have succeeded quite well. At other times, anonymity is less easy, especially if you are on a television series. But, I am happy to report, it is still possible for me to get lost in plain sight.

Since I came back to L.A., two years have passed. I am grateful for the experience of *Smash* but glad to be home and not under the corporate banner, where actors' opinions are not necessarily encouraged. When I was studying the art of acting, the objective was to form choices and to make decisions accordingly. Times have changed. Here in California, several years have passed in a winter's drought—blue skies and a cruel sun, no hint of rain. The Sierras that mark the horizon are without their snowcaps, gray-headed and bare, like old bald men.

The house and studio on Windward went into escrow four times and finally sold. Letting go was painful but necessary, and I moved out in less than two weeks. Now it, too, is consigned to memory.

I never thought I would get this far and have so many years behind me: life's kaleidoscope of colors, its sounds, emotions, and special effects, its memories receding like rainbows. I have no children of my own, but it is daunting to realize that by now I might be not only a great-aunt but a grandmother. I think of how children tie us to the earth, how hard it must be to parent them and then let them go.

I am reminded of an Irish phrase: When you are faced with an obstacle on the hunting field, it is said that you must first throw your heart over it before jumping.

I saw a medium recently. She said that Dad is happy in the afterlife because he likes alcohol and you can have a drink in heaven. She asked, "Who is the man with the goatee?" I said it was Bob. She said he tells me not to worry, that he is coming with me to the new house.

ACKNOWLEDGMENTS

To my brothers, Tony and Danny; my sister, Allegra; my extended family; and my excellent friends, thank you for providing the understanding, humor, encouragement, and steadfast loyalty that have carried us through the years, and for your company on life's journey. For my beautiful nieces and nephews, Laura, Matt, Jack, Stella, Rafa, and Jasper, who are proof of the love we siblings have shared, and some of whom already demonstrate that attribution to their own children, Noah, Sage, and Mathilda. In memory of my parents, whose voices still call me to reason, and in gratitude to the many people who raised me and showed me kindness—my Nurse, my teachers, and the many musicians, dancers, directors, actors, writers, designers, creators, artists, and others whose influence has inspired me, and who have led me to a deeper appreciation of the precious time we share, and to the miracles of our existence.

My thanks to those who have served me and cared for me. And to all of you who have made this book possible—Nan Graham, whose clarity and leadership are a force of nature, and all her colleagues at Scribner: Kathleen Rizzo, Kara Watson, Erich Hobbing, Daniel Loedel, Craig Mandeville, David Hillman, Brian Belfiglio, Alexsis Johnson, and Kate Lloyd, for her TLC and for looking after me on tour. To Elisa Shokoff, Chris Lynch, Ben Rimalower, and Sarah Lieberman at Simon & Schuster Audio. To Suzanne Baboneau at Simon & Schuster, London. To my editor, Bill Whitworth, for his calm overview, his knowledge, his devotion to the English language, and his valiant efforts to improve my grammar. To Bill Clegg, who gave me the title. To Chris Clemans, Fred Sanders, and Erich Rettermeyer. To my wonderful team—David Nochimson, Britt Bates and Nina Cancio, Ina Treciokas, and Christian Hodell. And everyone at WME—Claudia Ballard, Tracy Fisher, Kathleen Nishimoto, Amy Hasselbeck, Nancy Josephson, Scott Henderson, David Kalodner, Katrina Lebedeva, Izzy Arias, Alix Gucovsky, Tim Curtis, Deana Atwood, and Lisa Reiter.

Thanks also to Jack Nicholson, for allowing me to write about him and for always being a fair and true friend. To Boaty and Toni, two wonderful women. To Cici for sharing her memories, and to Annie Marshall for keeping a diary and being such a great ally throughout the years. To Mitch and Kelly, who always encourage me. To Rafi and Paulie for driving me. To Art Luna for his perfect haircuts. To the great instructors at Studio Surya Yoga in Venice and Uptown Pilates in New York City. To Trish Dean for keeping me adjusted and in line. To Blake for his talent in the kitchen. To Graydon Carter and Cullen Murphy for championing me in *Vanity Fair*. To Mike Nichols for being himself. To Joan Buck for our lifetime of friendship. To Jimmy and Jane Buffett for providing a home away from home and for their kindness and generosity.

Special thanks to Pammie; Laddie and Jake; Laila; Steven; Toby; Suze; Joe and A.M.; Sabrina; Earl; Mike and Irena; Larry; Philly; Whitey; Helena; Greta; Susan; Burke; Nona; Yachiyo and Yoshiko; Lillian and Erik; Lizzie; Emily; Bailey;

ACKNOWLEDGMENTS

Lois; Carey; Maude; Billy Al; Glenne; Julie; Jay; Jena; Doris; Mr. Ed; The July Girls; Noriko, Paul, and James; Lisa; Maya; Julie; Rebeca, Dora, Carlos, and Yolanda; and Johnny.

Thanks to the dear RAP, with love and appreciation. And to Jaclyn, whose sensitive awareness and devotion to our work continue to delight and astonish me.